EARLY AMERICAN
SILVER

Tankard, by Cornelius Kierstede (1674–1757), New York, c. 1700. Engraved with the Van Cortlandt arms and the initials I^{C}E for the original owners Jacobus and Eve (Philipse) Van Cortlandt who were married in 1691 (see Fig. 11). Height: 6½". Gift of Mrs. Augustus Van Cortlandt. *Courtesy, Museum of the City of New York*

EARLY AMERICAN SILVER

MARTHA GANDY FALES

Revised and Enlarged Edition

EXCALIBUR BOOKS

ISBN: 0-525-70096X

(*Front cover*). Tankard, by Benjamin Wynkoop (1675–1728), New York. Engraved with the Roosevelt arms and initialed for Nicholas and Heyltie Roosevelt, who were married in 1682. Height: 6½". Lent by The Roosevelt Hospital to the Museum of the City of New York. *Courtesy, Museum of the City of New York*

(*Back cover*). Paneled bowl, by Gerrit Onckelbag (1670–1732), New York, 1700–1710. Diameter: 9⅜". Bequest of Miss Charlotte A. Van Cortlandt. *Courtesy, Museum of the City of New York*

(*Title page*). Eagle-head finial for flagstaff, by Jesse Churchill (1773–1819), Boston, 1812. Presented by General Arnold Welles to the New England Guard in November 1812. Height: 7". *Courtesy, The Bostonian Society*

Illustrations inside the book's covers are courtesy of American Antiquarian Society, Charleston Library Society, The Historical Society of Pennsylvania, and The New-York Historical Society

MARTHA GANDY FALES served for many years as Assistant Curator and Keeper of Silver at The Henry Francis du Pont Winterthur Museum, Wilmington, Delaware. She has taught courses at Cooperstown Summer Seminars and has been a judge for Student Design Competitions sponsored by the Sterling Silversmiths' Guild. Now, in addition to being Honorary Curator of Silver at the Essex Institute, Salem, Massachusetts, she does consultant work and, with her husband, lectures on antiques and antique silver at many museums and historical societies. She has written articles for various publications, including *The Magazine* ANTIQUES and *The Connoisseur,* and two other books on individual silver collections.

Contents

v

Acknowledgments

In practically every sentence I have ever spoken or written on the subject of American silver, I have been indebted in some way to three people: John Marshall Phillips, the leading authority on the subject, whom I met only a few months before his untimely death in 1953; Kathryn C. Buhler, whose years of experience, meticulousness, and caution are evidenced in countless catalogues and articles, and whom I hold in special esteem; and Charles F. Montgomery, who first introduced me to the subject while I was a student at the Winterthur Museum and later encouraged my specialization as a member of the staff.

In the preparation of this particular book, I am especially thankful to the many willing and patient friends who are on the staffs of libraries and museums or who own American silver. They have taken a great deal of their time to answer necessary questions and arrange for photographs to be taken and processed. The names of the institutions and collectors who supplied the photographs are gratefully given in the captions accompanying the illustrations, but the people who represented them deserve personal acknowledgment:

Miss Gail E. Anderson	Mrs. Felice DeWitt
Miss Rose T. Briggs	Frederick J. Dockstader
David S. Brooke	Miss Louisa Dresser
E. Milby Burton	Miss Marie C. Eichelser
Mrs. DeForest Clarke	Leslie A. Elam
Kenneth C. Cramer	Henry N. Flynt
Mrs. Barbara S. Delaney	Daniel J. Foley
William de Matteo	Miss Jennifer Furkel

Mrs. Edith Gaines
Wendell D. Garrett
Miss Mary Glaze
John M. Graham
William H. Guthman
Philip H. Hammerslough
Mason Hammond
Thompson R. Harlow
Frank L. Harrington
G. Jeffries Harrington
Ashton Hawkins
Henry Hawley
Bartlett H. Hayes, Jr.
Graham Hood
The Rev. George M. Hooten, Jr.
Frank L. Horton
J. Stewart Johnson
James R. Ketchum
Mrs. Robert H. McCauley, Jr.
Marcus A. McCorison
Edgar deN. Mayhew
Edward Mayo
Miss Christine Meadows
Milo M. Naeve
Mrs. Margaret P. Nolan
Miss Margaret Olson
Mr. and Mrs. Richard Paine
Mrs. Gilbert R. Payson
John N. Pearce

Harold L. Peterson
Jules D. Prown
Ian M. G. Quimby
Norman S. Rice
Stephen T. Riley
Miss Caroline Rollins
Miss Virginia Rugheimer
Miss Vivian J. Scheidemantel
Henry H. Schnabel, Jr.
Mrs. Samuel Schwartz
Miss Carolyn Scoon
Mrs. James H. Shields
Walter E. Simmons, II
Glenn B. Skillen
Philip C. F. Smith
Miss Margaret Stearns
Theodore E. Stebbins, Jr.
Miss Lilly C. Stone
Kevin L. Tierney
W. Stephen Thomas
Leon de Valinger, Jr.
Nicholas B. Wainwright
Mrs. Frederick R. Walters
C. Malcolm Watkins
Mrs. Dean Webster
Gregor Norman-Wilcox
Miss Alice Winchester
Alfred J. Wyatt
Martin I. Yoelson

and a number of friends who, though they prefer to remain anonymous, are no less gratefully acknowledged.

Most of all, I am indebted to my husband, Dean, who has endured endless piles of papers and pictures, an often discouraged wife, rough copy served at breakfast, and hastily prepared dinners at night. Not that he has suffered in silence, but his good humor and encouragement have taken the edge off his caustic remarks!

Introduction

"If only everyone in Europe could see what I have seen today. We tend to think of America as a producer of Coke bottles and automobiles, and few of our people realize that there was a culture in America two centuries ago which was able to produce silver equal to that of their own country." These words were spoken to me one day long ago by Robert Kloster, an authority on Scandinavian silver, after studying one of the outstanding collections of American silver. His words still ring in my ears. It is not only Europeans but Americans as well who are unaware of our cultural heritage.

Silver represents the first important art form in this country. The historical events with which silver objects are associated represent major aspects of our development as a nation. American silver is therefore a subject of great interest and value. As such, it deserves to be brought to the attention of every American and should at least be taught in every course of American art history.

Until recent years, the artistry and historical significance of American silver were known only to a handful of collectors, curators, and antiquarians. The books written on the subject were mostly catalogues, published in small editions and sparsely illustrated. As general books began to be written, they stressed certain aspects such as chronological development, different forms made in silver, regional characteristics, and the silversmiths themselves.

The purpose of this book is to present all these different aspects with equal emphasis and to provide in one volume the most interesting and most essential information concerning American silver from the seventeenth century to the early nineteenth century. Little has ever been said in print about the proper care of silver, how to distinguish the authentic pieces from the forgeries which plague the field of silver, or how to read marks correctly, and this information is equally as important as matters concerning stylistic development and aesthetic qualities.

A great deal of thought has been given to the selection of the illustrations. An attempt has been made to obtain the most significant examples of American silver, as well as the best documented. Wherever possible, a representative range of the various geographical centers of silversmithing has been included. Because of their preeminence in production, Boston, New York, and Philadelphia are the most widely represented. Similarly, four museums with outstanding collections of American silver—the Museum of Fine Arts in Boston, the Garvan Collection at Yale, the Metropolitan Museum in New York, and the Winterthur Museum in Delaware—provided a large proportion of the illustrations. In addition, an effort was made to include some previously unpublished pieces, and objects which I have had an opportunity to study personally.

There are two stumbling blocks to the uninitiated which should be explained before a page is read. "Silver plate," or simply "plate," originally referred to solid silver and is used here in its traditional meaning. With the advent of Sheffield wares, the word "plated" came into use to designate silvered base metals. The other major confusion to the modern reader concerns the words "goldsmith" and "silversmith." Today it seems to many that these two words should designate two different occupations. In actuality, the two words were and are synonymous. Even though their work more often involved the less expensive metal, silver, these craftsmen were trained to work with gold as well, and until the eighteenth century "goldsmith" was the more common appellation.

The historical aspects of this craft have immense repercussions. Silver makes history come alive. But more than that, it represents one of our country's greatest cultural legacies. Family silver has always been the symbol of personal achievement, and so the nation's silver is a symbol of America's artistic and cultural inheritance.

I

ARTISTRY IN AMERICAN SILVER

Bowl, by John Coney (1656–1722), Boston, c. 1710–1720. Engraved on side with the arms of Walter Riddell, a member of the British Royal Navy who purchased the bowl while in Boston and took it back to England where it remained until 1972. Diameter: 9⅝". *Courtesy, Museum of Fine Arts, Boston*

CHAPTER ONE

Stylistic Development and Quality

THE brightness and beauty of silver has always attracted the attention of man and made the metal precious to him. It was the search for this lustrous metal which brought many adventurers to the New World. In fact, the reports of gold and silver mines which reached Europe in the sixteenth century were greatly exaggerated in an effort to encourage settlers to leave their homes and travel across a vast ocean in search of a better place to live.

In the hope of finding precious metals, as indeed the Spanish had found in South America, goldsmiths, jewelers, and refiners boarded the first English ships bound to North America, first to Virginia, then to Massachusetts, New York, Pennsylvania, and finally the entire eastern seaboard. So zealous were they in their pursuit of riches that it was reported in the *Proceedings of the Virginia Colony:* "the worst mischiefe was [that] our gilded refiners, with their golden promises, made all men their slaves, in hopes of recompense. There was not talke, no hope, nor worke, but dig gold, wash gold, refine gold, load gold. Such a brute of gold, as one mad fellow, desired to be buried in the sandes, lest they should by their art make gold of his bones." [1]

While these first settlers were destined to be disappointed in their quest for gold and silver mines, it was not long after, when the colonies had become rooted, that a need developed for the services of gold- and silversmiths. It had long been the custom for men of wealth to turn their coins into silver plate, which was not only an elegant reminder of one's station in life but was also useful and identifiable in case of loss

3

or theft. "I esteem it as well politic as reputable," wrote William Fitz-hugh from Virginia in 1688, "to furnish myself with an handsom Cup-board of plate which gives myself the present use and Credit, is a sure friend att a dead lift, without much loss, or a certain portion for a Child after my decease." [2]

Because plate was valuable and highly esteemed, it was natural that the purchasers of silver objects should desire them to be made in the newest style. Over and over again, the patrons requested the silver-smiths to make their silver in the latest fashion, and the silversmiths likewise advertised that their wares were suitable to the newest taste. As a result, American silver kept pace with styles abroad and showed clearly the influence and development of the major artistic movements in Europe. Silver, in fact, represented a fine art in the new country and progressed more rapidly than the arts of architecture, painting, or sculpture.

The styles that American silver followed were largely the styles of English silver, since most of the settlers were English and political control of the Colonies was maintained by England. In turn, the mother country followed the fashions of the Continent, particularly as they were translated by Dutch printed sources and immigrant Huguenot silversmiths. There was some direct Continental influence in the Col-onies from Dutch settlers in New York and Huguenot refugees, but for the most part it was imported English silver that set the mode.

In order to study the changes which occurred in American silver, it is convenient to group examples according to style and date. However, it must be remembered that such period classifications are somewhat artificial, that there are earlier and later examples of every style, and that fashions did not change overnight. Also, it is necessary to look at the objects which represent the highest style in order to see the ele-ments of each style. The result is that we become familiar with the fundamentals of good design and develop a sense of connoisseurship. We begin to understand what makes some expressions of style more successful than others, more enduring; what makes some design ele-ments more successful, more appealing; and ultimately, what makes one piece of American silver more beautiful than another.

THE LINGERING RENAISSANCE TRADITION (1650–1690)

By 1650, when the first American silversmiths found employment, the current vogue in England was in the late Renaissance tradition. There had actually been no radical changes in English silver since Elizabethan days, but with the restoration of Charles II to the throne in 1660, a rapid succession of innovations began to take place which corresponded exactly to the first important period in American silver. Derived as it was from the Renaissance movement of Italy, seventeenth-century silver design was architectural in nature, forms were basically rectilinear, and decoration included paneling, heraldic motifs, baluster shapes, and simplified ornamentation.

The earliest example of American silver expresses emphatically the stylized paneled decoration of the lingering Renaissance tradition. It is a tiny dram cup (Fig. 1) made about 1651 by John Hull and his partner Robert Sanderson for Ruth Brewster, who married John Pickett of New London, Connecticut, in 1651. Basically a simple form to execute in silver, it has twisted wire handles and a casually chased paneled design enclosing fleurs-de-lis. A heavy border of chased punchwork encircles the rim.

Slightly later is the beaker (Fig. 2) made by the same two silversmiths in 1659 for their church in Boston, The First Church. With straight sides and only the slightest amount of flaring at the rim, this beaker is extremely chaste in its design, and relies entirely for ornamentation on its wide band of matting, or granulation, laboriously pounced into the surface with a dotting tool to give a textural contrast to the metal. The initials of The Boston Church are simply placed in a shield-shaped tongue at the top of the band. In spite of being less than four inches tall, the beaker conveys a feeling of solidity and strength.

Equally expressive of the Puritan tradition, and elegant in its purity of line, is the standing cup (Fig. 3) which Hull and Sanderson made for the Newman Congregational Church at Rehoboth, Rhode Island, in 1674. The cup section has the same straight sides and slight flare at the rim as their beaker, both painstakingly hammered up from a single piece of silver without a seam. The shaft on which the cup is supported is shaped like the turned balusters found in architecture and furniture of the period, and is distinguished by the variety of shaping from the narrowest diameter to the greatest girth. Such variation delights the eye and adds to the overall effect of the piece. By exhibiting pleasing lines, a propriety to its purpose as a drinking vessel, and a suitability to the Puritan society for which it was intended, this standing cup exemplifies many of the features essential to good design.

It has been said that the chief characteristic of the best work of all great periods is that the work be "entirely of its own age."[3] A salver (Fig. 4) made by Timothy Dwight, working in Boston in the late Renaissance style, is definitely timely. Not only is it a type of footed tray which had only recently come into vogue, but it also represents its

[1] Dram cup, by John Hull (1624–1683) and Robert Sanderson (1608–1693), Boston, c.1651. Engraved RB for Ruth Brewster, who married John Pickett of New London in 1651. Width: 2⅞". *Courtesy, Yale University Art Gallery, Mabel Brady Garvan Collection*

[2] Beaker, by John Hull and Robert Sanderson, Boston, 1659. Pounced initials B^{T}C for The (First) Boston Church. Height: 3⅞". *Courtesy, Museum of Fine Arts, Boston*

[4] Salver, by Timothy Dwight (1654–1691/92), Boston, c.1680. Early pounced initials engraved over with initials T^{B}M for Thomas and Mary (Willoughby) Barton, who were married in 1710. Diameter: 11⁵⁄₁₆". *Courtesy, Museum of Fine Arts, Boston*

[3] Standing cup, by John Hull and Robert Sanderson, Boston, 1674. Gift of Captain Thomas Willet to Newman Congregational Church of Rehoboth (now East Providence), Rhode Island, in 1674. Height: 7¼". *Courtesy, Yale University Art Gallery, Mabel Brady Garvan Collection*

[5] Patch box, by William Rouse (1639–1704/05), Boston, c.1680. Engraved on base LF for Lydia Foster, who died before 1689. Diameter: 1$^{15}/_{16}$". *Courtesy, Yale University Art Gallery, Gift of the nephews of John Marshall Phillips*

[6] Tankard, by Robert Sanderson, Boston, c.1670. Pounced initials I^{V}M for Isaac and Mary Vergoose, who were married c.1668. Height: 6½". *Courtesy, Museum of Fine Arts, Boston*

[8] Two-handled cup, by Robert Sanderson, Boston, c.1675. Engraved on base T^{S}A for Thomas and Ann (Tyng) Shepherd, who were married in 1656. Height: 4½". Diameter of top: 4¾". *Courtesy, Henry Francis du Pont Winterthur Museum*

[7] Beaker, by Cornelius Vander Burch (1653–1699), New York, 1685. Gift to Robbert Sandersen in 1685 for his role as mediator in land transaction between Robert Livingston and the Mohawk Indians. Height: 8″. *Courtesy, Yale University Art Gallery, Mabel Brady Garvan Collection*

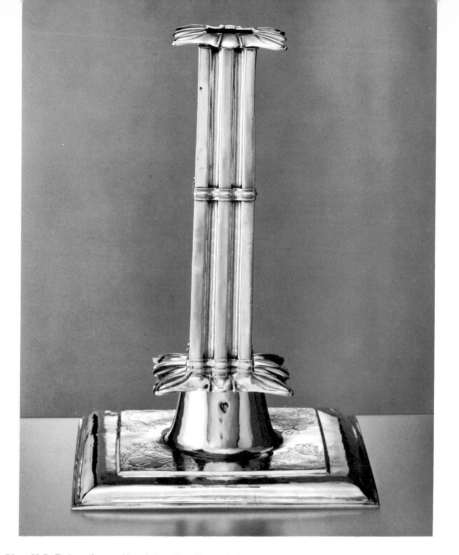

[9a, 9b] Pair of candlesticks, by Jeremiah Dummer (1645–1718), Boston, 1686. Engraved D^{J}E and made to commemorate the marriage of David Jeffries and Elizabeth Usher in 1686. Height: 10⅛". *Courtesy, Yale University Art Gallery, Mabel Brady Garvan Collection*

own age in the engraved border. Delineated around the broad rim, amid a running vine and flowers, are animals—not just a lion and a unicorn, but also an elephant and a camel. The latter designs were entirely dependent upon the newly opened East India trade, which had captured the imagination as well as the economy of the Western world in the last half of the seventeenth century.

While the forms in silver remained basically plain, there was an increasing amount of engraved ornamentation. The smallest objects as well as the largest show the general trends of the day. A tiny patch box (Fig. 5) made by William Rouse has the same kind of large round flower, like those popular in Stuart embroidery, engraved on its cover

that a tankard (Fig. 6) made by Robert Sanderson has on its lid. The long, thick rat-tail extending from the top of the handle down the body of the tankard, and repeated in the engraving both on the back of the handle and on the handle ending, is a feature frequently found on seventeenth-century silver.

In New York, the same basic features of simple rectilinear forms were followed, but in many cases there was a more abundant use of engraved ornamentation, as in Dutch silver. Cornelius Vander Burch's handsome tall beaker (Fig. 7) is expressive of its age, not only in form but also in its elaborate engraved designs, which were copied verbatim from Jacobus Cats's books of didactic verse, published in a folio edition in Amsterdam in 1658 and widely read by the Dutch.[4] The quality of the engraving is quite good. The lines flow smoothly; there is life and some tension to the figures and a sufficient amount of shading and tonal quality to give texture to the elements.

Even though vessels were basically rectilinear and often were as wide as they were tall, cups often were fashioned with curved sides, instead of straight sides (Fig. 8). The decoration could be in the form of chasing and rudimentary repoussé work rather than flat engraving alone. Increasingly, seventeenth-century silversmiths made use of repoussé designs, and often recessed areas were purposely tarnished to give added contrast and color. Curvaceous caryatid handles (or "ears," as they were called then) were more widely used in place of simple twisted or plain handles. Robert Sanderson, one of the first to use these features, made a caudle cup which had the turkey, an indigenous American fowl, modeled into the foliage of its sides. Similar cups were made in English silver during the period of Charles II.

Another form which followed the English fashions of the Restoration was the candlestick (Figs. 9a, 9b) made by Jeremiah Dummer of very thinly hammered sheets of silver. With a square base, the bound cluster of reeds form the column and provide in the shaft deep, dark recessed areas as well as raised, fully reflective bright areas. A shallowly modeled drip pan at the top and just above the base gives the same effect horizontally that the cluster-column achieved vertically.

THE ADVENT OF THE BAROQUE (1690–1720)

At the end of the seventeenth century, the style known as Baroque was introduced into American silver. It was a bold, contrasting, artistic style featuring massive, moving lines of curves and reverse curves, and florid three-dimensional details. Popularized for the decorative arts by the intricately drawn engravings of Jean Bérain, designer to the court of Louis XIV, the Baroque style placed the emphasis on complicated compositions and contrasting light and color, disregarding the former straightforward plan of designs.

Jeremiah Dummer, working with the new design elements, made a cup (Fig. 10) with patterned handles composed of leafy elements and graduated beading, and gadrooning on the body instead of repoussé decoration. Gadrooning was especially well suited to the Baroque tenets of richness, since its alternate reeds and flutes produced an effect of contrasting areas of alternating light and shade. In addition, the decorated area of the cup was itself set off by a band of perfectly smooth silver.

Equally pleasing in its brilliant Baroque effect is a covered cup (Fig. 11) made in New York by Jurian Blanck, Jr. The unique properties of silver are fully exploited in the contrast of the smooth, beautifully planished upper section of the body with the totally worked repoussé base, so freely executed that it makes the bowl appear to be nestling among the acanthus leaves. The design is balanced by the repetition of the repoussé ornament on the lid, where granulation is used to give further texture to the surface. The cast handles translate the leaf design from relief to full-round and are related to the body by the three knop finials on the lid, which serve to make the top into a footed tray when it is inverted. This interrelationship of parts causes the beholder's eye to move with delight from one section to another and around again. It is the engraved arms in the center, however, which provide the focal point. Without the arms, the eye would travel circuitously with nothing to lead it back to the center of the design.

One of the best ways for the silversmith to produce the richness inherent in Baroque art was to combine a number of methods of decoration in one piece. Edward Winslow's sugar box (Fig. 12) is not only an elaborately shaped piece, but its decoration is three-dimensional. The coils of gadrooning on the base and lid are augmented on the body by swirled reeds and flutes which are overscored with chased arcs. Bosses of repoussé work adorn the four sides, the one covering the hasp being decorated with a chivalric representation of a charging knight.[5] The acanthus leafage varies from broad flat leaves to delicate little tendrils and has been modeled with great skill. Supported by cast scrolled and trifid feet the box has a leafy scrolled handle which grows right out of the repoussé leafage of the lid, and both have been given texture by matting. The handle resembles the high crestings of the contemporary looking glasses and chairs of William and Mary furniture.

Scrolls, elaborate cast ornaments, repoussé acanthus leaves, and diversity of decoration were all Baroque features which penetrated the finest tankards (Fig. 13) of the late seventeenth and early eighteenth centuries. This richness of ornamentation is especially seen in New York tankards, where cut-card bands, engraving, spiral gadrooning, cast cherub heads, and pendent swags of fruit contrast handsomely with the smooth silver of the tankard body, which bears an enormous, elaborately engraved coat of arms on the front.

The best Baroque motifs were lavished on the cresting of a large punch bowl (Fig. 14) made by John Coney of Boston. The broken scrolled arches stand out boldly in silhouette, and the well-modeled cherubs' heads act as counterpoints to the deeply cut notches in the rim. So rich is the decoration of this piece, made in the full Baroque style, that the contrasting smooth surfaces of silver are reduced to

[10] Two-handled cup, by Jeremiah Dummer, Boston, c.1692. Engraved on base "Benjamin Coffin to R. G." for Ruth Gardner of Nantucket, who married James Coffin in 1692. Height: 3⅛". *Courtesy, Henry Francis du Pont Winterthur Museum*

[11] Two-handled covered cup, by Jurian Blanck, Jr. (1644–1714), New York, 1691. Engraved with the Philipse arms and I^{C}E for Jacobus and Eve (Philipse) Van Cortlandt, who were married in 1691. Height: 5½". *Courtesy, Henry Francis du Pont Winterthur Museum*

[13] Tankard, by Peter Van Dyck (1684–1751), New York, c.1705. Engraved with arms of the Wendell family and initials of Harmanus Wendell and his wife Anna, of Albany, who were married in 1699. Height: 7⅛". *Courtesy, Yale University Art Gallery, Mabel Brady Garvan Collection*

[12] Sugar box, by Edward Winslow (1669–1753), Boston, 1702. Engraved D^{O}E donum W.P. 1702, and given by William Partridge to Daniel and Elizabeth (Belcher) Oliver. Height: 5½". *Courtesy, Henry Francis du Pont Winterthur Museum*

[14] Monteith bowl, by John Coney (1656–1722), Boston, c.1710. Engraved with Colman arms in center for merchant John Colman. Diameter: 11″. *Courtesy, Yale University Art Gallery, Mabel Brady Garvan Collection*

narrow bands. The plain area of the bowl has been faceted into flat fluting, an almost two-dimensional version of the three-dimensional gadrooning on the base. This causes the light to be refracted in a different way at every slender angle, and indicates the direction of the newly developing dictates of fashion.

THE AGE OF HOGARTH (1720–1750)

The richness and heaviness of the Baroque style was bound to give way to greater simplicity, lightness of line, and restrained ornamentation. By 1720 the modifications of Baroque elements had been introduced into American silver and were beginning to form themselves into a style all their own. With an emphasis on contour, plain surfaces, and rhythmic curves, objects became basically circular, with little decoration other than engraving.

[15] One of a pair of candlesticks, by Nathaniel Morse (1685–1748), Boston, c.1720. Engraved with Faneuil arms on left side of base and later crest of Caulfield with motto on right. Height: 6⅛". *Courtesy, Henry Francis du Pont Winterthur Museum*

The octagonal shape shows the transition from rectilinear forms to circular forms graphically. A candlestick (Fig. 15), one of a pair made by Nathaniel Morse of Boston, is devoid of surface decoration, relying upon the contours of the shaped shaft and the facets of the octagonal base for success. Variety was achieved by dividing the shaft into many sections of unequal lengths, ranging from a wafer-thin disc to an elongated ogival curved section. The faceting of the base is repeated lightly in the slight faceting of the central section of the shaft, creating a pleasing repetition to unite the variations.

The octagonal shape was one of the most popular features of early eighteenth-century silver. An "Eight square Tea-Pot" was spoken of as "the newest Fashion" in 1727 when it was offered in the *New-York Gazette* as part of a prize made by Simeon Soumain.[6] Such a teapot (Fig.

[16] Teapot, by Peter Van Dyck, New York, c.1725. Engraved T^{W}I and P^{B}M on base. Height: 7⅛". *Courtesy, Yale University Art Gallery, Mabel Brady Garvan Collection*

[18] Sugar dish, by Simeon Soumain (1685–1750), New York, c.1736. Engraved on side of body and lid with cypher EC for the original owner, Elizabeth (Harris) Cruger, who had married Henry Cruger in 1736. Height: 4¼". *Courtesy, Yale University Art Gallery, Mabel Brady Garvan Collection*

[17] Salver, by Jacob Hurd (1702–1758), Boston, c.1730. Engraved in center with Clarke arms. Diameter: 12½". *Courtesy, Yale University Art Gallery, Mabel Brady Garvan Collection*

16) was also fashioned by Peter Van Dyck with an S-shaped spout and a C-scrolled handle.

A contemporary of Van Dyck, William Hogarth (1697–1764) of London, summarized the fundamental principals of the current style in his *Analysis of Beauty*.[7] Published in 1753, at the end of the period, this study of aesthetics is of special interest because Hogarth was himself trained as a silversmith and was an excellent engraver and a painter. One of his chief theories was that there was a fundamental S-shaped line of beauty or a line of grace which was shaped with just the proper amount of curvature; a line which was not too straight and not too exaggerated. This line appears repeatedly in silver made in the second quarter of the eighteenth century.

Another aspect of beauty which Hogarth discussed was the quality of

[19] Covered cup, by Jacob Hurd, Boston, 1744. Inscribed to Richard Spry, Commander of the *Comet Bomb*, which took a privateer, and presented by several Boston merchants. Height: 13⅞". *Privately owned*

[20] Coffee pot, by Jacob Hurd, Boston, c.1750. Engraved with Clarke arms. Height: 10¼". *Courtesy, Henry Francis du Pont Winterthur Museum*

fitness. There must be a fitness of the material for the purpose of the object. This is particularly true of the minor arts, where usefulness is a primary factor. There must also be a fitness of the material for the design: that is, the properties of silver should be considered and not be violated, a principle voiced earlier by Shakespeare: "o'er step not the modesty of nature." [8]

Silver was well suited to the brewing of tea. Furthermore, if the pot were in a pear-shape like the one by Peter Van Dyck, the tea would steep better because a maximum amount of water would be in contact with the tea leaves when they settled to the bottom of the pot. Tea was precious, and the early teapots were necessarily small so that small quantities could be brewed. However, the handle had to be of a certain size in order to be gripped by the normal-sized human hand. A curved handle fits the grip better than a squared handle. Since silver is highly conductive of heat, it is not suitable for handles, and wood was usually substituted. All these factors of fitness to function and beauty of line had to be taken into consideration by the silversmith.

To achieve variety in designs, several different curving lines were often joined together to form a continuous, smoothly flowing line. Engraved borders and embellishments of infinite variety were added. A tray (Fig. 17) made by Jacob Hurd has a border composed of many different motifs and textures, "to lead the eye a wanton chase," as Hogarth put it. Chief among these motifs were the delicate C-scroll, diapering, light curved leafage and flowers, and the scallop shell, which, with its many lobes, epitomized the desired roundness and united curved lines.

Engraved cyphers were well suited to the dictates of freely curving design with their circular and foliated script shapes of initials. Simeon Soumain made the cypher the chief form of embellishment on a sugar dish (Fig. 18). The engraving of the initials EC, contained within a circle on the side and just above on the lid, accentuates the roundness of the form itself and the circularity of the foot and reel top. The shape of the dish was taken from Chinese porcelain tea bowls, and Chinese design and decoration played an increasingly important part in the mid-eighteenth century.

One of the most impressive and lasting forms of this period is the covered cup (Fig. 19) made on several special occasions by Jacob Hurd for presentation to outstanding men. Although a large piece of silver, it has grace because of the simplicity of its curvilinear form. The expanse of the body is broken up by an elaborately engraved cartouche in the upper section, and by the proper placement of a mid-band, dividing the sections into pleasing proportions.

Jacob Hurd was a master of proper details and cohesive design. In a coffeepot (Fig. 20) he accentuated the roundness of the body with a domed lid and a round finial. Beneath the spout he added a drop, which is the same shape as the finial but only half-round. The same silhouette cut from a flat piece of silver was soldered just under the top of the handle. It is this thoughtful repetition of the same shape in different dimensions which gives the design interest and unity.

ELABORATION OF THE ROCOCO (1750–1775)

The fashions of Hogarth's day prepared the way for the Rococo style, which emerged in the middle of the eighteenth century. While the emphasis previously had been on forms and line, attention now became fixed on detail and surface ornamentation. Many of the old basic forms remained, but they were lightened by naturalistic flowers, leaves, and ruffles, which gave a gay, fanciful, feminine effect to the designs. Lines that had been simply curved before became doubly curved. C-scrolls became broken C-scrolls. The early symmetrical scallop shell was replaced by an asymmetrical or tattered shell. Where there had been smooth surfaces and some engraving, there was repoussé work, gadrooning, and cast ornament, all in great profusion. Hardly a spot of surface survived without some embellishment.

Because of its malleability, silver was very well suited to the enthusiasm for abundant decoration. A teapot (Fig. 21) made by Benjamin Burt shows the addition of chased and engraved ornamentation over the top surface of the body, spilling right over from the shoulders onto the flat lid, and hiding the flush hinge. Instead of a simple turned type of finial, a fat pineapple has been added. While the most popular shape for the earlier bodies of vessels was a pear shape or a globular shape, teapots and other forms now became apple-shaped or shaped like an inverted pear. This did away with the heavy, substantial-looking base of the Baroque form and created a lighter, less stable-looking object, bringing the delicacy of the Rococo style into the basic shape as well as its decoration.

These features can all be seen in three pieces (Fig. 22) made by Paul Revere in full Rococo style. Both the coffeepot and the sugar bowl are in the new inverted pear shape, which the silversmiths referred to as "double-bellied," as opposed to the "single-bellied" form. The lids of both pieces are doubly-domed, and capped with a pine cone finial. The repoussé ornament of the sugar bowl is a tangle of floral motifs, C-scrolls, and ruffles. The coffeepot has a double-scrolled handle, and a large cast shell has been added to the base of the spout. The top of the spout has an added furl, and the arms engraved on the side are enclosed in an asymmetrical cartouche. Gadrooning, which made its return to silver toward the end of the Rococo period, has been added to the edge of the lid and to the base. The tray also epitomizes Rococo design in its irregular border, emphasized by the reverberation in its molding, composed of conjoined S- and C-scrolls interrupted with alternating large and small tattered shells. The vocabulary of Rococo ornament has also been enunciated in the engraving of the delicate asymmetrical cartouche of the arms.

Outstanding among American examples of Rococo silver is the teakettle-on-stand (Fig. 23) made by Joseph Richardson of Philadelphia. Not only is the body of the teakettle double-bellied, but the frame on which it rests is festooned with floral garlands and ruffles. Even the

[21] Teapot, by Benjamin Burt (1729–1805), Boston, 1757. Engraved on base in script, M:ʸ Derby, for Mary Derby, who married George Crowninshield in 1757. Height: 5⅛". *Privately owned*

lamp underneath is ornamented, a feature rarely found in elaborate English silver. The naturalism of the Rococo can be seen in the animal's head, which is worked into the fantastic repoussé ornament at the top of the swirling cartouche, as well as in the bird's head which forms the lip of the spout. To achieve the fullness of the late Rococo style, Richardson had to combine chasing, engraving, repoussé, and cast ornament. An object of good design sits well in space and is equally as beautiful in the spaces it encloses as those that it occupies. The area enclosed by the raised handle is just as pleasing to look at as the whole shape of the piece.

The same shell foot found on the Richardson teakettle-on-stand was used by John David for a cruet stand and a pair of sauce boats (Fig. 24). In fact, shells and C-scrolls are everywhere in these pieces. The handles of the sauce boats are especially stylish since they are free-standing at the top and give the perilously-poised aspect of much Rococo design. The lightness and airiness which were accompanying features are evident in the cruet frame, which contains five glass cruets. Reverse scrolls, which look on the brink of toppling, support the asymmetrical frame of five lobes, and ruffled rings of gadrooning contain the bottles. The handle for the frame stands high and open, surmounted by a delicate furled shell. The piercings of the English caster tops give a further delicate swirling pattern to the composition.

Piercing was a form of decoration for silver which became increas-

[22] Coffeepot, salver and sugar bowl, by Paul Revere (1735–1818), Boston. The salver (diameter: 13⅛″) and sugar bowl (height: 6¾″) are engraved with the Chandler arms and were owned by Lucretia Chandler, who married John Murray in 1761. Revere recorded the charges for the sugar bowl in his accounts of that year. The coffee pot (height: 12¹⁵⁄₁₆″) was charged in 1781 to Paul Dudley Sargent and is engraved with the Sargent arms. *Courtesy, Museum of Fine Arts, Boston*

[23] Teakettle-on-stand, by Joseph Richardson (1711–1784), Philadelphia, c.1760. Engraved with Plumstead arms and made for the widow of Clement Plumstead, mayor of Philadelphia. Height: 14¾″. *Courtesy, Yale University Art Gallery, Mabel Brady Garvan Collection*

[25] Basket, by Myer Myers (1723–1795), New York, c.1765. Made for Samuel and Susan Cornell. Length: 14½". *Courtesy, The Metropolitan Museum of Art, Morris K. Jesup Fund, Purchase, 1954*

ingly popular in the late Rococo style. A large serving basket (Fig. 25) made by Myer Myers is an excellent example of the light, graceful, and airy effects that piercing could give an otherwise bulky piece of silver. The Gothic additions to Rococo design can be seen in the quatrefoil piercings, and the Chinese element, in the fretwork pattern of the base-band. Gadrooning edges the undulating rim of the basket in cusped sections and lightly outlines the diamond piercing of the handle. The total effect is like lace, and the pattern cast in the shadow is ephemeral and fleeting, as Rococo design was meant to be.

RETURN TO THE CLASSICAL (1775–1810)

The natural reaction to the freedom of the Rococo was a return to order and regularity. It was a calm, rational approach which replaced the turbulence and restlessness of the preceding style. While the Rococo style had emanated largely from France, with borrowings from the Chinese and the Gothic, the Classical style received its first major impetus from England and the genius of Robert Adam, who was in-

[24] Pair of sauceboats and cruet stand, by John David (1736–1798), Philadelphia, c.1765. Cruet stand (height: 10¾") engraved CR for the Ringgold family of New Jersey. Silver caps on glass bottles bear London hallmark. Sauceboats (height: 4¾") engraved TSC for Thomas and Sarah Cooch of Delaware. *Courtesy, Henry Francis du Pont Winterthur Museum*

[26] Urn, by Richard Humphreys (1749–1832), Philadelphia, 1774. Presented to Charles Thomson by the Continental Congress, which ordered on October 25, 1774, "a piece of plate for the Secretary £50 sterling." Engraved cartouche signed by James Smither, Sr. Height: 21½". *Courtesy, Philadelphia Museum of Art; lent by Dr. Charles T. Chamberlain; photograph by A. J. Wyatt, Staff Photographer*

spired by visits to ruins excavated in what had formerly been the Roman empire.

The new Classical style was characterized by simplicity and seeming correctness, by symmetry and proper proportion. It was restrained and orderly, and ornament was used discreetly. Classicism came quickly to American silver. No sooner had Robert Adam made his designs fashionable in London than Richard Humphreys produced a tall, elegant urn (Fig. 26) with such innovations as regimented acanthus leafage, beading and galleries for borders, and ball feet.[9] Only the asymmetrical Rococo cartouche surrounding its engraved inscription betrays the youthfulness of the new design. Because the Classical style was introduced just at the beginning of the American Revolution, it was not until after peace had been restored to the country that it became widely accepted. The urn was one of the chief features of the style, and the associations with classical Rome were appealing to a new nation that liked to draw its governmental inspiration from the same source.

By 1790 the engraving had become fully Classical in inspiration, too, with shield-shaped enclosures for the arms, bellflower and laurel swags, and much refined festoons of flowers suspended by rosettes and paterae. Reeding was a nice, orderly type of decoration and was added to edges or used as banding on the newly popular barrel form, a modified version of which became fashionable for tankards such as Joseph Anthony made (Fig. 27).

As the new Classical style developed, the effects of new machinery and the beginning of industrialization could be seen in the silver de-

[27] Hoop tankard, by Joseph Anthony, Jr. (1762–1814), Philadelphia, 1788. Presented by John Penn and John Penn, Jr., to Gunning Bedford. Height: 6⅞". *Courtesy, Philip H. Hammerslough*

signs. In Anthony's tankard, for instance, the flat piece of silver made available by rolling machines can be seen everywhere. The lid and the base were cut out of a sheet; the body was cut out in a long, rectangular section, forced into a circle, and seamed. The handle was square, since this would be easier to cut from several flat sections and solder together. Even the thumbpiece is simply cut out, like a jigsaw pattern, from the sheet metal. At this point, the machine gained the advantage over man. Before, the design had come first and then the method of executing the design was devised. But by the end of the eighteenth century, the machine became more important, and the design of the product began to be dependent upon what the machine could do.

The change was gradual, however, and the use of sheet silver is not so obvious in Paul Revere's tea set (Fig. 28). The sides of the pieces are

[28] Tea set, by Paul Revere, Boston, c.1795. Height of sugar urn: 9¼". *Courtesy, The Minneapolis Institute of Arts, Gift of Mr. and Mrs. James Ford Bell, 1960*

[29] Tray, by Paul Revere, Boston, 1797. Made for Elias Hasket Derby of Salem, who paid £14/13/10 for the silver, £12/6 for the making, and 15/ for the engraving. Length: 17". *Courtesy, Yale University Art Gallery* .

fluted to give a pleasing repetitive effect in the reflections. The shapes of all the vessels are Classical, from the urn-shaped sugar dish and the elliptical teapot and tea caddy to the creamer, which is shaped like an inverted Roman warrior's helmet. Instead of Rococo broken scrolls, the lines are barely curved and much simplified. Slightly scrolled French feet support the trays in place of the earlier shells or cabriole legs and claw-and-ball feet. A tiny bead has been added to the top of the cone finial, and the lids are only slightly domed. On other tea sets, silversmiths used the stylish pineapple finial (Fig. 136), occasionally made of ivory and with silver leaves.

The same oval form of the tea vessels was used by Revere in shaping a large tray (Fig. 29) and for enclosing the initials of its owner in a medallion lightly suspended by a fragile ribbon. Its modified roundness is emphasized by shallow lobings and vestigial shells. The total effect is one of great elegance and refinement.

[30] Sauceboat, by Anthony Rasch and Co. (w.1807–1825), Philadelphia, c.1810. Engraved with arms of the Carroll family of Baltimore. Length: 11⅞". *Courtesy, The Metropolitan Museum of Art, Sansbury Mills Fund, 1959*

THE REAFFIRMATION OF ANTIQUITY (1810–1840)

As the interest in Neo-Classicism progressed, styles became bolder and more strongly stated. The delicacy of the Adam shapes and motifs was replaced by the heavier forms and figures of monumental Egyptian, Greek, and Roman antiquities given vogue by the published drawings of Percier and Fontaine, who had accompanied Napoleon on his Egyptian campaign. France again led in the development of this new style, and because of the American alliance with France the innovations were eagerly received.

Not only were forms larger, the gauge of the silver was actually heavier. The scale was much bigger, and there was a greater emphasis on the horizontal axis of the design. Forms were generally simple and geometric, being semicircular, polygonal, or cubed. Vases and pitchers were sometimes modeled after Greek amphorae (Fig. 113). Greek and Roman vases, urns, and lamps served as models for other forms. The mixture of motifs was extraordinary, ranging from sphinx-like figures on heavy paw feet, to ram's heads and asps (Fig. 30). The previously delicate laurel vine became a stiff, milled border, and lotus blossoms and waterleaves became increasingly popular. The carved egg-and-dart moldings of ancient marbles were translated in silver into lobed borders and bases. Even in a relatively small object, such as an inkstand (Fig. 31) by Harvey Lewis, the monumental quality is apparent.

There is little doubt that one of the greatest contributions of this period is to be found in the beautifully sculpted cast decorations used for finials, handles, and caryatid supports. Because of the burgeoning patriotism, the American version of the eagle (Fig. 32) was often included in the repertoire of ancient motifs. Leaves abounded, sometimes in alternating layers of chased decoration, sometimes as cast or milled appliqués. In order to vary the machine-made ornament, more than one type of border embellished a single piece of silver, oak leaf and acorn borders being especially favored along with the sheaf of wheat, Greek-key, and geometric patterns.

As in the Baroque and late rococo periods, richness of design was achieved through a combination of many different techniques. Illustrative of various methods of embellishment, as well as heterogenous motifs, is the handsome candelabrum (Fig. 33) made by Andrew E. Warner of Baltimore. In its basic tripod structure the candelabrum is "antique," but within the center of the base there is also a cast full-length sculptural figure of Neptune, guarded by winged-caryatid supports on hoof-footed legs and festooned by opulent swags of fruit and flowers. The upper tier of the design contains a glass bowl for the centerpiece, held by a milled ring in a pierced rinceau pattern, and lighted by six candles held in leaf-bound branches. The effect is impressive and overpowering, as it was intended to be.

The antique style ran the gamut of designs and motifs until it exhausted itself. Finally, with the accession of Victoria to the throne of England in 1837, the severity of Neo-Classicism began to give way to Romanticism. In silver this meant a return to naturalism and, for the most part, a revival of mid-eighteenth-century Rococo decoration (Fig. 34). Gothic and naturalistic motifs returned. The forms ranged from bulky versions of eighteenth-century forms and even Classical shapes, to melon shapes and long lingering Empire forms (Fig. 35).

The Rococo Revival was succeeded in the 1860s by a Louis XVI revival, and in the 1870s by Neo-Renaissance and Neo-Greek revivals. Handwrought silver ceased to be the tradition and became the exception in a new age of machine production. By this time the skills of casting and chasing had been developed to such a point that details such as the bark of a branch used for a handle, or the mat surface of a leaf, were avidly incorporated into the mélange of ornaments. It was as

[31] Inkstand, by Harvey Lewis (c.1811–1825), Philadelphia, c.1815. Height: 3⁷⁄₁₆″.
Courtesy, Yale University Art Gallery, Mabel Brady Garvan Collection

if the repetition of designs made possible by machines required every ornament known to man to be included in a single object.

While a certain amount of variety is essential to good design, endless variation is exhausting, and some relief through the repetition of elements is necessary. The employment of novelty, variety, and inventiveness for its own sake, and without overall purpose or reason, calls attention to itself and shows its vulgarity. This is why much nineteenth-century art, with its indiscriminate borrowings from other ages and lack of assimilation, has been so widely criticized in the present day.

In any period of design, examples can be found which exemplify the finest qualities of the day. As the methods of manufacture change, so the basis of judgment must change. Throughout the fleeting fashions taken up by the early American silversmiths, however, certain fundamentals of good design can be seen. In objects of lasting beauty, quality

[32] Wine cooler, by Thomas Whartenby and Peter Bumm (w.1812–1818), Philadelphia, 1816. Presented to Commodore Decatur by the citizens of Philadelphia. Height: 15½″. *Courtesy, The Historical Society of Pennsylvania*

of workmanship is in balance with a familiarity of styles; mastery of techniques is in harmony with elements entirely of an age; variety and repetition are regulated by propriety and good proportion. It is the perfect combination of these elements which gives the best examples of American silver an ageless quality and universal beauty.

[33] Candelabrum, by Andrew E. Warner (1805–1870), Baltimore, 1817. Presented to Stephen Decatur by the citizens of Baltimore. Height: 20″. *Courtesy, Mrs. Edward Hopkinson, Jr.; photograph, courtesy, National Trust*

[35] Presentation set, by George K. Childs (w.1825–1850), Philadelphia, 1844. Presented to Gen. George Cadwalader for his abilities in suppressing the riots of May and July 1844. Heights: 31″. *Courtesy, Historical Society of Pennsylvania*

[34] Pitcher and tray, by Obadiah Rich (1809–1888), Boston, 1842. Presented to Uriel Crocker, Treasurer, by the Massachusetts Charitable Mechanic Association. Diameter: 13¼″ (tray). Height: 11½″ (pitcher). *Privately owned*

[35a] Beaker with handle, by Samuel Casey (c. 1724–c. 1770), South Kingstown, Rhode Island, c. 1766. Engraved with the initials of Thomas and Mary Vernon who were married in 1766. Height: 5½″. Marble Collection. *Courtesy, Los Angeles County Museum*

CHAPTER TWO

The Development of Forms

EVERY form in American silver felt the effect of the major stylistic changes which occurred in the arts, and it is interesting to see how the new fashions were adapted to the size, shape, and function of various types of silver, why certain new forms were developed or why certain old forms were discarded.

At the same time, it is essential to learn how each part of an object was formed, and which processes were involved in its manufacture. It helps to explain why certain forms, being difficult to make, were rarely produced in American shops, while other forms were very common. It is also necessary to discover the proper terminology, since many of the names originally applied to these objects are now archaic, and some of the modern names are misleading.

Since there are literally hundreds of different forms in American silver, it is best to consider the various items in groups arranged according to the purposes which they served. Drinking vessels, service objects such as tea sets and trays, and flatware constitute the major categories, but lighting devices and miscellaneous objects like sewing and writing equipment, toys, and little boxes deserve equal attention in their turn.

DRINKING VESSELS

CUPS

One of the first and largest groups of American silver consisted of the vessels used for drinking liquids. Among the earliest types was the little dram cup (Fig. 1) made by Hull and Sanderson, a small shallow dish, usually with two loop handles, still used by vintners and wine stewards today. Only two or three inches in diameter, these circular cups technically held just a dram of liquid. They had flat bottoms and slightly rounded sides formed by forging (see p. 204). The decoration usually consisted of simple chased panels containing stylized floral motifs. The handles were formed by putting a wire into a vise and twisting, and then shaping the wire into a curved handle which could be soldered to the body at top and bottom. In New York a larger version of this same form (Fig. 36) was made at the end of the seventeenth century and the beginning of the eighteenth century. Usually four to five inches in diameter, these drinking bowls occasionally had handles cut from a flat

[36] Drinking bowl, by Jacob Boelen (1659–1729), New York, c.1690. Diameter: 4⅛". *Courtesy, The Minneapolis Institute of Arts*

piece of silver in the same shape as the twisted wire handles. A round, shaped handle was used by John Coney on his dram cups (Fig. 37), which had curved sides and no paneling. By the second quarter of the eighteenth century, the form had become obsolete both in New York and New England.

Another seventeenth-century drinking vessel that did not survive long was the two-handled cup. Although used for various sorts of foods and drinks originally, these are referred to today as caudle cups (caudle was a type of thin porridge mixed with ale or wine and flavored with sugar and spice). The earliest American examples (Fig. 131), made by Hull and Sanderson, had gourd-shaped bodies supported by a narrow

[37] Early eighteenth-century Boston cups, left to right, by George Hanners (1696?–1746?), John Coney (1656–1722), and John Edwards (1671–1746). Diameters: 2¾", 2⅞", and 2¹⁄₁₆". *Hanners and Edwards cups, courtesy, Essex Institute; Coney dram cup, courtesy Mr. and Mrs. G. Jeffries Harrington; photograph by Richard Merrill*

ring of molding or a stepped base. They were decorated with chased panels in the lower section and pounced initials in the upper section. The ear-shaped handles either were twisted wires or were cast with leaf and beaded decoration. In the last quarter of the seventeenth century, repoussé decoration or gadrooning was sometimes substituted for the paneling in the base, or the cup was left plain so that engraved arms could decorate the sides (Fig. 38). Elaborate cast caryatid handles were added. Covers could accompany the cups to keep the beverages warm.

In New York a particular type of two-handled covered cup (Fig. 11) was developed which had three knop finials on the lid so that the cover could serve as a dish when it was inverted. Since a lump of sugar was

[38] Caudle cup, by John Coney, Boston, 1679. Engraved with Addington arms. Height: 6⅞". *Courtesy, Yale University Art Gallery, Mabel Brady Garvan Collection*

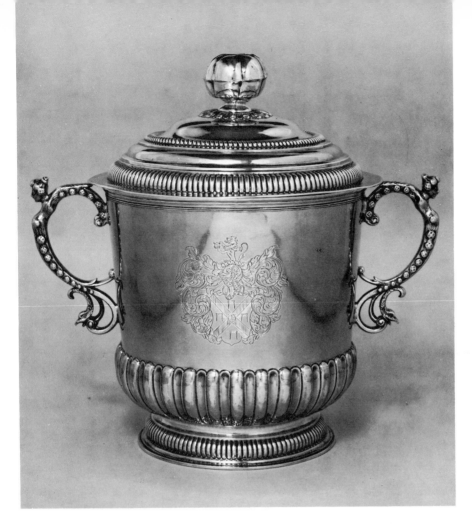

[39] Covered cup, by John Coney, Boston, 1701. Engraved with arms of Lieutenant Governor William Stoughton, who presented the cup to Harvard University. Height: 10". *Courtesy, Fogg Art Museum, Harvard University*

often served with the brandy, a dish was a very suitable accompaniment to the cup.

Such covered cups were used on special occasions, and as a result a larger version of this same basic form (Fig. 39) developed in the eighteenth century. Now known as grace cups or "loving cups," these communal covered vessels (Fig. 19) were given as special presentations. Because they were meant to be impressive, their shape changed quickly with the current fashion, from the circular body of the early eighteenth century to the urn-shaped body of the late eighteenth century, and finally into the "antique" form (Fig. 32) of the nineteenth century.

Cups supported on tall baluster bases and a round foot, imported as a form of domestic silver in the seventeenth century, were more often without a cover in this country (Fig. 3). Descended from the medieval hanap or wine cup, the standing cup also had a ceremonial connotation. In some instances the body of the cup could be made from a turned piece of maple or a hollowed-out coconut shell with silver mountings.

Until the Revolution, the goblet form was used more in churches than in homes. By that time the body of the cup had become less straight-sided and more oviform (Fig. 40), and the baluster more uniform in its shaping. The set of six goblets made by Paul Revere for Nathaniel and Mary (Lee) Tracy is particularly interesting because it was recorded in Revere's daybook on April 15, 1782, and is one of the few instances where the gilding inside the cups can be proven to be original. Revere charged eighteen shillings apiece for gilding them, three pounds each for making them, and six shillings each for engraving the Tracys' initials on them.

In the nineteenth century, the oviform cup continued and the bases became even plainer and smoother in their shaping. Beading and engraved borders were used around 1800, and leafage and Neo-Classical motifs were introduced shortly thereafter.

BEAKERS AND TUMBLERS

While there is some confusion in terms, cups without baluster supports were usually referred to as beakers if they had flat bases, tumblers if they had rounded bases, and simply as cups if they had handles. Beakers, which derived from earlier horn vessels, were frequently shorter in New England than in New York. Some were made without a base molding, like the example made by Hull and Sanderson in 1659 (Fig. 2). The seventeenth-century beakers were usually straight-sided or tapered slightly in their cylindrical form, while in the eighteenth century the body became more curvilinear and was shaped like an inverted bell. Samuel Casey of Rhode Island made a plain pair of footed beakers with curved lips for Esther Helme, and Daniel Christian Fueter made a similar footed beaker (Fig. 125) which was elaborately engraved with contemporary political cartoons.

At the end of the eighteenth century, the bodies had become straight-sided again, as indicated by those made by Richard Humphreys of Philadelphia for George Washington (Fig. 41). In 1780 Humphreys made a set of six large "Camp Cups," as he called them, as well as a pair of small ones.[10] In 1795 Paul Revere made a set of eight beakers and engraved them to match a French example (Figs. 122, 123) for Elias Hasket Derby. It is this basic beaker form, with the addition of a molded rim and foot band, which continued in the nineteenth century and remains popular today as the famous "mint julep cup" of the South.

Technically, tumblers have rounded bases and were made of thicker silver. The form became popular in England toward the end of the seventeenth century, but in America their popularity seems to have been confined chiefly to New York and only until the middle of the eighteenth century. One of the most handsome examples (Fig. 42) was the work of an unidentified New York maker and is engraved with the Van Schaik arms in heavily foliated mantling.

SMALL CUPS

Ordinary cups, three or four inches high, smaller and lighter than canns or mugs, were made in all periods and with many variations. Frequently they took the form of a caudle cup or else a beaker with a single handle added on the side. At first the handles were flat strap handles (Fig. 37), but this changed to a cast C-scroll handle with occasional graduated beading or, by the mid-eighteenth century, to acanthus leafage at the top. By the nineteenth century, the cups were made of seamed silver and in enormous quantities for presentation to children. They reflect clearly the successive stylistic changes from the Classical beading and refined moldings of about 1800 to the more ornate leafage of the 1820s and the Rococo Revival ornamentation of the 1840s.

A specialized version of these little cups, used for feeding children or invalids, was the spout cup (Fig. 43). A seventeenth-century form, spout cups usually had a thin curving spout placed at right angles to the handle, and often had a lid with a finial. The shape of the earliest American spout cups was like that of sixteenth-century German stoneware jugs, with a globular body and wide, reeded neck. An example made by Jeremiah Dummer is unusual in having two handles. Most examples of this short-lived form seem to have been made in New England, although rare Philadelphia and New York specimens have survived. In the eighteenth century the spout cup was replaced by the pap boat, a shallow, boat-shaped, elongated bowl with a wide lip at one end. Being without a foot or cover, and having no surface ornamentation, the pap boat is a rather awkward and undistinguished form.

MUGS AND CANNS

Large cups with single handles were called either mugs or canns. The two terms were used interchangeably in the eighteenth century, but

[40] Pair of goblets, by Paul Revere, Boston, 1782. Engraved with initials of Nathaniel and Mary (Lee) Tracy, who paid £38/10/8 for six goblets on April 15, 1782, of which £5/8 was for gilding inside the cups and £1/16 for engraving the cyphers. Height: 5⁵⁄₁₆″. *Courtesy, Museum of Fine Arts, Boston*

[41] Cup, by Richard Humphreys, Philadelphia, 1780. Made for George Washington and engraved with his crest. Height: 1¹¹⁄₁₆″. *Courtesy, Yale University Art Gallery, Mabel Brady Garvan Collection*

[42] Tumbler, by unidentified H.H., New York, c.1695. Engraved with arms and initials of the Van Schaik family. Height: 2⅝". *Courtesy, Yale University Art Gallery, Mabel Brady Garvan Collection*

[43] Spout cup, by Jeremiah Dummer, Boston, c. 1700. Engraved D^{H}E for Daniel and Elizabeth Henchman, who were married in 1713. Height: 5⅝₆". *Courtesy, Museum of Fine Arts, Boston*

[44] Mug, by Francis Richardson, Sr. (1681–1729), Philadelphia, c.1728. Made for Phebe Sharples as a bequest from her betrothed, Josiah Hibberd of Chester County. Height: 5⅛". *Courtesy, Henry Francis du Pont Winterthur Museum*

today a mug generally refers to a straight-sided or slightly tapering vessel with a molded base, while a cann refers to a tulip-shaped vessel with a rounded base on a domed circular foot.

The earliest mugs (Fig. 44) were almost as wide at the top as at the bottom, and had widely scrolled handles made of two flat pieces of silver, upper and lower, which were soldered along the two sides and finished at the end with a flat, shield-shaped terminal. The upper rim had a molded edge or was grooved to look like molding, and the base was supported by a wide, splayed molding. An alternate type of handle was the flat strap handle with reeding or graduated beading running from top to bottom. The bodies were left plain or had wide bands of circumferential multiple reeding. By the second quarter of the eighteenth century, a single mid-band was used, at first placed rather low on the body but gradually rising to the midsection. Cast scrolled handles replaced the earlier handles, and simpler base moldings were used.

Toward the end of the century, cylindrical mugs hooped like a barrel came into fashion, with squared hollow scrolled handles.

The cann form with a rounded body made its appearance about 1720; it was usually supported by a circular domed foot. At first rather bulbous (Fig. 45), it often had a heavy drop placed under the top of the cast scrolled handle and a flat furl placed on top. By mid-century the body had become more pear-shaped (Fig. 203) and the handle more elaborately scrolled, with an acanthus leaf instead of a flat furl at its top. While the engraving of arms on the front of these canns changed from Rococo to Classical at the end of the century (Fig. 122), the basic form did not change much; and by the nineteenth century, with the increased manufacture of both ceramic and glass drinking vessels, silver mugs and canns began to disappear from the scene.

TANKARDS

The same general development of form and fate can be seen in the tankard, which was a lidded version of the mug. The earliest tankards, like the one made by Robert Sanderson (Fig. 6), had almost straight

[45] Cann, by John Cowell, Boston, c.1728. Engraved on handle T^{I}M. Height: 5½". *Courtesy, Heritage Foundation, Deerfield, Mass.*

sides, a very flat lid, a cusped thumbpiece, and a widely sweeping handle made in two sections, like those on mugs. A generation later, the tankard made by Jeremiah Dummer (Fig. 46) had only a slightly higher stepping to the lid and a tiny bit of crenelation to the lip, but a huge and handsome cast lion that rested on a ridged rat-tail spine served as a thumbpiece, and the decoration on each side of the pinned hinge was much more elaborately crenelated. The only other American tankard with a lion thumbpiece, fashionable in English silver from about 1670 to 1685, was made by Dummer's contemporary Timothy Dwight, who also decorated the base with elaborate repoussé acanthus leafage. Cut-card decoration on the lid or behind the handle (Fig. 134), gadrooning around the step of the lid, and reeding or graduated beading down the length of the handle were other forms of decoration added to tankards at the end of the seventeenth century. Cast cherub's heads were used as handle terminals, and the rat-tail spine underneath the handle began to diminish in length. The crenelated lip at the front edge of the lid became more widely scalloped. The most typical thumbpiece was a scrolled one resembling a ram's horn, but there were variations such as the dolphin-and-mask thumbpiece used in Massachusetts and the co-coon-shaped thumbpiece used in New York.

Because the handles were made in two sections, there is an air vent cut into them on the underneath side, usually under the terminal decoration but occasionally under the top of the handle. This was to allow for the escape of air when the handle was heated and soldered to the body. The presence of the opening has given rise to the fiction that this was a whistle used to call for another drink. While this story is false, some early tankards did have short pegs affixed at proper intervals down the inside of the body to indicate how much of a drink was to be taken when a tankard was passed round the table. An example made by Cornelius Kierstede of New York has five shaped pegs placed inside on a vertical line with the handle.

Coins and medals were sometimes set into the lid or were used as handle terminals. This, as well as the pegs, was a common tradition in Northern Europe and Scandinavia, and it occurred more frequently in New York silver than in New England. The European practice of setting coins into the sides of the body of a tankard was evidently not taken up in America, although the engraving of cyphers in circlets on the front of tankards gives the impression of imitating inset coins or medals.

In the eighteenth century, tankards (Fig. 141) grew taller and had much more taper to the body. The handles were less widely scrolled and had a simple cast drop at the top and a mask or a plain oval handle

[46] Tankard, by Jeremiah Dummer, Boston, c.1685. Originally owned by William Foxcroft. Engraved with Foxcroft arms. Owned by Phoebe Foxcroft, who married Samuel Phillips in 1773. Height: 8″. *Privately owned*

terminal. Underneath the top of the handle, the rat-tail disappeared altogether, leaving a plain rounded joint. The base moldings became wider and a mid-band was added. The lids became domed and then doubled-domed. In New England the lids were tightly fitted, often with a finial added to the top.

Tankards with rounded bodies were made during the mid-century (Fig. 112). Philadelphia particularly favored this type of tankard, frequently in combination with an open thumbpiece and a heart-shaped handle terminal. Although the earlier, flat-lidded type of tankard persisted in New York until after the Revolution, the rounded-body form was finally taken up there as well, with an open thumbpiece and with a tapering molded handle terminal.

By the end of the eighteenth century, when the tankard had begun to decline in popularity, one final innovation in form was introduced. This was the hooped tankard (Fig. 27), in fashion in Philadelphia in the 1780s after English styles and continued into the nineteenth century, when Samuel Williamson made a hooped tankard with a domed lid and eagle finial.

PORRINGERS

Another form which paralleled tankards in popularity and duration was the porringer. The earliest American porringers (Fig. 47) were simply formed, with flat bottoms and almost straight sides to the circular bowls, resembling an inverted skillet cover, with a single flat handle soldered horizontally on one side. The handles, which were frequently engraved in the center with the owner's initials, were cast in a sand mold, even though the pattern looks as though it had been cut with a file. The piercings of the seventeenth-century porringer handles were geometric, and heraldic in nature. In New England, circular openings were combined with crescents, tablets, and crosses. In New York, more complicated arrangements of diamonds, hearts, and crosses were used (Fig. 48).

By the eighteenth century the bowls had become shaped with rounded sides and an everted narrow lip. The bases were flat around the outer circumference, but were slightly domed in the center. Several variations in handle piercings were developed. In New England, a pattern known as crown-cresting was made by several Boston silversmiths, and in New York, a handle with three large openings was used.

By 1725 the keyhole piercing had come into vogue, distinguished by the shape of the opening at the tip of the handle (Fig. 49). This pattern became universally popular and could be found on porringers in every colony. It is the pattern which is still favored today for reproductions. So traditional did the keyhole handle become that very few innovations were made after its appearance, except in New York, where a large diamond piercing was used during the late Rococo period and a script-initial piercing during the Classical period.

On rare occasions, covers accompanied the porringer (Fig. 48), in the tradition of the French *écuelle* (a large covered porringer form which had two flat handles instead of a single one). Style changes can be seen in the lids: the early examples were flat, while the later lids were domed and occasionally had a cast finial.

Usually made in pairs or sets, porringers were available in many different sizes, pint and half-pint sizes being most popular. They could be used for anything for which the modern cereal bowl can be used. As the name implies, the form was primarily for eating porridge, but Dr. Alexander Hamilton, while traveling in the colonies in 1744, drank a porringer of milk, and at least one colonial lady left a record of using her porringer to mix her rouge.[11]

In England the single-handled shallow bowl which we know as a porringer is generally called a cupping or bleeding bowl, while the English porringer is the two-handled cup known as a caudle cup in American silver. Since the English porringer had declined in popularity early in the eighteenth century, the development of this form in American silver was in a sense unique, owing to its enormous popularity here as a useful article and also to the special designs developed here for the handles.

FLATWARE

KNIVES AND FORKS

American silver-handled knives are unknown until the nineteenth century, and forks were only rarely made here before that time. The few colonial forks that were made were usually short (Fig. 54) and were probably used for dessert or sweets. The earliest examples have only two tines; the third tine was added in the eighteenth century, and a fourth tine in the nineteenth century (Fig. 56).

Occasionally, in the seventeenth century, the fork was conjoined with a spoon (Fig. 50) to form a sucket or sweetmeat fork. The fork end was used for eating preserved plums and grapes, and the spoon end for the thick syrup in which they were served. Not many sweetmeat or sucket forks were made by American silversmiths, because the fashion

[47] Porringer, by John Hull and Robert Sanderson, Boston, c.1655. Engraved A^M I for Arthur and Johannah Mason of Boston, who were married in 1655. Diameter: 4¾". *Courtesy, Museum of Fine Arts, Boston*

[48] Covered porringer, by Jan Niewkerk (w.1708–1716), New York, c.1710. Length: 11¼". *Courtesy, The Metropolitan Museum of Art, Bequest of A. T. Clearwater, 1933*

[49] Porringers (left to right), by Jeffrey Lang (1707–1758), Salem, c.1745, diameter: 5"; Edward Winslow (1669–1753), Boston, c.1700, diameter: 4¾"; Joseph Foster (1760–1839), Boston, 1791, gift of Joseph Hiller to S. Foster, diameter: 5¼". *Courtesy, Essex Institute, Salem, Mass.; photograph by Richard Merrill*

[50] Set of four sucket forks, by Bartholomew Le Roux (1663–1713), New York, c.1710. All engraved GS for Gertrude Schuyler, and two, E^{P}L for Peter and Elizabeth Lansing of Albany. Length: 4¾". *Courtesy, Heritage Foundation, Deerfield, Mass.*

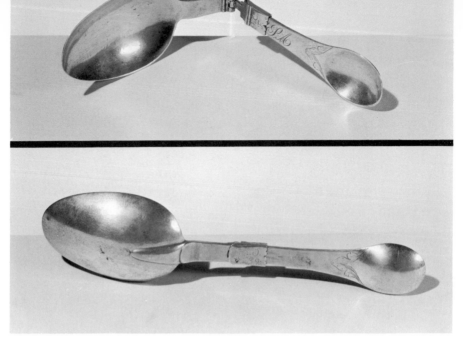

[51] Folding spoon, by Caesar Ghiselin (1670–1734), Philadelphia, c.1700. Length: 7⅛". *Courtesy, Philadelphia Museum of Art; photograph by A. J. Wyatt, Staff Photographer*

was limited and did not last long after 1700. Examples by William Rouse of Boston, by Jesse Kip and Bartholomew Le Roux of New York, and by Johan Nys of Philadelphia are known today, and all have the rat-tail drop on the back of the spoon bowl which is characteristic of spoons in the late seventeenth and early eighteenth centuries. By 1790 the form was so little known that "½ dozen Sweetmeet Silver Spoons, with Round Ladle Bowls, twisted Shafts, & two pronged forks on the Handle" were described as an oddity by the Reverend William Bentley when he saw them at a friend's house in Salem, Massachusetts.[12] Another oddity of the seventeenth century was the folding spoon (Fig. 51), a single example of which survives from the hand of Caesar Ghiselin.

SPOONS

Spoons had been made for centuries with fig-shaped bowls, straight stems, and decorative finials at the end. No examples of the "Apostle" or "seal top" spoons, so popular in seventeenth-century England, are known by American silversmiths. The earliest colonial silver spoons were made by Hull and Sanderson. An example of the "slip-end" type current about 1660, at Yale, features a fig-shaped bowl with a V-shaped drop on the back. The handle is slender and polygonal, with the end chamfered so that it looks like a slipped stalk (hence the name "slip-end"). Another early type, known as a "Puritan" spoon and popular in the 1660s, had a flattened handle with a squared end and a generous, more ovoid bowl.

Toward the end of the seventeenth century, the trifid handle was introduced (Fig. 53), with the flattened end split into three parts. At this time, the back of the bowl was hammered into a swage to give it a relief decoration of leafage and graduated beading in scrolls around a long, ridged rat-tail drop.

Early in the eighteenth century, the handle was shaped into a wavy end (Fig. 54) and there was only a plain rat-tail on the back of the bowl. It was only a short step from this type of spoon to the rounded handle ending known as spatulate (Fig. 55), which is one of the most popular patterns ever devised. The handle has a ridge running down the center

[52] "Slip-end" spoon, by John Hull and Robert Sanderson, Boston, c. 1665. Engraved with initials of William and Hannah Brown of Salem, who were married in 1664. Length: 6⅞". *Courtesy, Essex Institute, Salem, Massachusetts; photograph by Richard Merrill*

[53] Trifid spoon, by John Edwards, Boston, c.1695. Engraved on back I^{G}M. Length: 7¼". *Courtesy, Henry Francis du Pont Winterthur Museum*

of it, and the thickened end turns up slightly and curves in to meet the ridge. The rat-tail on the back of the bowl continued for a while and then began to disappear about 1725, when a spatulate drop or a shell drop was used instead. The attention to details and the engraving of family initials on the back of these spoons is explained by the fact that they had been placed face down on the table. Only in rare instances (Fig. 130) was a swage design used on the front of the handle ending, repeating the shell on the back, with scrolls and perhaps a floral motif.

By mid-century there was a great deal of variety in the decoration of spoons. Different types of rococo shells and floral or furled leaf designs were used in different areas. A plain double drop was an alternative decoration for the back of the bowl (Fig. 56b). A new kind of handle was introduced in the 1760s which is known today as the Onslow pattern, consisting of a handle which turned back and ended in a volute. Edmund Milne of Philadelphia advertised that he had imported such "fluted and polished sauce spoons, with scroll heads," and a few large spoons and ladles were made by American silversmiths in this design.[13]

[54] Spoon and fork, by John Coney, Boston, c.1700. Length: 4½″. *Courtesy, Museum of Fine Arts, Boston*

[55] Set of gold spatulate teaspoons and strainer spoon, by Simeon Soumain, New York, c.1730. Made for Hugh Hall of Barbados and Boston, and mentioned in an account he took of his plate June 25, 1750. Length: 4¹⁄₁₆″ (teaspoons), 4⁹⁄₁₆″ (strainer) spoon. *Courtesy, Yale University Art Gallery, Mabel Brady Garvan Collection*

Spoons with turned-back handles had completely replaced the earlier spatulate design by 1783, when William Haverstick of Philadelphia announced that he had two tablespoons suspected of being stolen which had "handles turned the old fashion way and marked with two letters on the back of the handles." [14] With the new handles (Fig. 56c) a change had occurred in the placement of engraved initials and crests on the front instead of the back, indicating a change also in the way the spoons were placed on the table. The front of the handle was often further ornamented with a sort of gadrooned border or "feather edge." Drops on the back of the bowl ranged from a simple rounded single drop to the design of a bird with an olive branch (Fig. 178), sometimes sitting on top of an open cage with a banner proclaiming "I Love Liberty."

Toward the end of the eighteenth century, the spoon handles became much more pointed and the bowls more ovoid in shape (Fig. 56e). A bright-cut border was substituted for the feather-edge and the initials, usually in script, were placed in a faceted oval or shield-shaped enclosure with a bow knot or delicate flowers surrounding it and running down the length of the handle. A variation in the shape of the handle ending was provided briefly around 1800 by the so-called coffin handle (Fig. 56g), with canted corners instead of the oval tip.

An innovation to the other end of the handle, in the form of projections near the juncture of the bowl, was introduced at the end of the eighteenth century but did not come into general fashion until early in the next century (Fig. 56h). By that time the bowls had become wider and more pointed on the end. The backs had lost their drops completely or had only a vestigial V-shaped outline. Engraved script initials were often placed lengthwise on the handle, which was now shaped like a fiddle. A variety of stamped Classical designs was used to decorate the end, including baskets of fruit and flowers, sheafs of wheat, and even profile busts of Washington.

During the Rococo Revival, shell motifs reappeared and the handle returned to a spatulate design, although the mid-rib was lacking this time. Occasionally, the shape of the handle was outlined with single or double ridging (Fig. 56i). This "threaded" pattern was made as early as the 1790s but enjoyed rather limited success here, although it was very popular in English silver. The more widely accepted pattern in the 1830s was the plain spatulate design, fashioned from very thin sheet silver, with incurving sides to the handle ending and rounded shoulders near the juncture with the bowl.

The mid-nineteenth century saw a variety of patterns—acorns and oak leaves abounded, formed with machine dies (Fig. 56 l)—as well as

[56] Series of American spoons and a fork, by various makers, showing the development from about 1740 to about 1860, from (a) upper left to (l) lower right. *Privately owned; photograph by Richard Merrill*

greater variation in the shapes of the handles. The shaft of the spoon tapered very thinly just before it joined the bowl. The shoulders disappeared, and there was a return to the pointed handle elaborately engraved with the Victorian version of Rococo and other eclectic ornament.

SPECIALIZED SPOONS

The variety in size and specialized functions of spoons had changed enormously from the seventeenth century, when one medium-sized spoon was considered a luxury and was used for many different things. Early in the eighteenth century, large serving spoons supplemented the ordinary tablespoon, and small spoons were made for eating custard and pap and for drinking tea and chocolate. In the mid-eighteenth century, strainer spoons (Fig. 55) were also occasionally made to clear leaves and other debris from tea or punch. In place of the spatulate handle, these so-called mote spoons were often fashioned with a very thin, pointed handle which could be used to free the strainer in the base of the teapot spout from clogged tea leaves. Because of the thinness of the handle and the piercing in the bowl, strainer spoons are rarely fully marked, either here or in England, and American examples are therefore hard to substantiate.

Toward the end of the eighteenth century, American silversmiths on occasion made caddy spoons (Fig. 28) to scoop tea out of tea caddies. These were often shaped as scallop shells. Another type of scoop was the marrow spoon (Fig. 57), which had a long narrow channel in the handle and a slightly wider and shorter scoop where the bowl would have been. These were used for retrieving the marrow from bones, marrow being considered a great delicacy by the eighteenth-century diner. Although in 1765 Joseph Edwards, Jr., of Boston charged Joshua Green for a marrow spoon (see page 243), relatively few were made by American silversmiths. However, early in the nineteenth century there was a minor fad for this form in Albany, where several marrow scoops were made, usually with a diamond-shaped mid-section.

[57] Marrow spoon, by Shepherd and Boyd (1806–1830), Albany, 1815. Made for Anne Stevenson (1774–1821), second wife of Pierre van Cortlandt II, at a cost of $3.50. Length: 9^{11}⁄₁₆″. *Courtesy, Museum of the City of New York, bequest of Joseph B. Brenauer*

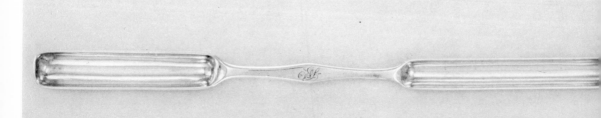

[58] Early nineteenth-century teaspoons, salt and mustard spoons, and ladles, by John Vogler (w.1803–1827), Winston-Salem, North Carolina. *Courtesy, Old Salem*

Salt spoons only a few inches long were made by American silversmiths from the second quarter of the eighteenth century on, although few of the early shovel-shaped examples have survived. The handles of salt spoons (Fig. 58) followed the style of larger spoons, but the bowls were wider and much rounder, often shaped like a shell. In the nineteenth century similar spoons with very long, thin handles became popular for serving mustard; they can usually be distinguished by their badly tarnished bowls.

LADLES

Gravy or sauce spoons and small ladles are easily recognized by their large round bowls and the exaggerated curvature of the handles. A large ladle used for punch, or more often perhaps for soup, could have a silver handle like spoon handles, or else its silver bowl could be attached to a long twisted whalebone or turned wooden handle. It is not unusual to find that the bowl was made from a single silver coin, such as the punch ladles "out of Dollars" advertised by Charles Harris of Charleston, South Carolina, in 1768.[15] During the Rococo period, punch ladles often had scalloped bowls, which became more widely fluted and oval in shape in the Classical period. The nineteenth-century ladles had almost circular bowls, very plain, and their silver handles were more widely curved.

FISH SERVERS

Fish slices or fish servers were made in the late eighteenth century but did not gain in popularity until the early nineteenth century. While they were sometimes triangular in shape, like modern pie servers, they were made of thin silver and were elaborately pierced and engraved, often with a fish delineated in the center.

SKEWERS

Skewers were not often made in American silver, and, unlike modern skewers, they were flat instead of round and had a good deal of taper to their length, going from perhaps an inch at one end to nothing at the other end. The circular opening at the wide end, used as a handle, was usually left plain but in a few instances was shaped along its outer edge.

TEA TONGS

Tea tongs were introduced in the second quarter of the eighteenth century, the earliest examples being shaped like scissors with a flat circular hinge and with plain or scalloped shell-shaped nippers. In the Rococo period, the arms were made of conjoined sections of curves and furls (Fig. 59), and a double hinge was used to conceal the joint. By the 1760s a new, bow-shaped type of tongs was introduced. The long straight arms were cast and chased in an intricately pierced pattern and soldered to a hammered arch to form "spring tongs." In the Classical period, these were made from one piece of silver (Fig. 28) cut out from a thin sheet of metal and decorated with bright-cut and other engraving down the long tapering arms to the oval or acorn grips. This same form continued into the Victorian period with suitable changes in the engraved ornamentation.

PUNCH STRAINERS

Punch strainers were introduced into American silver in the mid-eighteenth century. The earliest examples were simple round pieces of silver, with a shallow shaping, piercings in a geometric pattern, and a plain hook-type handle. In the Rococo period, two handles were used and became long enough to bridge the top of a punch bowl. They were elaborately shaped, somewhat like a porringer handle although open in the center (Fig. 60). The rims of these punch strainers were frequently gadrooned to match the carving on the scrolls of the handle. In the Classical period, the strainers had beaded decoration and the handles were formed of thinner, barely curved elements.

SERVING PIECES

SALTS

To the colonists table salt was as precious a commodity as it had been in the old country. The processing of this now common household item was laborious and costly. It is no wonder that when it was placed at the table it was located at first nearest the most important people and in very fancy receptacles. From this practice has derived the phrase "below the salt" to describe lesser people.

The Elizabethan salts had been diminutive versions of the great standing salts, which had been the single most important piece of domestic plate in the Middle Ages. At the time the first American examples were being made, the form had a circular base, a trumpet or spool-shaped body, a shallow well, and four scrolled knop finials which may have supported a napkin as a cover or a dish. During the Baroque period, the bases and upper sections became octagonally shaped, and bands of gadrooning and a molded mid-band were added (Fig. 61).

By 1700, in England the standing salt had given way to a salt half the size, as salt was no longer so dear and people in great houses no longer dined altogether at one long table. These smaller salts were called trencher salts, since they were placed beside each guest's trencher, or plate. American examples in the Baroque style were made in both Boston and New York with gadrooned borders at the top and bottom of their bell-shaped bodies. In the second decade of the eighteenth century, the American trencher salts were often octagonal in shape (Fig. 62).

By the mid-eighteenth century, the bodies of the salts had become

[59] Scissors tongs, by Charles Oliver Bruff (1735–1817), New York, c.1765. Length: 5". *Courtesy, Henry Francis du Pont Winterthur Museum*

[60] Punch strainer, by Jonathan Clarke (1706–1766), Newport and Providence, R.I., 1766. Made for Jabez Bowen, Providence January 17, 1766. Length: 11⅞". *Courtesy, Yale University Art Gallery, Mabel Brady Garvan Collection*

[61] Standing salt, by Edward Winslow, Boston, c.1710. Engraved I^{E}M, and with lion head. Height: 5½". *Courtesy, Museum of Fine Arts, Boston*

circular and were supported by three or four cast feet on incurved legs, with a convex design like a shell on the knee (Fig. 63). This design continued with little change, except the addition of repoussé to the body or gadrooning to the edge, until the Classical period, when oval, pierced salt cellars with colored-glass linings and beaded edges were introduced. Glass linings had been used during the preceding period as well but became much more common after the Revolution. Another type of salt which became popular around 1800 was boat-shaped and was supported on a single oval or rectangular foot. Occasionally, two handles were added to these salts to make them easier to pass. In the second quarter of the nineteenth century, salts often reverted to earlier Rococo forms or revived the Classical oval beaded designs of the immediate past.

CASTERS AND CRUET STANDS

The shakers which we think of today as being used for salt were originally used to serve mustard, pepper, and sugar. They were usually made in pairs, or sets of three if the larger container for sugar was included. This form, used for "casting" condiments on food, was not

[62] Trencher salt, by Jacob Hurd, Boston, c.1730. Height: 1⅜″. *Courtesy, The Metropolitan Museum of Art, Rogers Fund, 1943*

introduced generally as a separate item of English silver until the last quarter of the seventeenth century.

The first American examples were made about 1700 and were straight-sided cylinders with gadrooning around the lower edge of the body and top (Fig. 64). The two parts were held together by a bayonet joint on each side. A mid-band, cut-card decoration, a finial, and perhaps a coat of arms further added to the decoration of the piece. The piercings of the lid were the most distinctive part of the decoration. (Often the piercings of the lid of the dry-mustard caster were only simulated and were left blind.) Other early eighteenth-century casters had a much lower, domed lid with simpler piercings and a single scrolled handle, more like what we think of today as a kitchen dredger. These became octagonal in shape about 1725, and frequently there was an engraved device on one of the octagonal sections of the lid's bezel, corresponding to a similar marking on one section of the body, to indicate exactly which way the lid fit. Occasionally, the caster was raised up on three feet, but more often it had a molding for a base. Casters soon lost their handles and took their place along side the developing pear-shaped caster, until they were finally given up in the mid-eighteenth century. One of the earliest pear-shaped casters was made by John Coney with a plain curvilinear body, compass-patterned piercings in the lid, a large, circular finial, and bayonet fastenings (Fig. 65). Mid-bands were soon added to this form, the pear-shaping became more accentuated, and the middle section above the bulge of the caster became more attenuated (Fig. 66).

After 1750, the lid also became taller in proportion, the area around the piercings was engraved with alternating sections of diapering and foliated designs, and a bell or pine cone finial was added. About the time of the Revolution, the body of the caster became shaped like an inverted pear, and was formed of two separate pieces, as some of the earlier casters had been; that is, the neck was formed from a shaped piece of silver seamed vertically which was soldered to a forged base, the horizontal joint being covered over by a mid-band. Domed circular feet supported these casters. This type of caster continued into the Classical period, and it was not until the end of the eighteenth century that the urn-shaped caster with urn finial was introduced, with a deeper body, shorter neck, and reduced lid. Circular or oval domed feet or square plinths supported these casters. This was not a very pleasingly proportioned form and in the nineteenth century was shortly replaced by glass casters with silver lids.

Often the casters were combined with cruets, the glass bottles which held vinegar and oil, and were fitted into a footed tray with a long

[63] Pair of salts, by Charles Le Roux (1689–1745), New York, c.1745. Height: 1$\frac{13}{16}$″. Engraved I^{S}A, probably for John and Ann Schuyler, who were married in 1737. *Courtesy, The Metropolitan Museum of Art, Dodge Fund. 1935*

[64] Caster, by Peter Van Dyck, New York, c.1715. Engraved with Schuyler arms. Height: 7½". *Courtesy, Yale University Art Gallery, The Mabel Brady Garvan Collection*

[65] One of a pair of casters, by John Coney, Boston, c.1710. Height: 5". *Courtesy, Museum of Fine Arts, Boston*

[66] Set of casters for sugar and two spices, by Adrian Bancker (1703–1772), New York, c.1730. Height: 7⅛″ (center) and 5¾″. *Courtesy, Museum of the City of New York*

[67] Cruet stand, by Thomas Fletcher and Sidney Gardiner (w. 1808–1827), Boston and Philadelphia, c. 1820. Weight: 62 oz. 5 dwt. Height: 11″. Diameter of base: 11½″. *Courtesy, Charles V. Swain*

central handle. Such caster stands or cruet stands had been introduced into American silver during the Rococo period, but while the frame might have been made in this country, the bottles were imported (Fig. 24). American examples in the Empire style were made in Philadelphia by John McMullin and by Fletcher and Gardiner (Fig. 67). Of unusually heavy silver, the Fletcher and Gardiner example weighs slightly over sixty-two ounces, excluding the glass containers. Casters in cruet stands were usually for Jamaica and Cayenne pepper, and in some instances there was also a caster for sugar or salt.

The container for the mustard took a very different course in the Classical period. It became a mustard pot, a straight-sided pot with an opening in the lid for a small long-handled spoon. Often made like the hooped tankard of the Classical period, it was referred to as a mustard tankard. Since mustard tarnishes silver very badly, these containers were fitted with glass liners. The American silversmiths had ordered glass liners for mustard containers from England prior to the Revolu-

[68] Mustard pot, by Baldwin & Co., Newark, N.J., c.1830. Glass liner not original. Height: 3¾". *Privately owned*

tion, and in the Classical period the silver became pierced so that the glass liners would show through on the sides. In the nineteenth century, the whole body was made of glass inset, with a hinged lid, and a frame supported by four legs formed of very thin soldered sections of silver and cast ornament (Fig. 68).

CHAFING DISHES

Chafing dishes, or braziers, as we would call them today, were used to keep food or liquids warm at the table. It is mildly horrifying to think of putting hot charcoals in the center of these pierced pans, but actually the charcoal did not create heat intense enough to damage the silver. Most of the chafing dishes in American silver date from the first half of the eighteenth century (Fig. 69). Often made in pairs, they usually had a single heavy turned wooden handle and three silver knops around the top to support the kettle or dish being warmed. There were usually three legs, the earliest being in the form of a bird's-claw foot clutching a wooden ball. By the second quarter of the eighteenth century, C-scrolls were used instead of the bird's claw, with or without the practical wooden ball feet. The sides of the dish were pierced to allow the heat to escape, at first just around the outer rim, in the center bottom, and around the base, and later around the sides of the body as well. The piercings follow general stylistic trends, with an interlaced heart pattern being favored for early examples and elaborate foliate and diaper patterns for Rococo examples. The form, which had never been very popular in England, does not seem to have been made in the Classical period here, although a much reduced version was used in the early nineteenth century as a pipe lighter and a container for burning charcoal.

SKILLETS AND SAUCEPANS

Skillets and saucepans were also used for serving hot food at the table. The skillet was a straight-sided vessel, supported by three cast feet, made in England in the second half of the seventeenth century. Only two examples of American skillets are known today. One made by William Rouse of Boston was fashioned with a hollow, tankard-type of handle on the body and a lid with a single flat horizontal handle, so that the lid could serve as a porringer when it was inverted (Fig. 230).

In the eighteenth century, the most popular shape for the saucepan was bulbous, curving in rather abruptly at the top, with a long turned wooden handle (Fig. 70) placed at right angles to the spout, and sometimes with a silver lid. An example by Gerrit Onckelbag of New York has a long hollow silver handle. Its lid was fashioned by another New York silversmith, Jesse Kip. While some examples of this form were large enough to be stewpans, others were small and may have been used for warming brandy or mulled wine. The saucepans were apparently referred to as panakins sometimes by the early silversmiths, and are called pipkins today. By the last quarter of the eighteenth century, the form became straight-sided with molded basebands. Beading was added to the edges in the Classical period, and there was less variety in the turnings of the handles.

SAUCEBOATS

Sauceboats, or butter boats, as they were sometimes called, were introduced into American silver in the first half of the eighteenth century. One of the earliest examples was made by Charles Le Roux and was fashioned in a boat shape with spouts at each end and with a handle in the center of each side. The more common form had only a single long pouring lip at one end and a scrolled handle at the other end

[69] Pair of chafing dishes, by John Coney, Boston, c.1700. Engraved with Hutch-inson crest. Length: 15″. *Privately owned*

[70] Saucepan, by James Geddy, Jr. (1731–1807), Williamsburg, Va., c.1750. Made for Colonel Preston. Handle is an early replacement. Length: 6⅞″. *Courtesy, Colonial Williamsburg; photograph by Delmore Wenzel*

(Fig. 24). With gracefully scalloped upper rims, the boats were supported by three curved legs with pad or shell feet and knees. In the
Rococo period the handles were often free-standing, but in the Classical
period they became simply curved.

By 1800 a single oval foot or only a molded base-band was used for
support and beading or a wire border decorated the smooth upper rim
of the boat. The sauce tureen with a shaped lid was introduced about
this time; it sometimes had an opening in its edge to accommodate the
handle of the sauce ladle (Fig. 71). There were two handles to facilitate
passing and serving. The decoration of the sauce tureen followed the
same designs as the large soup tureens, and they frequently were made
in sets of two or four to match. Sauce boats continued to be made at the
same time, and became very ornate in their "antique" decoration. The
free-standing handle could be in the shape of an angry asp (Fig. 30) or
a pendant lotus blossom. The four cast feet were frequently either
eagles or sphinxes. Occasionally a matching tray was made to hold the
boat to take care of the dripping from the lip.

SOUP TUREENS

When John Singleton Copley was in Paris in 1774 he was much
amazed to see "Soupp . . . in Silver Turenes." [16] It was not until about
1800 that silver tureens were made in his native America. Such large
and heavy pieces as tureens were not very practical in silver until thinly
rolled metal became readily available. With two large cast handles on
each side and a similar handle placed upright on the lid, the pair of
soup tureens (Fig. 72) made by Joseph Lownes for Benjamin W. Crowninshield were fashioned in an oblong shape, decorated with milled shell
borders, and supported by eagle claw-and-ball feet.

BREAD BASKETS

Another large form of serving silver was the bread basket, or cake
basket, as it is called today. A few Rococo examples are known in
American silver, all made in New York, with pierced sides, bail handles
and either four scrolled feet or a pierced base-band (Fig. 25). It was not
until the early nineteenth century, however, that this form was made in
any quantity, and even then they were considered very special. Dorothy
Quincy Hancock Scott noted in her will in 1830 that her large silver
cake basket was used at weddings, and she hoped that it would continue
to be used.[17] While some of these baskets were made with bail handles,
more often the handles were placed at, or were simple extensions of, the
narrow ends of their solid oblong bodies. A rectangular or oval domed

[71] Pair of sauce tureens, by Andrew E. Warner, Baltimore, Md., 1817. Presented by the citizens of Baltimore to Stephen Decatur. *Courtesy, Eliot D. Hawkins; photograph, courtesy, National Trust*

[72] Soup tureen, by Joseph Lownes (w.1780–1816), Philadelphia, c.1810. Originally owned by Secretary of the Navy Benjamin W. Crowninshield, and engraved with his initial C. Length: 16¾". *Privately owned; photograph by Richard Merrill*

foot with milled borders supported the deep body, and cast or engraved decoration ornamented the rim. Occasionally the rims were fashioned from a lattice of wire and regularly placed flat cast leaves.

TOAST RACKS

Another form constructed largely of molded wire and cast ornament was the toast rack (Fig. 73). Introduced into English silver about 1770, it was not until the early nineteenth century that the toast rack was made in American silver, and even then the number of examples is limited. A very practical and strikingly modern piece of silver, it frequently is used today to hold letters at a desk, but it was originally intended to keep toast from getting soggy at the table.

DISH RINGS AND DISH CROSSES

Dish rings, used to support hot dishes and protect the table, are rare in American silver. Wrongly thought to be Irish in origin and misnamed "potato rings," the form appeared in English silver at the beginning of the eighteenth century. More elaborate versions were made by the 1730s in Ireland, with intricate pierced designs. The only American example known today (Fig. 74) was made by Myer Myers about 1770, when the form reached its height of popularity abroad.

At the same time, a new type of dish stand was introduced which was formed of two adjustable cross-arms with a spirit lamp in the center. These were advertised as early as 1763 by Edmund Milne as "ex's, with sliders and lamps for dish stands." [18] Many dish crosses (or table crosses, as they were also called) were imported, and few were made here, although several have been attributed to New York makers.

SALVERS OR TRAYS

Flat trays designed to hold other vessels were originally referred to as salvers. When the form was first introduced in England, it was described in 1661 by Thomas Blount in his *Glossographia* as "a new fashioned piece of wrought plate, broad and flat, with a foot underneath, and is used in giving Beer or other liquid thing to save the Carpit or Cloathes from drops." The terms "server" and "weighter" or "waiter" were apparently used interchangeably in the eighteenth century, but the word "tazza" is a modern misnomer for this form.

The earliest of these salvers were supported on a central trumpet-shaped foot, as is found on Timothy Dwight's example (Fig. 4) made in

[73] Toast rack, by John Taylor and Horace Hinsdale (w.1804–1830), New York, c.1825. Length: 8¾". *Privately owned; photograph by Richard Merrill*

[74] Dish ring, by Myer Myers, New York, c.1770. Made for Samuel and Susan Cornell. Diameter: 8¹⁵⁄₁₆". *Courtesy, Yale University Art Gallery, Mabel Brady Garvan Collection*

the 1680s. At first the rims were simply reeded, but in the Baroque period a gadrooned border was added to the edge of the tray and around the foot.

Salvers were circular until the early eighteenth century, when a variety of shapes was introduced. Edward Winslow made a trefoil salver, while John Burt made an equally rare hexafoil salver (Fig. 75) about 1725. At this time the salvers were usually plain with molded rims. One of the most typical borders was scalloped with incurving corners and sides (Fig. 17). During the Rococo period, the rims were formed by a series of conjoined curves with applied cast borders of scallop shells or gadrooning. The supports for the salvers, too, had changed early in the eighteenth century from the single trumpet-shaped base to three or four little cast feet. The shape of these changed from a scrolled-knop sort of foot to a scroll-and-pad foot, and finally, in the Rococo period, to a cabriole leg, with a claw-and-ball foot or a shell foot (Fig. 76.). Toward the end of the eighteenth century, a French foot was substituted on small trays (Fig. 77), and large tea trays were more practical with no feet at all.

While the first trays had been quite small, a wide assortment of sizes was available after the Revolution, with oval shapes (Fig. 29) being especially favored around 1800, and circular or rectangular trays with canted corners (Fig. 156) supplementing the elliptical designs. The borders in the Classical period usually were decorated with beading, but occasionally one finds an example of the pierced rims so popular in English silver at that time (Fig. 77). In the nineteenth century, the edges might be enriched with machine-formed borders of stamped decoration or gadrooning (Fig. 137). Cast feet in a design of scrolls and paws or an eagle supported the trays. Large cast handles were often added to the heavier trays to make them easier to carry.

PLATES, PLATTERS, AND DISHES

Plates and dishes are rare in American silver until the nineteenth century. One of the few early examples is a plate made by John Coney with a very broad brim and reeded edge (Fig. 78), which was ornamented with tulips, sunflowers, pinks, and cherubs' heads. It is not until about 1810, however, that sets of plates are found in American silver. A pair of plates (Fig. 79) made by Fletcher and Gardiner of Philadelphia about 1815 are very plain, with rather narrow rims and gadrooned edges. Platters in this same design, but oval instead of circular, were made by the same silversmiths in graduated sizes for the service (Fig. 137) presented to Commodore John Rodgers by the citi-

[75] Salver, by John Burt (1692/3–1745/6), Boston, c. 1725. Owned by the Dennis, Day, Dodge families. Diameter: 5¾". *Courtesy, Mr. and Mrs. Frank L. Harrington*

[76] Salver, and a detail showing leg, by Bancroft Woodcock (1732–1817), Wilmington, Del., c.1760. Engraved in script CSM. Diameter: 9". *Courtesy, Henry Francis du Pont Winterthur Museum*

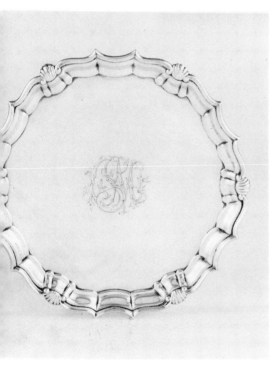

[77] Salver, by Joseph and Nathaniel Richardson (1777–1791), Philadelphia, c.1785–1790. Engraved MP for Mary Pemberton. Length: 7½". *Privately owned*

[78] Plate, by John Coney, Boston, c.1685. Engraved C^{R}E. Owned by Benjamin Pickman of Salem at his death in 1819. Diameter: 11⅛". *Courtesy, Museum of Fine Arts, Boston*

zens of Baltimore in 1817. In the same year Andrew E. Warner made a service for Baltimore citizens to present to Stephen Decatur which included "2 – 23 Inch Oval dishes 270 oz" and two sixteen-inch oval dishes weighing ninety-six ounces, with cast emblematic borders.[19]

One type of serving dish that was made occasionally in the eighteenth century by American silversmiths was the baking dish, or strawberry dish, as it is sometimes called today because of its resemblance to English dessert dishes. A circular shallow dish with scalloped or fluted sides, it was made of one solid piece of silver with no soldered additions so that baking in a moderate oven would cause no damage to the piece. Myer Myers, Daniel Christian Fueter, and Joseph Richardson, Jr., are among the few American silversmiths known to have produced this form.

TEAPOTS, COFFEEPOTS, AND CHOCOLATE POTS

Nothing has ever influenced the development of forms so much as the introduction of exotic beverages. It is hard to imagine a way of life without tea, coffee, chocolate, and even punch. Nevertheless, it was not until the middle of the seventeenth century that these beverages came

[79] Pair of plates, by Thomas Fletcher and Sidney Gardiner (w.1808–1827), Boston and Philadelphia, c.1820. Diameter: 9⅞". *Privately owned. Photograph, courtesy, S. J. Shrubsole*

[80] Teapot, by John Coney, Boston, c.1710. Engraved with arms of Jean Paul Mascarène. Height: 7⅛". *Courtesy, The Metropolitan Museum of Art, Bequest of A. T. Clearwater, 1933*

upon the London social scene, and probably not until close to 1700 that they were enjoyed in the Colonies with any frequency.

One of the earliest references to the use of a special form to accomodate tea drinking is found in Boston in Lieutenant Governor Stoughton's will in 1701, where particular mention is made of "my silver teapot." [20] New York, perhaps because of the influence of the Dutch East India Company, seems to have preceded Boston in the production of the new specialized forms. A globular teapot with a straight spout and a low domed lid with gadrooning was made by Jacob Boelen probably before the end of the seventeenth century. It had a C-shaped wooden handle and ball finial, and an ornamented base-band. Early in the eighteenth century, John Coney fashioned a small teapot following English silver of the Queen Anne period, with a rather squat pear shape, a curved spout set close to the body, a wide C-shaped wooden handle, and a high domed lid with a silver ball finial (Fig. 80).

By 1725, the teapot had become more commodious and could be made in the popular octagonally shaped pyriform (Fig. 16) or in a circular shape, with a more widely extended S-shaped spout and a slightly domed foot, instead of the earlier simple base-band. Teapots of the mid-eighteenth century were often apple-shaped with the lid flush with the shoulders of the pot (Fig. 81) and ornamented with a band of engraved patterns. Rococo examples are often double-bellied and have a slightly domed lid (Fig. 135). More elaborate ornamentation was to be found, such as gadrooning on the foot, a pine cone finial, furls and scrolls on the spout, and often repoussé work on the lid and shoulders of the body (Fig. 82).

During the Classical period, the form of the teapot was radically changed to an oval-shaped or drum-shaped pot with a straight spout, and a D-shaped wooden handle (Fig. 83). Often flat-based without any foot or base molding, these teapots were raised up from the table sur-

[81] Teapot, by Jacob Hurd, Boston, c.1735. Engraved with arms of father of Sir William Pepperell. Height: 5″. *Courtesy, Yale University Art Gallery, Mabel Brady Garvan Collection*

[82] Teapot, by Paul Revere, Boston, 1773. Engraved with initials of Lois Orne and Orne arms. Height: 6⅝". *Courtesy, Worcester Art Museum*

[83] Teapot and stand, by Paul Revere, Boston, 1799. Presented to Edmund Hartt, constructor of the frigate *Boston*. Length of tray: 6⁵⁄₁₆". *Courtesy, Museum of Fine Arts, Boston*

[84] Tea set, by Baldwin Gardiner (w.1814–1847), New York, 1827. Presented to Capt. Thomas Bennett by the passengers on the *Packet Ship* in October 1827. Height (teapot): 9¼". *Courtesy, Society for the Preservation of New England Antiquities; photograph by Richard Merrill*

face by a small, close-fitting tray or stand which had four diminutive claw-and-ball feet or the more appropriate French feet. During the last few years of the eighteenth century, fluting (Fig. 28) became very popular for a decade, but a return was soon made to a heavier, melon-shaped teapot with an exaggerated scrolled spout, four ball feet, and a rectangular or cast animal finial. Antique ewer forms with animalistic spouts, feet, and finials were popular in the second quarter of the nineteenth century. Acorns and oak leaves and heavy milled borders decorated the pots, which were supported once again by domed feet (Fig. 84) or on a plinth with four eagle or sphinx feet. Silver handles with ivory insulating rings were occasionally introduced.

Coffeepots and chocolate pots followed the same general stylistic development, with the major difference that they were usually tall and cylindrical. Probably the early coffeepots were also used for serving

[85] Chocolate pot, by John Coney, Boston, 1701. Made for Mrs. Tailer from a legacy of £ 12. Height: 7⅞″. *Courtesy, Museum of Fine Arts, Boston*

chocolate, but the unmistakable evidence of a chocolate pot is the small opening in the lid, covered over by a removable finial, which allowed a long stirring rod to be inserted to mix up the chocolate that invariably settled to the bottom of the pot. Chocolate pots are rare in American silver, one of the earliest being an example by John Coney with a Chinese-vase-shaped body, a spout at right angles to the handle and cut-card ornament at the base of the handle (Fig. 85). Edward Winslow provided his chocolate pot with a chain to make sure that the removable finial would not be lost (Fig. 86). By the mid-eighteenth century, Zachariah Brigden had fashioned chocolate pots in the identical cylindrical form used for coffeepots, but with a removable finial fitted into the top as a bobeche fits into a candlestick (Fig. 87).

Octagonal, pear-shaped, or inverted pear-shaped coffeepots (Fig. 88) were made to accompany similar teapots, but because of their large size, the lids were more highly domed, and the handles often were made with an additional curve at the bottom to extend their length sufficiently. With the abrupt change in the Federal period, coffeepots became urn-shaped with a plinth foot (Fig. 136). Whether fluted or plain, these were very heavy pots, and by 1810 the shape had returned to a more manageable melon- or vase-shaped body on four feet. By this time chocolate pots had taken on the form of the hot-water jug, with the spout shaped out of the upper corner of the lip and a fitted lid shaped to cover both. A special type of coffeepot was developed about 1799, with a strainer built into it to filter the coffee. Named after the inventor, George Biggin, by 1804 "Silver Coffee-pots and Biggins"

[86] Chocolate pot, by Edward Winslow, Boston, c.1705. Made for the Hutchinson family. Height: 9½". *Courtesy, The Metropolitan Museum of Art, Bequest of A. T. Clearwater, 1933*

[87] Chocolate pot, by Zachariah Brigden (1734–1787), Boston, c.1760. Engraved with arms of Thompson impaling Dering. Height: 10⅝". *Courtesy, Heritage Foundation, Deerfield, Mass.*

were advertised among items "made to any pattern, on the shortest notice," by New York's Thomas Warren, but none are known to have survived.[21]

TEAKETTLES AND URNS

Large kettles on a stand with a lamp to keep the liquid hot were rare in American silver but were introduced in the early eighteenth century. Generally following teapot shapes, their chief distinction was the large bail handle affixed to the top; it was made of wood or was originally wrapped with wicker to protect the server's hand (Fig. 89). The stand was made with a circular ring on which the kettle rested, with three or four legs between which the circular spirit lamp was attached, concealed in some cases by an ornamental skirt (Fig. 23). By the Classical period, the form had been transformed into an urn with handles on each side and a spigot with a tap placed horizontally on the front of the body (Fig. 158). Made with and without lamps concealed in the base, these urns were raised up from the table by four ball feet and were further ventilated with piercings in the upper part of the foot. In the nineteenth century this basic form continued but became more ponderous. During the Rococo Revival, the teakettle-on-stand was revived, but lacked its former styling.

PITCHERS AND JUGS

Large pitchers apparently were not made in American silver until about 1800. Undoubtedly the most famous of all designs for this form was that translated into silver by Paul Revere from the Liverpool ceramic pitchers (Fig. 129). Barrel-shaped pitchers were also popular, and were made with a lid fitting over the triangular spout (Fig. 167). By 1820, lidded pitchers with open spouts were made in bulbous, lobed forms with gadrooning and milled borders. Heavy cast ornament decorated the handles (Fig. 90). At the same time, open pitchers were fashioned in antique ewer forms with leaf decoration on the body, and often a snake formed the handle (Fig. 113).

[88] Coffee pot, by John David, Philadelphia, c.1765. Engraved with arms of John Dickinson of Delaware. See end paper. Height: 11¾". *Courtesy, John Dickinson Mansion and Delaware State Archives*

[89] Teakettle-on-stand, by Jacob Hurd, Boston, c.1740. Engraved with Lowell arms quartering Leversedge. Height: 14⅜". *Courtesy, Museum of Fine Arts, Boston*

MILK POTS AND CREAM URNS

In the seventeenth century it was not customary to serve milk or cream with tea, but early in the eighteenth century small pitchers began to be made in silver, and were referred to as milk pots. The earliest of these were pear-shaped with a triangular spout and a domed lid and foot (Fig. 91). A thin cast scrolled handle served the body and a small cast finial made a handle for the lid. By mid-century, an elongated curved lip replaced the triangular spout and the body of the pot was lifted off the table by three little curved legs (Fig. 197). By 1765, double-bellied pots were made with domed feet and often were embellished with gadrooning or heavy pearling (Fig. 135).

The biggest change occurred about 1770, when milk pots began to be called cream urns and were shaped like an urn or an inverted helmet (Fig. 28). These were supported on a plinth or an oval foot and were decorated with beading and engraved ornament. A very unusual form, advertised as early as the 1770s among imported wares, was the cream cow, which was shaped exactly like a cow with a lid in its back for filling; the cow's mouth served as the spout. A single example from Philadelphia has been noted in American silver.[22]

In the 1790s, the terms for this vessel were quite descriptive too, such as cream pitcher (shaped like the larger pitchers), cream ewers, cream pails, and cream buckets. In spite of these special shapes, creamers, as they came to be called in modern times, were most often made to match the large tea sets, following the basic shape of the coffeepots and teapots, but retaining their elongated curved lip (Fig. 84).

SUGAR BOXES AND BOWLS

Elliptically-shaped boxes with hinged lids and hasps, used to contain sugar and perhaps spices and sweetmeats as well, were introduced into English silver in the middle of the seventeenth century. Sugar was often

[90] Pair of pitchers, by John B. Jones (1782–1854), Salem, 1823. Presented by Insurance Companies to Capt. Nathaniel Garland, who defended the schooner *Tatler* from a piratical assault by the crew. Height: 10″. *Courtesy, The Peabody Museum of Salem.*

served with wines. Its primary purpose was to smooth out the uneven
quality of some of the liquors, but Sir Francis Bacon harbored the
opinion in 1626 that "wine sugared inebriateth less than wine pure" as
well.[23]

Nine American sugar boxes of this shape have survived, the earliest
four of which were made by John Coney (Fig. 92). Remarkably similar
to the London prototypes made about 1675, these boxes were designed
with large bosses and either repoussé leafage or rings of gadrooning. On
top of the lid, a snake was coiled to form a handle.[24]

Edward Winslow also used a coiled-snake handle for one of the four
sugar boxes he made, but soon he changed to a leafy-scrolled handle

[91a] Covered milk pot, by Jacob Hurd, Boston, c. 1735. Height: 4⁹⁄₁₆". *Courtesy,
The Cleveland Museum of Art, Gift of Hollis French.* [91b] Milk pot, by Jacob
Hurd, Boston, c. 1750. Engraved with view of Castle William in Boston Harbor.
Height: 4". *Courtesy, Yale University Art Gallery*

[92] Sugar box, by John Coney, Boston, c.1680. Length: 8⅞". *Courtesy, Currier Gallery, Manchester, N.H., given in memory of H. Ellis Straw; photograph by Frank A. Kelly*

(Fig. 12). The body of Winslow's boxes was designed with swirled gadrooning interrupted by flat acanthus repoussé and bosses containing a plain heraldic shield or the figure of a knight in combat. Two of Winslow's boxes were inscribed with the date of 1702.

The only other American sugar box of this type was made by Daniel Greenough of New Hampshire for his wife's parents. Presumably it could not have been made before 1706, when Greenough was twenty-one years old, and is the latest example of the group. The form was soon given up entirely in favor of the sugar bowl used at the tea table.

Sugar bowls or dishes, as opposed to the casket-shaped sugar box, had not been used in the seventeenth century. Early in the eighteenth century, they were introduced for use at the tea table, and were fashioned in a circular or octagonal shape. Their fitted lids had a reel-shaped top or a molded band around the top (Fig. 93) so that it was possible to invert the lid and make a small salver of it. The reel-top was continued in the second half of the eighteenth century in New York, but in New England and Philadelphia a cast finial gradually replaced it. By 1755, the body of the sugar bowl was fashioned in an inverted pear-shape, often with elaborate repoussé decoration or gadrooning (Fig. 135), but this style was soon given up for the slender urn-shaped sugar dishes with high conical lids, urn or pineapple finials, and square bases (Fig. 28).

By 1800 this form was supplemented by a lower oval or boat-shaped dish on an oval foot, and occasionally with two handles. Sugar baskets with bail handles, pierced sides, and glass liners were rarely made in American silver, although they were popular in England during the Classical period. However, fluted baskets were made occasionally and were fashioned with an elliptical fluted foot during the last few years of the eighteenth century. The nineteenth-century sugar dishes followed the shapes of the teapots and other forms in the large sets that were fashionable and usually were made with two handles and a cover (Fig. 84).

TEA CADDIES

Tea caddies, introduced about 1725 for storing tea, received their name from the Malay word *kati*, meaning the measure of weight by which tea was originally sold. Not often made in American silver, the few surviving tea caddies exhibit a variety of shapes, but compared to English examples are modestly plain. The earliest were rectangular-shaped boxes with incurved corners and a circular bottle-neck lid (Fig. 94). Often they were made in pairs and were engraved with the name of the tea kept within, such as "Green" or "Bohea" tea and later "Hysom" or "Black" tea.

From the second half of the eighteenth century, they were shaped like the Chinese porcelain tea caddies (Fig. 95) or like a tea chest. Fashioned with individual locks to guard against pilfering of the precious tea, chest-like caddies were divided into compartments inside to contain different varieties (Fig. 28). A basket-type of tea caddy was made in the first quarter of the nineteenth century, but with the greater availability of tea, this form gradually disappeared from silver tea sets.

SPOON TRAYS

Small oblong trays were introduced into English silver in the early eighteenth century to hold teaspoons. While there are records showing that this form was made by American silversmiths, none are known today. By the mid-eighteenth century, even in England, porcelain spoon trays had replaced the silver ones altogether.

SLOP BOWLS OR WASTE BOWLS

By the middle of the eighteenth century, small circular or octagonal bowls were added to the equipment necessary for the serving of tea.

[93a] Sugar dish by Joseph Richardson, Philadelphia, 1736. Engraved with initials of Oswald and Lydia Peel. *Courtesy, Mr. and Mrs. William H. Potter; photograph, courtesy, Smithsonian Institution.* [93b] Charge for sugar dish recorded in Richardson's account book. *Courtesy, The Historical Society of Pennsylvania*

[94] One of a pair of tea caddies, by Thauvet Besley (w.1727–1757), New York, c.1740. Engraved on base with initials of Catherine McPheadres, who married Robert Gilbert Livingston in 1740. Height: 5⅞". *Courtesy, Museum of the City of New York*

Slop bowls, as they were then inelegantly called, were used for pouring out the remaining cold tea in a cup before pouring another. It was not until the second half of the eighteenth century that the form became standard equipment at the tea table. In the Classical period they became designated as slop basins, and in general were fashioned with a large basin form supported on a pedestal base (Fig. 136). In the nineteenth century, the slop bowl continued as a circular basin without any handles or lid, and was almost twice as large as the sugar bowls in teasets. Often it had a wide projecting rim at this period, a practical measure taken against splashing during use.

PUNCH BOWLS

Large circular bowls used for preparing and serving punch came in several varieties. In the seventeenth century, a bowl by Jeremiah Dummer had rather straight sides with two large handles and a low shaped base (Fig. 96). The body was decorated with chased floral vines. New York examples were lobate in form and had chased panels containing

[95] Pair of tea caddies, in inlaid mahogany stand, by William Moulton (1772–1861), Newburyport, Mass., c.1810. Engraved PBC for Paulina Bass Coney. Height: 4½". *Privately owned; photograph by Richard Merrill*

floral designs (Fig. 132). By the mid-eighteenth century the bowls were rather plain in form, following closely the style of Chinese porcelain bowls (Fig. 97). A circular domed foot was used instead of the baseband.

One of the most interesting types of punch bowls had a deeply notched rim, often removable, and was called a monteith. Anthony à Wood in 1683 described this as "a vessel or bason notched at the brim to let drinking glasses hang there by the foot so that the body and drinking place might hang in the water to cool them. Such a bason was a 'Monteigh,' from a fantastical Scot called 'Monsieur Monteigh' who at that time or a little before [in Oxford] wore the bottome of his cloake or coate so notched." [25] The monteith was first produced in American silver in Boston in the early eighteenth century (Fig. 14) and a modified version (Fig. 98) was fashioned as late as 1771. It was not until the second quarter of the nineteenth century that the form was revived, this time in Baltimore, with a rim so widely scalloped that glasses could not have been suspended, and with a high domed cylindrical foot (Fig. 99).

BOTTLE STANDS

Bottle stands, or coasters, were introduced to hold decanters or

[96] Bowl, by Jeremiah Dummer, Boston, 1692. Engraved R^PH. Diameter: 6¾".
Courtesy, Yale University Art Gallery, Mabel Brady Garvan Collection

[97] Bowl, made by John Heath of New York and charged to Pierre Van Cortland in extant bill, c.1760. *Courtesy, Yale University Art Gallery, John Marshall Phillips Collection*

[98] Monteith bowl, by Daniel Henchman (1730–1775), Boston, 1771. Presented by Governor John Wentworth of New Hampshire to the Reverend Eleazer Wheelock at the first Commencement of Dartmouth College. Diameter: 10¾". *Courtesy, the Trustees of Dartmouth College*

[99] Monteith bowl, by Gould, Stowell & Ward (w. c.1855–1858), Baltimore, c.1855. Diameter: 9". *Privately owned; photograph by Richard Merrill*

bottles in use at the table in the last half of the eighteenth century. Imported "neat pierced and polished silver coasters or bottle stands" were advertised as early as 1764 by Edmund Milne in Philadelphia.[26] A pair of coasters by Myer Myers have pierced and undulating rims with turned wooden bases, but American examples of this form are rare (Fig. 220c).

BOTTLE TICKETS

Little silver labels were engraved with the names of various wines and were suspended on chains around the necks of bottles and decanters toward the end of the eighteenth century. In 1772, Paul Revere recorded in his accounts that he made a silver label for Claret, and about 1810 Louis Boudo of Charleston fashioned a Madeira label.

WINE FUNNELS AND SIPHONS

Wine funnels to strain and decant wine may have been made by American silversmiths at the end of the eighteenth century, although none have yet been positively identified. In the early nineteenth century, siphons were made by American silversmiths in various sizes and degrees of elaboration.

MISCELLANEOUS OBJECTS

BOXES

Throughout the colonial period and well into the nineteenth century, boxes were made of gold and silver, and sometimes of shells, to contain tobacco or snuff and the small beauty patches fashionable among women during the early part of this period (Fig. 5). The tobacco boxes (Fig. 164) were sometimes several inches in length and were shaped so that they could be held comfortably in the hand. Patch boxes were smaller and do not show the discoloration inside which tobacco caused.

Sponge boxes or vinaigrettes were made with perforated tops to allow the aroma to escape from a sponge concealed within, which had been soaked in vinegar or smelling salts. These, along with toothpick cases, were recorded in the accounts of American silversmiths but have not yet been completely identified. Nutmeg graters were also occasionally made here, and these small boxes had a grater just inside the cover, which lifted up so that the nutmeg could be stored in the lower part of the box (Fig. 100).

[100] Nutmeg grater, by Andrew E. Warner, Baltimore c.1840. Length: 3″. *Privately owned; photograph by Richard Merrill*

BOATSWAIN'S WHISTLES

Silver whistles or calls (Fig. 101) were made in the last quarter of the eighteenth century and in the nineteenth century for the boatswains on ships to pipe calls when directing work on board sailing vessels. These have a special shape consisting of a long curved reed with a bulbous ending, open at the top, and a rudder-like base with a ring by which the whistle was suspended. Edward Lang recorded making a number of these for the ships which sailed out of Salem in the 1780s, and John F. Vent made some at the end of the eighteenth century for a Boston firm which he described as "manufactured in a stile at once novel and elegant." [27]

TOYS AND MINIATURES

For the child born "with a silver spoon in his mouth," American silversmiths also made rattles of silver or gold in the eighteenth century. Fashioned with a whistle in one end, a coral in the other end for teething, and rows of bells around the middle of a shaped shaft, these delightful objects were suspended from the child's neck or waist by a chain or a ribbon (Fig. 102). Many more coral-and-bells, or whistles-and-bells, as they were variously called, were imported from England than were made here, and by the nineteenth century few if any were made by American silversmiths.

By that time little sets of tiny silver spoons were being made for children to play with. Frequently referred to in the silversmith's accounts as "Child's spoons," these followed the fashions of parents' spoons and sometimes were engraved with the little girl's name or initials (Fig. 103). Some miniature silver had been made in the late seventeenth century, usually in the shape of cups. A few examples (Fig. 104) are attributed to Boston makers but, being very small, they do not bear maker's marks.

WRITING EQUIPMENT

Silver inkstands, or standishes, were only occasionally made by American silversmiths. These were trays which held the equipment necessary for writing. Most frequently they held an inkpot, a container for seals, a pounce or sand caster for blotting the ink, and a place to put the pens (Fig. 105). There was also a vertical handle on some to

[101] Early nineteenth-century boatswains' whistles. Top one marked with pseudo-hallmarks used by Valentine Martin, Boston, c.1840. Length: 5¼″. *Courtesy, The Peabody Museum of Salem*

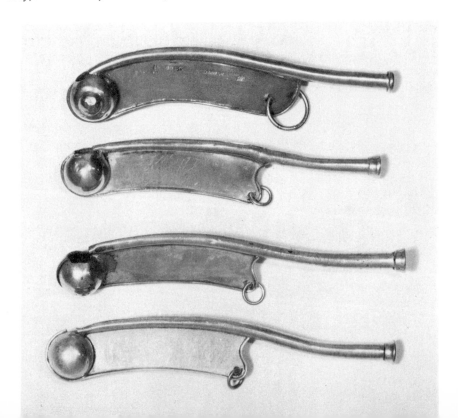

[102] Coral and bells, by Thomas Edwards (1701–1775), Boston, c.1730. Engraved with Fayerweather crest and initials IF. End of coral broken off. Length: 4½″. *Courtesy of The Art Institute of Chicago*

make them more easily portable, so that the ink would not be so apt to spill when the tray was moved (Fig. 146). On rare occasions, a candlestick or a taperstick was incorporated into the design (Fig. 106). Tapersticks were miniature candlesticks used in affixing seals, as were wax jacks, stands which held a reel of taper; but these are unknown in American silver.

SEWING EQUIPMENT

Many of the small objects used in sewing, such as gold or silver thimbles, hooks, and needlecases, were made by American silversmiths, but due to their size they rarely bear maker's marks. A few eighteenth-century bodkins are marked on their flat shank. These were used to pull tapes through hems, and were designed with eyelets in the ends. Later bodkins had eyelets in one rounded end and had a pointed shape to the other end (Fig. 103). The bands which encircled pin-cushion balls, and the chatelaine hooks (or harts, as they were called because of their shape), from which other sewing equipment such as scissors were suspended by chains, were also made by American silversmiths.

LIGHTING DEVICES

It is hard for us to imagine what a problem lighting was before the

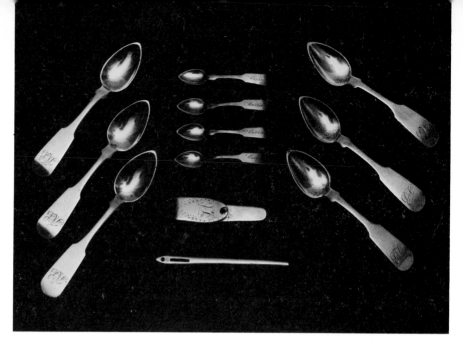

[103] Children's spoons, chatelaine hook and bodkin, early nineteenth century, American. Smaller spoons 2" long, larger spoons 4⅛" long. *Privately owned*

[104] Miniature caudle cup, attributed to John Edwards, Boston, c.1700. Height: 1". *Courtesy, Museum of Fine Arts, Boston*

[105] Inkstand, by John Coney, Boston, c.1710. Made for Governor Jonathan Belcher and engraved with Belcher crest. Height: 4¼". *Courtesy, The Metropolitan Museum of Art, Bequest of Charles A. Munn, 1924*

[106] Inkstand with candlestick, by Obadiah Rich, Boston, c.1835. Candlestick probably a replacement. Height: 6⅝". *Courtesy, Yale University Art Gallery, Mabel Brady Garvan Collection*

[107] Candlesticks and snuffer stand, by Cornelius Kierstede (1674–1757), New York and New Haven, c.1705. Engraved with initials of John and Elizabeth Schuyler. Height (sticks): 11½", 11¾". *Courtesy, The Metropolitan Museum of Art, Gift of Robert L. Cammann, 1957, Gift of Mr. and Mrs. William A. Moore, 1923, Gift of Mrs. Clermont L. Barnwell, 1964*

invention of electric lights. For centuries man struggled along with messy, smoky, reeking fat lamps and candles. Base metals such as iron and tin were more suitable holders for the crude materials used to create light, and brass and bell metal were frequently used to hold the dripping candles. By the seventeenth century, as candles became somewhat refined, silver candlesticks were made in England and occasionally in the Colonies. At least one fine pair of American candlesticks survives from every early period.

The earliest American candlesticks known today are a pair made by Jeremiah Dummer (Fig. 9). Fashioned like their English Stuart counterparts, Dummer's candlesticks have large bases and wide drip pans to catch the grease. Instead of acanthus decoration, which often appeared on English sticks, the American version has only a suggestion of leafage on the drip pans.

Similar in form, but more ornate, are the candlesticks made by Cornelius Kierstede of New York (Fig. 107). Stop-fluted columns have been substituted for the square cluster columns, and Baroque richness of decoration, in the form of gadrooning and chinoiserie engraving, indicates an early eighteenth-century date. A matching accessory to the candlesticks, and also a rarity in American silver, is the upright snuffer stand with an embossed and matted baluster support for the box which held the snuffers. A doubleheaded eagle embellishes the side of the container, and graduated beads garnish the loop handle on the side.

A contemporary of Kierstede, John Noyes of Boston, made a pair of candlesticks with stop-fluted shafts, bands of gadrooning, and chamfered corners on the bases and drip-pans. By 1716, octagonal candlesticks devoid of Baroque decoration were being made by John Coney (Fig. 155) and Nathaniel Morse (Fig. 15) for wealthy Boston patrons. Most candlesticks by this time were cast, requiring a great deal of silver. They were, therefore, quite expensive, and it is not surprising that so few were made and that even fewer survive today. Imported silver or even brass candlesticks could be used as patterns for the molds, so American candlesticks followed the foreign examples faithfully. The castings were made in short longitudinal halves which were soldered vertically, the sections then being joined together. "Candlestick moulds" were listed in the inventory of John Coney's estate in 1722, and both octagonal-based (Fig. 155) and circular-based candlesticks are known to have been made by him.[28]

In Coney's day, the large drip-pans were no longer used. The columnar socket at the top of a baluster shaft might or might not have a removable bobeche. The same type of socket was used on a pair of sconces made about 1735 by Jacob Hurd (Fig. 108). American silver sconces are extremely rare, only one other, marked by Knight Leverett, also of Boston, being known. With a simple circular-shaped drip-pan and an S-shaped arm which pivots in the hinge of its shaped silver back plate, these sconces were affixed to the wooden frames of quill-work pictures. The scrolled bits of metal and sprinkles of mica dusted over the surface of the picture behind the glass sparkled effectively in the light of the candle.

In the second quarter of the eighteenth century, John Burt fashioned a pair of candlesticks (Fig. 109) which had cusped corners in the base and an echo of the pattern on the shoulders of the baluster shaft. What is more unusual is the pair of snuffers with their nicely formed tray in a matching pattern. The scissors-like snuffers were not used for putting out the candles, as many people now think, but were used to cut and trim the burnt wick, which fell safely into the compartment on the

[108] One of pair of candle sconces, by Jacob Hurd, Boston, c.1730. Quill work in frame done by Elizabeth Hunt of Boston, who married Jacob Wendell in 1733, and after his death married the Reverend Thomas Smith of Falmouth, Maine. Length of arm: 4¾". *Courtesy, Henry Francis du Pont Winterthur Museum*

side, the word "snuff" meaning the discarded portion of anything. The pointed end was used to pry out the remaining stub of the candles.

During the Rococo period, candlesticks became more florid in their decoration, had narrow edges of gadrooning, and had lobed and curly bases (Fig. 110). A leafy bobeche was again added to the top of the socket to protect the table or cloth from the hot wax. A set of four such candlesticks made by Thomas Dane of Boston about 1765 are fully as elaborate as their English counterparts. Myer Myers of New York made a pair in the same period with shells in the lobes of the base and an ornate companion tray with snuffers.

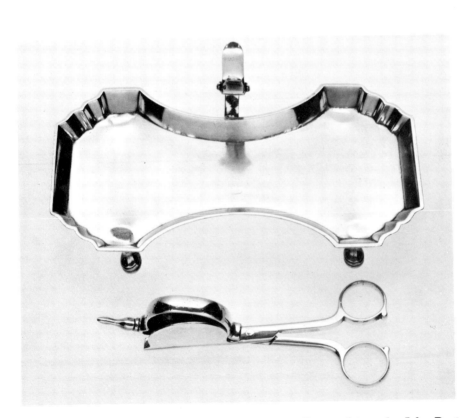

[109a, 109b] Pair of candlesticks and matching snuffers and tray, by John Burt, Boston, c.1730. Engraved with initials of Daniel and Sarah (Hill) Warner, who were married in 1720. Height: 7³⁄₁₆". Length of tray: 7¼". *Courtesy, Henry Francis du Pont Winterthur Museum*

[110] Set of four candlesticks, by Thomas Dane (1726–1795?), Boston, c.1765. Listed in inventory of Benjamin Hallowell in 1773. Height: 8⅞". *Courtesy, Heritage Foundation, Deerfield, Mass.*

[111] Candlestick, snuffers, douter, and tray, by Joseph Lownes, Philadelphia, c.1800. Length of tray: 9⅝". *Courtesy, The Metropolitan Museum of Art, Bequest of Charles Allen Munn, 1924*

By nature, candlesticks lent themselves to the designs of architectural columns, and with the revival of interest in Classical forms at the end of the eighteenth century, candlesticks were shaped like fluted or reeded columns, usually on square bases. The socket and bobeche blended into a smoothly flowing urn shape, and the shaft often was tapered like a Classical pedestal. Joseph Lownes of Philadelphia combined a short candlestick with a snuffer tray of elliptical shape (Fig. 111). The snuffers were supported by a plain columnar shaft and were balanced on the other side by a douter, a small cone-shaped object used for extinguishing the candle flame. Save-alls, another piece of equipment used with lighting devices, were described by Samuel Johnson in his *Dictionary* as "A small pan inserted into a candlestick to save the ends of candles." These tiny objects, weighing less than an ounce, were also made by American silversmiths, according to their account books, but none have been identified.

By the nineteenth century, all-silver candlesticks, as well as the plated ones, were more widely made and used, along with more readily available and better types of candles. Branched candlesticks and candelabra were occasionally produced (Fig. 33), the example made by Andrew E. Warner of Baltimore for Stephen Decatur in 1817 being the earliest American candelabrum known.

[111a] Trade card of William and John H. Hamlin, Providence, c. 1809–1819. Engraved by William Hamlin, showing an early nineteenth-century style candlestick among the silver he and his son sold. *Courtesy, American Antiquarian Society*

[111b] Watercolor drawing by Hugh Bridport (1794–c. 1868), Philadelphia, of one of a pair of covered urns, made by Thomas Fletcher and Sidney Gardiner, Philadelphia, 1824–1825, presented to De Witt Clinton by the Pearl Street merchants in New York City. The urn form is derived from the Warwick Vase (Fig. 115). The views of the Erie Canal delineated in the panels on the sides of the vase are based on engravings of the official drawings for the Erie Canal geological survey made by James Eights (1798–1882) of Albany. Height of urn: 24″. *Courtesy, The Metropolitan Museum of Art*

CHAPTER THREE

Design Sources

THE sources of design for silver in America were as diverse as the people who inhabited the new world. The ultimate design source might be said to be the life and the thought of the day. More specifically, however, it could be a timely original drawing, an engraved design, an actual piece of silver, or any one of the other arts.

While the greatest goldsmiths and the innovators of design may have started their work with an original drawing, most American craftsmen probably used finished pieces of silver as working objects or made life-size working sketches. Very few such drawings are known. The folio of William Faris of Maryland is a remarkable eighteenth-century exception. Among the drawings (Fig. 112) are accurate sketches of various forms, from tankards to soup ladles. Not only are these drawn to scale, meaning that the silversmith could actually measure with his calipers the piece he was making against the drawing, but also they show the important details such as the exact shape of moldings, the design of cast ornament, and the size and location of hinges.[29]

Early in the nineteenth century, Thomas Fletcher, of Boston and Philadelphia, also left a set of drawings for his work in silver. One design is for two ewers, or pitchers, with a detail of the shape of the lip on one of them (Fig. 113). Other designs include a presentation piece for a Baltimore insurance company, a chalice and paten for a Boston church in 1818, a covered vegetable dish with a cast handle, a wine cooler, lovely little casters, a coffee urn, and a triangular-shaped object described as a "Corner dish & cover."

115

[112] Design for a tankard, by William Faris (1728–1804), Annapolis, Md., c.1770. *Courtesy, Maryland Historical Society*

Engraved designs provided inspiration to American silversmiths. Undoubtedly one of the most important sources in this category was the engraved trade cards and bill heads (Fig. 114) of English goldsmiths, who sent these paper advertisements along with their shipments of wares to America. The Philadelphia silversmith Joseph Richardson mentioned in his letter book in 1758 that he had received such a shop bill from George Ritherdon, a London goldsmith.[30] Frequently these trade cards had borders composed of the latest designs in silver of all sizes, from the largest teakettle-on-stand to the smallest buckle or étui case. The American silversmith could keep well informed of the latest London styles and the newly introduced forms in this way.

There were no eighteenth-century printed design books for American silversmiths equivalent to Chippendale's *Director* for the cabinet-maker. However, in the early nineteenth century, engraved designs were more frequently published which could serve as sources for the silversmith. Many of these were printed catalogues of Sheffield wares or else engravings of marble vases which had been unearthed in the ever-increasing excavations of classical ruins (Fig. 115). Henry Moses published in London in 1814 *A Collection of Antique Vases*, which included the famous Warwick Vase, the design source for both Ward &

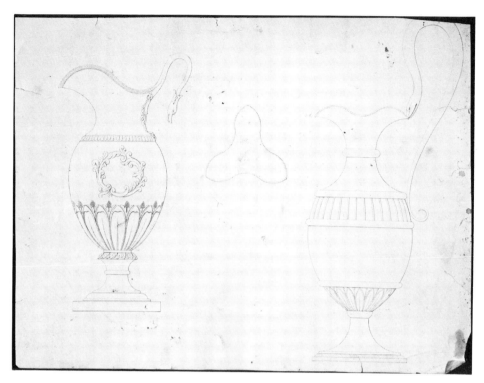

[113] Design for pitchers, by Thomas Fletcher (1787–1866), Boston and Philadelphia, c.1818. *Courtesy, The Metropolitan Museum of Art, Whittelsey Fund, 1953*

Rich in the Daniel Webster Vase (Fig. 116) of 1835 and Fletcher & Gardiner in the pair of urns presented to De Witt Clinton a decade earlier.[31]

By far the most common design source, however, was another piece of silver, either brought to this country with other possessions or imported by silversmiths for resale. Church silver (see pp. 151–158) shows many examples of foreign silver serving as models for American-produced silver. John Andrew's copy of the English flagon (Fig. 143) for The First Church in Salem is identical with the original in its dimensions, basic design, and in such distinctive details as the asymmetrical drop at the base of the spout and the leafy scroll beneath the hinge at the top of the handle.

By using imported models for their work in silver, the American craftsmen could produce wares that were just as fashionable as those being made in London. It only took a few months to send a letter to England ordering a shipment of plate, and to receive the goods. This meant that there was not always such a time lag in the designs as might be expected, or indeed as is actually encountered with the other arts. The First Church flagon bears a London date-letter of 1767–68, and John Andrew's flagon was made in 1769. Similarly, the candlesticks

[114] Engraved trade card of London goldsmith John Fossey, 1748. *Courtesy, The British Museum*

[115] Engraving of the Warwick Vase, published by Henry Moses, in *A Collection of Antique Vases*, London, 1814. Courtesy, *The Metropolitan Museum of Art, Rogers Fund, 1952*

made by John Coney for Tutor Flynt in 1716 (Fig. 155) have their counterparts in English silver of the same year.

This is not to say that a time lag did not exist at all in American silver. There are occasions when a design was continued or revived many years after the original model was made. An example of this can be seen in a comparison of a rare group of three-legged coffeepots. Coffeepots supported by three scrolled legs are by no means common even in English silver, although they are more frequently found on the Continent. Only two extant examples are known in American silver, one (Fig. 117) made by Paul Revere in 1772; both of them were owned in Salem, Massachusetts. The design source of this unusual form is to be found in a third three-legged coffeepot (Fig. 118) made in London in 1759 but owned in the same town of Salem by Mary Vial, who married Dr. Edward Augustus Holyoke late in that year. While the overall design is basically the same, Revere updated his version by changing the body of the pot from a single-bellied form to a more stylish double-bellied design.[32]

The patron obviously played some part in the choice of design and might prefer a piece of silver to be made like that belonging to a friend. In New York, the De Peyster family owned a salver made in London in 1766–67 (Fig. 119) which had a cusped and gadrooned border with an unusual ruffled inner border interrupted alternately by a rosette and a leaf. This undoubtedly was the design source for several salvers fashioned with the same border by New York silversmiths for the Schuyler family (Fig. 120) in the 1760s and the Clarkson family in the 1770s.

[116] Vase designed after the Warwick Vase, by Obadiah Rich and Samuel L. Ward, Boston, 1835. Presented to Daniel Webster by citizens of Boston on October 12, 1835. Height: 13¾″. *Courtesy, Boston Public Library*

[117] Coffeepot, by Paul Revere, Boston, 1772. Purchased for £6/3/4 by Richard Derby and engraved with the initials of his son John and John's second wife, Elizabeth, who were married in 1787. Height: 12″. *Courtesy, Mr. and Mrs. Charles Townsend; photograph, courtesy, Museum of Fine Arts, Boston*

[118] English coffeepot, by Arthur Annesley, London, 1759–60. Given by Jonathan Simpson to his niece Mary Vial, who married Edward Augustus Holyoke of Salem in 1759. Height: 11¼″. *Courtesy, Mrs. Ernest Brooks*

Sometimes American silversmiths were asked to make other pieces to match a teapot or coffeepot. Oliver and Abigail Whipple of Portsmouth, N.H., had David Tyler of Boston make a creamer to match the tea urn, chocolate pitcher and sugar basin made for them by the London goldsmiths John Schofield and William Plummer in 1786. Early in the nineteenth century, Ebenezer Moulton was employed to make a teapot and sugar bowl following the design of a coffeepot and cream pitcher (Fig. 121) made in 1799 by the Batemans of London.

French silver also served occasionally as a design source, particularly at the end of the eighteenth century, when our ties with France became stronger, and anything in the French taste seemed more fash-

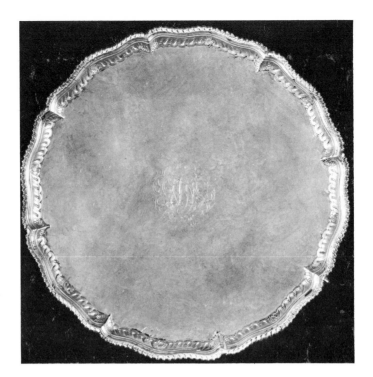

[119] English salver, by Thomas Hannam and John Crouch, London, 1766–67. Owned by the De Peyster family. Diameter: 15½″. *Courtesy of The New-York Historical Society, New York City*

[120] Salver, by John Heath (w.1761), New York, c.1770. Engraved with Schuyler arms. Diameter: 15″. *Courtesy, Henry Francis du Pont Winterthur Museum*

[121] Coffeepot and cream pitcher, by Peter, Ann, and William Bateman, London, 1799, and matching teapot and sugar bowl by Ebenezer Moulton, Boston and Newburyport, c. 1800. Originally owned by Thomas and Ann Perkins of Boston. Height: 12″ (coffeepot). *Courtesy, The Towle Company*

ionable. Joseph Cooke advertised in the *Federal Gazette* in Philadelphia in 1792 that he had "formed such connections as to forward him immediately the most fashionable, &c. as soon as they appear in London or Paris . . ."[33] A vivid illustration of Parisian influence is to be found in the silver owned by Elias Hasket Derby, who had Paul Revere copy a French tumbler made by Denis Colombier (Figs. 122, 123). The unusual engraved border of the French example is identical in pattern in the Revere versions, even though it is less detailed in execution.

A typical French form is the beaker (Fig. 124) made in St. Malo, France, early in the eighteenth century and engraved by Joseph Leddel of New York in 1750. Not only the shape but also the dramatic political engraving around the sides was emulated by Daniel Christian Fueter of New York a few years later (Fig. 125). The engraving itself probably found its source in one of the many political cartoons circulating at

[122] Two canns and four cups, by Paul Revere, Boston, bought by Elias Hasket Derby in 1783 and 1795 respectively. Height: 6½″ (canns), 2¹³⁄₁₆″ (cups). *Canns, courtesy, The Metropolitan Museum of Art, Sansbury Mills Fund, 1958; cups, courtesy, Mrs. Russell Sage Gift, Purchase, 1958*

that time. The same French form without the cartoon-work was also made by Samuel Casey of Rhode Island.

Dutch silver (Fig. 126) made equally important contributions to American silver because of early Dutch settlement of New York and the fact that many of the silversmiths in that area were Dutchmen who had actually served their apprenticeships in Holland. Dutch customs prompted such forms as ceremonial bowls (Fig. 132) and ceremonial spoons (Fig. 152), the latter following, quite exactly, Dutch prototypes.

Dutch design sources affected the decoration of silver even more than the forms. In New York, tankards, which were basically English forms, were given more elaborate cast ornamentation, derived from the designs in brass pattern books published in Holland in the late seventeenth century. A greater abundance of engraved decoration is logically found in New York silver, since Dutch silver is especially noted for its superb engraving. In one case (Fig. 127), the New York silversmith copied his engraved motifs from Jacobus Cats's book of didactic verse, which was published in Amsterdam in the seventeenth century.

All of the other arts provided design sources for American silver, too. Motifs were taken by silversmiths from current architectural patterns. Jeremiah Dummer made use of the cluster-column for a pair of candlesticks (Fig. 9) similar to columns and chimneys of the seventeenth

[123] French cup by Denis Colombier, Paris, 1789. Owned by Elias Hasket Derby and used as a model by Paul Revere. *Courtesy, The Metropolitan Museum of Art, Purchase, Mr. and Mrs. Marshall P. Blankarn Gift Fund, 1967*

▼ [124] French beaker, by unknown maker, St. Malo, France, early eighteenth century. Engraving signed by "Joseph Leddel Sculp. 1750." Height: 3¹⁄₁₆". *Courtesy, Museum of the City of New York, on loan from collection of Mrs. L. W. Hussey*

[125] Beaker, by Daniel Christian Fueter (1720–1785), New York, c.1754–1779. Fashioned after French beaker and engraved with same contemporary political cartoons of the Devil, Pope, and Pretender. Height: 3³⁄₁₆". *Courtesy, Henry Francis du Pont Winterthur Museum* ▲

[126] Dutch beaker, by I. G., Amsterdam, 1637. Engraved with initials of American silversmith Robert Sanderson and his wife Elizabeth, who bequeathed it to The First Church of Boston at her death n 1694. Served as model for several beakers made by Hull and Sanderson (Fig. 139), and similar to those which inspired New York beakers (see figure 7). Height: 6⅞". *Courtesy, Museum of Fine Arts, Boston, and The First Church*

[127a, 127b] Detail of engraving on beaker (see Fig. 7) by Cornelius Vander Burch, New York, c.1685, and source of design, engraving illustrating didactic verse of Jacobus Cats, published in Amsterdam in 1658. *Courtesy, Yale University Art Gallery and The Folger Shakespeare Library*

272

NESCIT HABERE MODVM.
XLVI.

OVID.10. *Nec modus aut requies, nisi mors, reperitur amoris,*
METAM.
SEN.Oct.*Amor perennis conjugis castæ manet.*
ACT.I.
AVSON. V*xor vivamus, quod viximus, & teneamus*
Nomina quæ primo sumpsimus in thalamo;
Næve sit ulla dies ut commutemur in ævo.
Quin tibi sim juvenis, tuque puella mihi, &c.

[128] Liverpool creamware pitcher decorated with patriotic American emblems, verses, and heroes. Made in England and owned in Boston, dated 1802. Height: 9⅓". *Courtesy, Society for the Preservation of New England Antiquities; photograph by Richard Merrill*

century. When caryatid supports became fashionable in the early nineteenth century, this design was incorporated by Andrew E. Warner into the candelabrum presented to Stephen Decatur in 1817 (Fig. 33).

Sculptural forms found their way into American silver. The carved swags of fruit and flowers took the form of cast ornament on tankard handles (Fig. 13) or repoussé decoration. The lions so frequently found supporting English monumental sculpture found their way into American silver, as they did into English silver, in the guise of a cast thumbpiece on a tankard (Fig. 46), or as supporting members of an imposing inkstand (Fig. 105). The sculptural influences are even more evident in the nineteenth century, when sculpture in America began to come into its own. Many of the cast handles and feet of silver are based directly upon sculptural counterparts, and the American sculptor Horatio Greenough is believed to have been the one who supplied the design for an inkstand (Fig. 106) made by Obadiah Rich of Boston.

Of all the minor arts, ceramics probably had the closest design relationship with silver. The kinship is an obvious one since both materials were used for making the same forms. When the first European porcelain factory began in Meissen in 1709, it was a goldsmith who was employed to make the designs. It is sometimes difficult, therefore, to tell which came first, the silver design or the ceramic design. In general, the ceramic designs which originated in Chinese porcelain preceded and actually influenced the European and American silver designs. This would include such forms as the reel-top sugar bowl (Fig. 18), bellied or pear-shaped mugs, and the earliest designs for teapots.

As the English potteries in the Staffordshire area began to grow, they also exerted their influence upon silver designs. A Liverpool pitcher of Classic shape such as was owned in Boston in 1802 (Fig. 128) served as the design source for the famous pitchers made by Paul Revere (Fig. 129) and now known by his name. In turn, American as well as English potteries shared similar designs with American silver.

Furniture, too, had a logical influence upon silver designs. Carvers of

[129] Pitcher, by Paul Revere, Boston, 1806. Fashioned after Liverpool pitchers and presented to Samuel Gilbert, Secretary, by the Mechanic Association. Height: 6". *Courtesy, The Paul Revere Life Insurance Company, Worcester, Mass.*

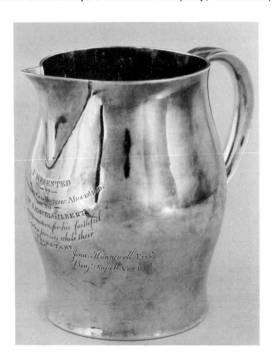

furniture sometimes carved the patterns used in casting, just as they carved the handles for teapots and coffeepots, so it is not surprising to find the same shell so popular in Queen Anne furniture also introduced as cast ornamentation in silver in the second half of the eighteenth century. Since silver trays were meant for use upon tables, they often followed the shape of current designs for table tops. Mid-eighteenth-century salvers consequently have the same shape as the piecrust tables on which they sat, as well as the same gadrooned edges that were carved into the edges of the table tops at that period (Fig. 165). In the Classical period, not only the tray but also entire tea services took on the shape of the sash-cornered tables newly introduced into furniture (Fig. 28).

Flame finials found on New England tankards, but not common to English tankards, are cast in the same design as the finials carved by New England cabinetmakers for tall chests and clocks. In New York, the same diamond-shaped piercings found in chair splats and fretwork on desks is found in pierced porringer handles (see p. 139) and in the reticulation of silver serving baskets (Fig. 25).

[130] Spoon, by Samuel Casey (c.1724–c.1770), South Kingstown, R.I., 1751. Made for Ann Hurd, daughter of Jacob Hurd (to whom Casey was apprenticed), and fashioned after a pattern of Hurd's. Length: 4⅝". *Courtesy, Museum of Fine Arts, Boston*

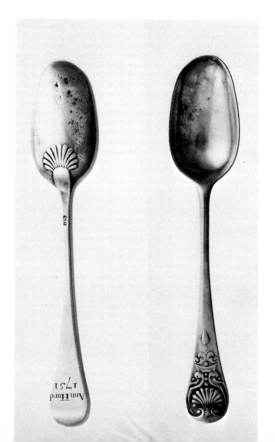

[131] Caudle cup, by John Hull and Robert Sanderson, Boston, c.1652. Initials ED pricked on one side, BB on other. Height: 3³⁄₁₆". *Courtesy, Museum of Fine Arts, Boston*

A comparison of Chippendale furniture made in Newport and a silver creamer (Fig. 131b) made by Samuel Casey of South Kingstown, Rhode Island, reveals similarities of design, not only in the use of scalloped edges and claw-and-ball feet, but also in the surface decoration. In this creamer, another design source for silver is also apparent. Samuel Casey's work is very similar to a creamer made by his master, Jacob Hurd.[34] In another instance, Casey copied a design for a spoon from one Jacob Hurd had made (Fig. 130). The borrowing of the master's designs was especially apt to occur whenever actual patterns were needed in the process of manufacturing, as in the case of the swage work on the spoons or in applied cast ornaments. The swages and molds were relatively expensive and each one was used as much as possible. An apprentice might be taught to make a copy of the mold for his own use, or in some instances he may have purchased or inherited another silversmith's molds. Such was the case with Jeremiah Dummer, who had served his apprenticeship with Hull and Sanderson and who continued to use the same pattern for the handles on his caudle cups that his masters had used (Figs. 10, 131).

Whether the design source was determined by an engraving, another piece of silver, a patron's whim, or a master's instruction, every time the American silversmith made an object, he had to decide which features to include and how elaborate the decoration should be. By so doing he created a new object with its own particular design. It is especially interesting to see which forms and which features were taken up in this country and which were eliminated or avoided, because it was in this process of selection that the special qualities of American silver were developed. It was in the deviation from the design source that American silversmiths developed their own style, and through them that this new nation made its contribution to silver design in general.

[131a] Mahogany gaming table made in Newport, c. 1760. Height, 27". *Courtesy, Henry Francis du Pont Winterthur Museum.* [131b] Cream pot, by Samuel Casey, South Kingstown, Rhode Island, c. 1760. Height: 4". Both the claw-and-ball feet and the type of decoration executed in carving and repoussé work show the interdependence of the design of silver and furniture. *Courtesy, Museum of Fine Arts, Boston*

Regional Contributions

JUST as one looks at a group portrait of parents and children and sees certain family resemblances as well as individual differences, one sees in American silver certain regional characteristics which distinguish the product of one area from that of another. In both instances, it is a combination of heredity and environment which caused these family traits. We have already seen how the apprenticeship system and common design sources produced particular forms or specific features in the silver of a single town. But there were other causes as well, some ethnic in nature, some social, and some dependent upon the other arts.

In Boston in the early years, when most of the people living there were English, the silver naturally followed English traditions. In New York, on the other hand, the Dutch traditions of its early settlers persisted long after the English took over the city. As a result, New York silver in general seems to be more substantial in line, more capacious, while New England examples appear more delicate and somewhat restrained. In the same way, the areas around a major city like Boston, New York, and Philadelphia tended to produce silver similar to that of the most dominant metropolis in the vicinity.[35]

Baltimore silver closely resembles the silver of Philadelphia, the city upon which Baltimore was economically dependent for its first hundred years. The silver of Connecticut, situated as it is half way between two cities, was buffeted by influences from both Boston and New York. New Jersey likewise was influenced by New York and Pennsylvania. The

133

island of Nantucket received its stimulus more from Providence, Rhode Island, than from Boston because of the ease of shipping between the first two, and the consequent ready communication.

The inherited traits in silver make themselves known in many different ways. Perhaps the most obvious appearance is in forms peculiar to a particular area. The little spout cup (Fig. 43) used for feeding invalids or children generally can be considered a New England form. Only one New York and one Philadelphia example are known, while dozens of New England spout cups are in existence. The standing salt (Fig. 61) is another form apparently restricted to New England manufacture, since all the early New York salts seem to be of trencher form.

Church silver reveals regional preferences for certain forms. In New England, the standing cup (Fig. 3) was the most often used type of communion vessel at first, while in New York, the characteristic communion vessel was a tall, highly engraved beaker with a slight flare at the top (Fig. 7). Not surprisingly, these New York beakers follow closely Dutch examples, which had the same interlaced bands, birds, and swags of fruit.

It is somewhat surprising, however, that one of these Dutch beakers was presented to the First Church of Boston in 1694 by Elizabeth Sanderson, the widow of the silversmith Robert Sanderson (Fig. 126). Their initials, R^{S}E, are engraved on the base, and the beaker bears the marks of an unknown Amsterdam goldsmith, with the date-letter for 1637. The presence of this Dutch beaker in Boston and actually in the possession of Robert Sanderson explains the otherwise puzzling appearance in the work of Hull and Sanderson of a beaker in this same style (Fig. 139). The New England example makes use of a Dutch-type band around the base, but the engraving is more in the English tradition. Probably because of the lack of a substantial Dutch element in the Boston area, this form did not establish itself there, and the Dutch-type beaker (Fig. 7) is rightly considered characteristic of such Dutch goldsmiths in New York as Cornelius Vander Burch and the Boelens.

Another form that emanated from New York was the large paneled drinking bowl (Fig. 132). For years, scholars have been intrigued to discover how this form came to be popular in New York. Two-handled bowls were popular in Dutch silver but normally they had flat handles, like a porringer or *écuelle*, at the top of the bowl. The panels of floral ornament also occur in Dutch silver but in forms other than bowls, such as beakers. So it appears that silversmiths of Dutch origin created this "sport" in the silver of New York.[36]

These large handled bowls were used as ceremonial bowls and were filled with brandy and raisins on special occasions. The Dutch custom

[132] Bowl, by Benjamin Wynkoop (1675–1728), New York, c.1710. Originally owned by Nicholas and Hilletje Roosevelt, who were married in 1682. Diameter: 8″. *Courtesy, Mrs. Jack R. Hovey; photograph, courtesy, Smithsonian Institution*

was that each guest had a silver spoon and helped himself to the liquor and then passed the bowl on to the next person. It is this social custom which explains why in America ceremonial spoons (Fig. 152) were made only in New York, for weddings, christenings, and funerals, following closely Dutch examples of the mid-seventeenth century.

Other forms associated with New York particularly are sucket forks (Fig. 50), gold freedom boxes (Fig. 164), and gold rattles. Little spoons of gold are rare, but a number were made by New York silversmiths. They were made as early as 1700 by Jacobus Vander Spiegel and a little later by Simeon Soumain, curiously enough for a Bostonian, Hugh Hall, who mentioned them in an account he took of his plate on June 25, 1750 (Fig. 55). A late example can be found in a fiddle-handled gold spoon made about 1850 by John L. Moffat, a "forty-niner," and inscribed as having been made of native gold by Moffat & Company in San Francisco, after Moffat had moved there from New York.

Several other forms are known only in New York. The large cake or bread basket (Fig. 25) is unknown elsewhere in the mid-eighteenth century, although by 1800 this form was being made everywhere. An earlier form restricted to New York at the end of the seventeenth century is the two-handled cup (Fig. 11) with a low knopped cover, made by Jurian Blanck, Jr., and also by Gerrit Onckelbag. Even though this is a purely English form of design, it seems to have been made in this country only in New York, and no examples of it have been found in New England, where one might expect such an English form.

New England had its preferences for such forms as sugar or sweetmeat boxes and monteith punch bowls (Figs. 12, 14), and these fol-lowed English fashions in a very literal way. In Boston, the large two-handled covered cup (Fig. 19) became especially popular as˙ a presentation piece. Most of the known examples were made by Jacob Hurd and were fashioned along the same lines as a London-made grace cup owned by Lydia Hancock and later by her nephew John.

Often it is in the details rather than in the overall form that regional contributions can be seen in silver. In New York, the reel-type lid was especially popular for sugar bowls, and in the Rococo period, silver-smiths there often used a ruffled edge for the decoration of the reel (Fig. 135). On their creamers of the same period, they used a type of triple-scrolled handle (Fig. 135) which is a certain indication of New York influence.

Philadelphia, too, had its preferences for certain details, although it shared common bonds with New York in such forms as pear-shaped tankards. While much of the Quaker silver was quite plain, the silver made for other Philadelphians is among the most elaborate in the country. Especially during the Rococo period, when Philadelphia was second only to London in the English-speaking world, her metropolitan pretensions can be seen in elaborately embossed silver teakettles (Fig. 23) and trays. In the Classical period, Philadelphia silversmiths began decorating their tea sets with a pierced gallery at the top of the sugar urns and teapots (Fig. 136). The reason for the great popularity of this motif has never been explained, but it was transmitted by Philadelphia silversmiths to New Jersey and Maryland, and even to Bermuda.

Tankards in Philadelphia followed English imported models very

closely. One detail particularly favored in that area was a horseshoe-shaped thumbpiece which terminated in a scroll (Fig. 185). This same feature is to be seen on the flagon (Fig. 138) presented to Christ Church, Philadelphia, by Queen Anne in 1708, which was made by

John East of London, as well as on the duplicate flagon made in 1712 by Philip Syng, one of the city's earliest silversmiths. Another type of tankard based on English models which became especially popular in Philadelphia was the hooped tankard (Fig. 27). Introduced as early as 1788, this special design found favor there into the nineteenth century.

New York tankards were often more elaborately engraved and heavier in stance than those of other areas. The decorated base-band found on the Dutch-derived beakers in New York was repeated on the tankards of that area (Figs. 13, 133). On the lid there was a widely overhanging lip, usually crenelated and sometimes even engraved. Tankards actually are a rare form in Dutch silver, and apparently it was the English domination of New York which caused the form to be made there at all, but with its inset coins, applied cast decoration, and cocoon-shaped thumbpiece, the New York tankard is distinctly different from the tankards of other Colonies.

In New England, tankards had special features too (Fig. 134). While they copied English designs for the most part, the silversmiths in that area soon developed their own innovations. A mask-and-dolphin thumbpiece was often substituted by Boston makers about 1700 for the more usual cusped thumbpiece. In the mid-eighteenth century, in addition to putting a mid-band on the body of the tankard, they also added a

corkscrew finial, which silversmiths of other areas did not use. Instead of the flat, widely overhanging lid continued by New York silversmiths, a domed and closely fitting lid was used (Fig. 141).

[133] Tankard, by Cornelius Kierstede, New York, c.1725. Engraved R^{S}I and owned by the Sill family. Engraved with the arms of Lady Jane Still. Height 7½". *Courtesy, Henry Francis du Pont Winterthur Museum*

[134] Tankard, by Jeremiah Dummer, Boston, c.1700. Given by Mary Cook to her nephew Dr. Thomas Williams of Deerfield in the mid-eighteenth century. Height: 6¾". *Courtesy, Heritage Foundation, Deerfield, Mass.; gift of Mrs. Williams Hartigan*

Porringer handles show the same kinds of differences as tankard details throughout the Colonies. Early New England examples have simple geometric piercings (Fig. 49b), while early New York porringers had more elaborately pierced handles with intricate designs of hearts, crosses, diamonds, and crescents (Fig. 48). Boston silver-

smiths like John Edwards and William Cowell developed a type of porringer handle known as "crown and cresting," and New York silversmiths such as Adrian Bancker and Elias Pelletreau countered with a broad porringer handle with only three large piercings. By the last part of the century, the keyhole type of porringer handle had become universal, but a few New York makers such as Cary Dunn, Hays and Myers, and Andrew Billings used an interlaced type of design which relates to the carved diamond-shaped fretwork in New York furniture of the same period.

The backs of spoons, especially the design on the bowl, also reveal regional differences. The shells on the bowls of Boston spoons in the Rococo period often had webbing between the lobes. This design differs markedly from the Philadelphia type of drop, with unattached lobes and a separated arc-shaped design above a round drop.[37]

Whether in a detail as small as a drop on the back of a spoon or in the larger general preference for a particular form, the regional contributions of American silver are distinct. Such variations are the chief reward of a handicraft tradition. By the nineteenth century and the machine age, with closer communication between areas and the mass-production of both forms and decorative details, these individual differences began to disappear forever. For handwrought silver, however, regional developments are most important indications of America's contributions to the artistry of silver design.

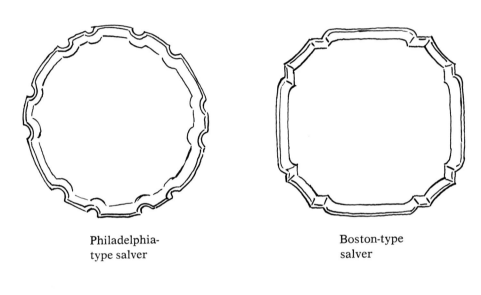

Philadelphia-
type salver

Boston-type
salver

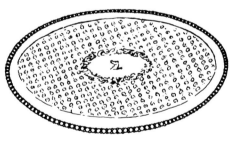

Baltimore-type tray

THE

HISTORICAL

SIGNIFICANCE

OF AMERICAN

SILVER

[134a] Teakettle, by Cornelius Kierstede, New York and New Haven, c. 1715. Made for the De Peyster family. Height: 10¼". *Courtesy, The Metropolitan Museum of Art, Bequest of James Stevenson Van Cortlandt, 1917*

CHAPTER FIVE

Domestic Silver

IN addition to its artistic value, American silver has enormous historical significance. Not only are the major events in our nation's history recorded in silver, but our economic, religious, institutional, and social development can be traced through these lustrous objects.

On the domestic scene, when the settlers came to this country they were somewhat limited in the amount of household goods they could bring with them. The ships which carried them were not very large and had to bring enough provisions to keep them in food until crops could be planted and harvested. While kettles and tools were among the items recommended to be brought by every colonist, family silver was not. Furthermore, there were few among the first settlers who might have owned any silver. While some were well-to-do, most of the founding fathers were from the lower middle classes and yeomanry of the English provinces, or else tradesmen and craftsmen of the cities, so that they were not likely to have had much silver to bring with them.

Family riches would have been out of place in the first decades, anyway: Captain Nathaniel Butler reported in 1622 of Virginia that the "Howses are generally the worst that ever I sawe, the meanest Cottages in England being every waye equall (if not superior) with the most of the best." Twenty years later the situation had vastly improved. Edmund Johnson observed in his *Wonder-Working Providence* that "the Lord hath been pleased to turn all the wigwams, huts and hovels the English dwelt in at their first coming, into orderly, fair and well built houses, well furnished many of them." [38]

By 1647, when William Clarke died in Salem, Massachusetts, he left a house of two stories with a garret, a cellar, and a kitchen in addition to three bedrooms, a parlor, and a great room, or hall. The house was undoubtedly of simple frame construction, with exposed beams and plastered walls, little windows, and large fireplaces. The oak or pine furniture was rectilinear in design, and was largely made up of joint stools, benches, tables, and trunks, although there was also a court cupboard. Nevertheless, William Clarke managed to have six silver spoons and two small pieces of plate valued at 3 pounds in one of his closets.[39]

In the second half of the seventeenth century, the situation began to improve more dramatically. In England as well as in the Colonies, a rising middle class began to be able to provide itself with more silver tableware. Spoons of silver were the first items which they indulged in, but soon there were added silver bowls, salts, cups, beakers, tankards, and porringers. The value of family plate steadily increased in the inventories taken of the estates of the colonists. Whereas the Reverend Nathaniel Rogers of Ipswich left a little over £35 in plate in 1655, Cornelius Steenwyck, Mayor of New York, left 723 ounces of silver plate valued at £216/18/– in 1686, and Sir William Phipps, Royal Governor of Massachusetts, left 1,240 ounces in 1696.[40]

Much of the silver in the first homes was imported or, more likely, was brought with the colonists when they came. The trade statistics of the Public Record Office in London show that in 1698 only £28 worth of plate were imported from England to Colonial America.[41] By 1728, this amount had increased to £1,265. Merchants had become prosperous as the population increased and commerce became established. Ties were close with England; there was frequent travel between the Colonies and the mother country, and the weekly list of ships arriving in port was long indeed. In Boston, David Neal found that by 1718 "The Conversation in this Town is as polite as in most of the cities and towns of England . . . so that a Gentleman from London would almost think himself at home in Boston when he observes the Numbers of People, their Houses, their Furniture, their Tables, their Dress and Conversation which perhaps is as splendid and showy, as that of the most considerable Tradesman in London."[42]

By the second quarter of the eighteenth century, the houses had larger, glassed windows, four or more rooms to a floor, wainscoted walls, and were furnished with handsomely designed walnut chairs, chests, tables of various sizes, desks, looking glasses, and pictures. A much greater variety of form was to be found among the silver furnishings than had existed in the preceding century. In 1728, Colonel

Thomas Lee's house in Virginia was robbed; among the interesting forms which were stolen were caudle cups, a chocolate pot, a coffee-pot, a teapot, three casters, four salts, a plate, a tumbler, four candle-sticks, canns, a funnel for quart bottles, and a pair of snuffers and stand.[43]

In the same year in New York, Colonel Abraham de Peyster died, leaving seven tankards, ten mugs, seven porringers, a large silver punch bowl and spoon, seven large and small salvers, six candlesticks, three pairs of snuffers and snuff boxes, two basins, two cordial cups, two large spice boxes, three sugar casters, a coffeepot, a teapot, a milk pot, three plates, a chafing dish, and three tumblers. This was in addition to smaller items such as eleven salt cellars, six small salt spoons, thirty-six forks, thirty-five spoons, two large ladles, four small forks, fifteen small teaspoons, a small spoon dish, and a worn candlestick. This was in addition still to a silver gilt salver and plate, a large cordial cup, another salver, another plate, a large tankard, a mug, a porringer, a salt cellar, a pepper box, and a ladle! [44]

The same year in Boston, Governor William Burnet died, and he rivaled de Peyster's estate with plate consisting of:

12 candlesticks, 2 branches for 3 lights, 1 snuff dish and snuffers, 3 stands and 3 pair snuffers, 3 castors and crewit stand, pepper box, 8 salts, 2 canns, chaffendish and plate, a large Square Salver, 4 small ditto, 1 shaving basin, 2 two-handled porringers, 1 Sangarey [punch] Cup and cover, 1 Mountef [Monteith], 2 large decanters, 2 coffee pots, Teapot, small panneken with wooden handle, 2 doz. and 16 spoons, 8 teaspoons, tea tongs, 3 soup ladles, 1 punch spoon, pr. spurs, 2 pr. shoe buckles, 2 pr. garter buckles, child's spoon, toothpick case, large silver gilt salver, 4 silver gilt antient family Cups with Covers, 6 gilt tea spoons, pr. tongs and strainer, doz. spoons, doz. knives, doz. forks, for a Desert, three cases containing 3 doz. knives and 3 doz. forkes with silver handles.[45]

Some of these forms, like the pistol-handled knives and forks, were invariably imported from England, but by this time there were a sufficient number of silversmiths in this country who were able to produce most of the objects a rich merchant might require. It was the ceremony surrounding the tea table that caused the biggest boon to the local silversmith's business. At first, a tradesman might request only a little silver milk pot, or teaspoons, strainer, and tongs to be used with a china tea set, but by 1748, Anthony Morris of Philadelphia had purchased from Joseph Richardson a teapot, a weighter, a sugar dish, a milk pot, and a slop bowl, all at one time.[46]

At first it was not necessary for all the pieces in a tea set to be of the same style, but by the mid-eighteenth century, matching teapots, sugar bowls, and milk pots were being made (Fig. 135). By this time, too, the amount of imported plate had reached an all-time high, with over

[135] Tea set, by Peter de Riemer (1738–1814), New York, c.1760. Engraved with Van Rensselaer crest and initials of Philip Schuyler Van Rensselaer, Mayor of Albany. Height (teapot): 6¾". *Courtesy, Museum of the City of New York*

£4,700 worth of wrought silver being imported from England to the American colonies both in 1760 and again in 1761. Patriotism and pride ultimately caused Daniel Henchman to protest in Boston in 1773 against "those Strangers among us who import and sell English Plate to the great Hurt and Prejudice of the Townsmen who have been bred to the Business." [47]

Not only the very wealthy wanted silver objects. The butcher, the baker, and candlestick maker were all among the customers of Joseph Richardson. The mid-eighteenth-century houses of tradesmen had become much finer. The walls were prettily paneled and painted, or else covered with imported wallpapers. The ceilings might have been decorated with moldings or stucco work. Some of the windows were hung with curtains, there were imported rugs on the floor, and the houses were filled with richly carved Chippendale-style mahogany furniture. The silver might have been displayed in an open or glassed shell cupboard to the side of an elaborately embellished fireplace over which a landscape painting might hang in carved framework.

The most common forms found among the household plate at this time, in addition to the objects associated with tea drinking, were canns, porringers, salts, casters, tankards, ladles, and, of course, spoons. A great many smaller items were available in silver now, and jewelry and buckles to adorn one's person were also eagerly sought by rising middle-class patrons.

The Revolutionary War called a temporary halt to the importation of silver from England and greatly curtailed the activities of many of the American silversmiths. Some were forced to flee to the country, and Tories all over the eastern seaboard carried what family plate they could when they sought refuge in Nova Scotia or England, some never to return again. However, as soon as hostilities were officially ended in 1783 and the new nation became constitutionally established, Americans found themselves free to trade not only with England, but wherever they pleased. Many felt, however, that they did not want to buy anything abroad that American workmanship could produce. As a result, importation was renewed with England and begun with France and other countries, but at the same time the American silversmith was patronized as he never had been before.

To go with newly constructed and lavishly furnished mansions, a great variety of silver forms were made available, and were supplemented by quantities of Sheffield and plated wares. Complete tea sets were ordered at one time, at a cost of over £100. Joseph Richardson, Jr., of Philadelphia, made dozens of silver services like the one, bought by Lydia Spencer on October 19, 1796, which included a coffeepot, teapot, sugar dish, slop bowl, cream pot, a dozen teaspoons, and a dozen tablespoons (Fig. 136).[48] Tongs, strainers, caddies, and urns were

[136] Tea and coffee service, by Joseph Richardson, Jr. (1752–1831), Philadelphia, c.1790. Part of a nineteen-piece set, including teaspoons and tongs. Height (coffeepot): 13″. *Courtesy, Henry Francis du Pont Winterthur Museum*

other items which were now deemed essential for the proper serving
of tea. One visitor to this country was so impressed with the amount
of tea drinking done here that he deduced that Americans must feel it
was their patriotic duty to drink tea! [49]

The tea was served from trays, in a large room—a room much larger than was
common at that age. The service was more splendid than I had before seen. It
stood under the mahogany table,—it was the fashion, then. A silver tea-kettle
stood on a silver chafing-dish. Coal might be placed in the chafing-dish and that
kept the water hot. A large tea-urn of silver and a silver waiter stood on the table,
with a silver teapot, sugar dish and milk pot surrounded by an elegant set of
china service. I had never seen so much silver service and it was regarded as an
evidence of ancient wealth and family.[50]

Such was Mrs. Anstis Lee's recollection of the urbanity and dignity of
the tea ceremony at Colonel Wyllys' mansion in Connecticut in 1791.

Service at the dinner table had also become more elaborate in America. The sideboard had been introduced in the Federal period as a new
piece of furniture, and soon the silversmiths were advertising sideboard
sets in addition to tea sets. Moreau de St. Méry, a French bookseller
who lived in Philadelphia during the 1790s, remarked that the Americans followed English custom in that "all the silver one owns is displayed on the sideboard in the dining room." [51] Decorative pieces were
soon added to the essential plate on the dining room table.

The fact that the seat of Congress was then in Philadelphia and that
the President's House was in that city undoubtedly influenced society
and its fashions. According to John F. Watson's *Annals*, President Washington gave dinner parties every Thursday evening. "He had a silver pint
cup or mug of beer placed by his plate, of which he drank; . . . There
were placed upon his table, as ornaments, sundry alabaster mythologi-
cal figures of about two feet high. The centre of the table contained five
or six large silver or plated waiters. The table itself was of an oval
shape; at the end were also some silver waiters of an oval form." [52]

Washington had been at great pains to have appropriate silver for his
table. Tobias Lear had written for him in 1789:

The President is desireous of getting a sett of those waiters, salvers, or whatever
they are called, which are set in the middle of a dining table to ornament it—and
to occupy the place which must otherwise be filled with dishes of meat, which
are seldom or never touched. Mr. Morris & Mr. Bingham have them, and the
French & Spanish Ministers here, but I know of no one else who has . . .[53]

The following spring, Washington received the new table ornaments
from France and called them by their proper name, *plateaux*. Only a
few were ever made by American silversmiths, and the three surviving
examples, by New York silversmiths, were made shortly after 1800.[54]

They were designed with varying lengths of flat glassed sections so that the center surface was a mirror. A gallery formed a rim around the entire length. In the case of the Forbes plateau now at the White House, the gallery was decorated with raised figures of Flora and Pomona surmounted by American eagle finials.

Drawing of plateau and photographic detail showing classic ornament, by John W. Forbes (w. 1802–1838), New York, c. 1803. Drawn by Edward Mayo. Length: 88″. *Courtesy, The White House Collection*

In New England, millionaire merchant Elias Hasket Derby built an elegant house in Salem and furnished it handsomely. When he died in 1799, the inventory of his household goods rambled on for fourteen pages and listed over a thousand dollars' worth of silver, some of it old and some of it new. There were two mahogany, urn-shaped knife cases, designed for the sideboard and inlaid with his initials, which contained eight silver spoons, two carving knives and forks, and ninety-six knives and forks. There was a gold-washed silver punch urn, a basin, two pitchers, two coffeepots, three butter boats, two tankards, two pairs of canns in different sizes, a dozen tumblers (Figs. 122, 123), four pepper and mustard pots, three porringers, two bowls, a spout cup, four salts, a waiter (Fig. 29), a sugar urn, a teapot and stand, two cream pitchers and a cream pail, three sets of casters, a sugar pail and tongs, a punch strainer, and dozens of spoons and ladles of various sizes. Furthermore, Derby had not scorned the new plated wares, and had fruit baskets, caster sets, candlesticks, snuffers and a tray, a spice box, and a fish knife made of silver-plated copper.[55]

By the beginning of the nineteenth century, the variety and size of silver objects available was enormous. Whole dinner services were made with silver plates and pitchers of graduated sizes (Fig. 137). Huge silver tureens graced the sideboard, and for the center of the table towering candelabra were made to serve as both impressive ornamentation and useful illumination. Matching tea sets continued to be

[137] Dinner service, by Thomas Fletcher and Sidney Gardiner, Philadelphia, 1817. Part of fifty-two piece service costing $4,000, presented to Commodore John Rodgers for his defense of the city by the citizens of Baltimore on the third anniversary of the bombardment of Fort McHenry, September 12–13, 1814. Largest platter: 22¾" by 17½". *Courtesy, Maryland Historical Society*

made with all the necessary accouterments and were, now more than ever, generous in their proportions. The cream pot in these tea sets had grown almost as large as the earliest teapots. The smallest and most insignificant trifle might now be made of silver, and the innovation in forms seemed unlimited.

Even in rural areas, where conditions were more primitive and more like the days of first settlement, where previously only a few families had had silver spoons or possibly a tankard, a cann, or a porringer, there were now plated tea sets, at least, and small silver cups in many of the farmhouses. The transformation from the struggling settlements of the seventeenth century to the established affluence of the nineteenth century had been dramatically achieved, and there was now no end to the demand for domestic silver in the rising American democracy.

CHAPTER SIX

Church Silver

CHURCHES have been instrumental in preserving one of the largest and most significant groups of American silver. As soon as the country was settled, churches were established, and vessels were needed for the service of communion and for baptism. While pewter was used in the poorer parishes, most of the early American churches aspired to silver vessels. In many cases these were given by members of the congregation or purchased by the church with funds given for that purpose.[56]

During the Colonial period, and especially with the founding of the Society for the Propagation of the Gospel, whole sets of silver were occasionally given by the British monarchs to certain American churches. Trinity Church in New York has three services of royal plate, given by William and Mary, Queen Anne, and George III. Queen Anne gave Christ Church in Philadelphia a flagon (Fig. 138), a chalice, and a paten; George II gave Christ Church and Trinity Church in Boston the same forms and an alms basin as well; and George III gave Bruton Parish Church in Williamsburg a chalice, a flagon, and a basin. These royal services were invariably made by English silversmiths, but for the most part, the silver in American churches was made by American silversmiths.

Perhaps the earliest donation of silver to an American church was that given by Mrs. Mary Robinson of London in her will, dated 1617. She bequeathed for "the helpe of the poore people in Virginia, towards

151

the building of a Church & the reduceinge of them to the knowledge of God's word, the sum of two hundred pounds." With this money, the Hampton Church in Virginia procured two patens and a chalice made during the following year in London. In Boston, members of the congregation gave to their churches English-made standing cups, such as the one John Winthrop brought with him, which bears the London date-letter for 1610–11, and which is the earliest piece of silver among the forty-five pieces belonging to The First Church.

The earliest silver in American churches was English-made, and rarely departed from English tradition and forms. The Reformation of the Church of England, which took place during the century preceding American colonization, had caused a complete change in church silver. In an effort to rid the reformed church of the old ritualistic elements of the service, the Reformation leaders wanted the medieval chalice of the Catholic Church to be replaced by a secular form of communion cup. The new cups were the same as the domestic cups used in homes, just as the new churches were meeting houses rather than cathedrals. Even in the Anglican Church, where the break with Catholic tradition was less severe, an injunction was issued by the Archbishop of Canterbury that each parish should have its chalice changed into a "decent communion cup." [57]

In general, the silver in the early New England churches was puritanically plain and chaste in its design. In the second half of the seventeenth century, when John Hull and Robert Sanderson began to make silver for The First Church in Boston, of which both were members, they followed the general form of the most recently presented London examples. When the Newman Congregational Church in Rehoboth (now East Providence, Rhode Island) received a legacy of five pounds from Captain Thomas Willet in 1674, they had Hull and Sanderson make the standing cup similar to an English cup which had been given by Noah Newman (Fig. 3). As late as 1772, The First Church in Marblehead had Joseph Smith of Boston copy an English beaker which had been made a hundred years earlier and had been part of that church's silver since at least 1728 (Fig. 139).

Beakers were another form of domestic silver which became suitable for use in reformed churches. The earliest dated example of work by Hull and Sanderson is the beaker (Fig. 2) they made for The First Church, Boston, in 1659. With its broad band of granulation, it follows the pattern of the upper section of a standing cup given that church by Jeremy Houchin, which was made in London in 1639–40.

In New York, the beaker was the most important early form for the Dutch Reformed Church. In the Collegiate Church, which was founded

[138] Flagon (left), by John East, London, 1707–08. Given by Queen Anne to Christ Church, Philadelphia, in 1708. Flagon (right), by Philip Syng (1676–1739), Philadelphia, 1712. Given by Col. Robert Quary to Christ Church on October 29, 1712. Height: 11″. *Courtesy, Christ Church; photograph, courtesy, Philadelphia Museum of Art*

[139] Beakers (left to right) by Jeremiah Dummer, Boston, c.1675; T.C. or C.T., London, probably 1671–72; Joseph Smith, Boston, c.1772; and Hull and Sanderson, Boston, c.1675. Heights: 6″, 5½″, 5½″, 6″. *Courtesy, The First Church of Christ, Marblehead, Mass.; photograph by Richard Merrill*

in 1628, there were three beakers, two of which were made in Haar-
lem, Holland, and one of which was made in this country. These beakers differ from the first New England beakers in that they are quite tall
and elaborately engraved with strapwork and vignettes of emblems
such as Faith, Hope, and Charity. These also were domestic drinking
vessels, such as the example made by Cornelius Vander Burch for presentation to Robbert Sandersen (Fig. 7).

A Dutch beaker made in Amsterdam in 1637 was given to The First
Church in Boston by the widow of the goldsmith Robert Sanderson, and
undoubtedly had inspired the beaker he and John Hull made which
became part of the communion silver in The First Church of Marblehead (Figs. 126, 139). The more usual form of beaker in New England
remained the plain beaker (Fig. 139) with molded base-band and
slightly flaring lip, such as that made by Jeremiah Dummer. At the end
of the seventeenth century, the base became rounded and bands of
baroque reeding and fluting were introduced into the design of both
beakers and standing cups (Fig. 140).

Caudle cups were also used as communion vessels in American
churches as early as 1676 when John Coney began making this form
for the First Parish in Concord. In the eighteenth century, a combination caudle cup and beaker was also made, which was a tall beaker
with two handles.

Mugs or canns, although less popular, were also domestic forms of
silver used for communion. Like the other forms of church silver, they
followed the same changes in style that domestic plate did. The most
widely used type, however, was the bellied mug. Salem churches especially made use of this type of cup. Over half the known examples in
American churches were in Salem in the second half of the eighteenth
century.

Tankards were also used as sacramental cups. Samuel Sewall refers
in his diary to the use of personal tankards at the communion table, and
the Reverend Samson Stoddard bequeathed his tankard to the church
in Chelmsford, Massachusetts, in 1740 for use at the communion table.
One of the earliest tankards made by an American silversmith for
presentation to a church is a tankard at Winterthur made in 1676 by
Jeremiah Dummer to fulfill the legacy of Richard Russell to the church
in Charlestown, Massachusetts. In its design it follows closely an English tankard of 1674–75 owned by Charles Frost and given by him to the
church in Berwick, Maine, in 1725. By the eighteenth century, with the
growth in size of the congregations, it was necessary for the third
church in Brookfield, Massachusetts, to purchase a set of six matching
tankards (Fig. 141) from Paul Revere.

Flagons have been called "tankards-gone-to-church," since they follow the general design of tankards. They differ in having elongated bodies and handles, and much wider base moldings, and in being used to fill the communion vessels instead of serving as the communion cup. The flagons in American churches were more frequently used in Anglican services, particularly in the seventeenth century. However, in the mid-eighteenth century, the Burts of Boston were making flagons for The First Church (Congregational) in Marblehead (Fig. 142), and in Salem John Andrew was employed to copy an imported English flagon given The First Church there by Samuel Browne (Fig. 143).

In the Anglican Church, the cover of the communion cup, which before the Reformation was generally surmounted by a cruciform finial, was usually fashioned so that when it was taken off and inverted it became a small paten on a reel-shaped foot which could serve as a plate for the bread. In America, the paten was restricted to Episcopal churches for the most part. In the reformed churches, shallow plates were preferred until the nineteenth century, when bread baskets came into use. At first the plates were plain and generally footless, but these became more elaborate in the eighteenth century and often followed the design of domestic salvers.

Baptismal basins or plain bowls of silver were generally introduced into American churches early in the eighteenth century. An exceptionally early example is one made in 1694 by Jacobus Vander Spiegel which follows a Dutch design. Philip Syng made a basin of the very deep variety with a narrow rim in 1712 for Christ Church, Philadelphia. The more typical form was the less deep bowl with broad brim and reeded edge made by William Cowell, Sr., for the Brattle Street Church in 1716, and by Paul Revere (Fig. 142) in 1773 for The First Church in Marblehead. A unique design was fashioned by Daniel Russell in 1734 for Trinity Church in Newport. It has a deep oval body on a molded foot and two ring handles.

Alms basins or dishes did not differ much from the broad-brim-type of baptismal bowl, although they might have been a little shallower. Not every church had an alms basin, since this form, when it is found, is usually part of Anglican or Episcopal church plate. The example given by George II to Christ Church in Boston in 1733 was referred to at the time as a "Receiver." Perhaps the lack of alms dishes in most churches can be explained by the records of Collegiate Church in New York: ten silver plates were ordered in 1791 so "that as soon as the plates are obtained the alms shall hereafter be collected in plates instead of the Bags hitherto used . . ."

Spoons or ladles, used in the preparation of communion, sometimes

[140] Four beakers, by Jeremiah Dummer, Boston, c.1700. Spoon, by Andrew Tyler (1692–1741), Boston, c.1720. Height (beakers): 4½". Length (spoon): 5½". *Courtesy, The First Church of Christ, Marblehead, Mass.; photograph by Richard Merrill*

[141] Set of six tankards, by Paul Revere, Boston, 1772. Bought by the Third Church of Brookfield, Mass., with legacy of Mary Bartlett, who died in 1768, and charged in Revere's accounts in 1772. Height: 8¼". *Courtesy, Henry Francis du Pont Winterthur Museum*

[142] Four flagons by Samuel Burt (1724–1754) and Benjamin Burt (1729–1804), Boston, 1748 and 1759. Engraved with arms of donors. Height: 13″. Baptismal basin, by Paul Revere, Boston, 1773. Engraved with Lemmon arms and given by Dr. Joseph Lemmon in 1773. Diameter: 12⅞″. *Courtesy, The First Church of Christ, Marblehead, Mass.; photograph by Richard Merrill*

[143] Flagon (left), by W. and J. Priest, London, 1767–68. Gift of Colonel Samuel Browne, 1731. Flagon (right), by John Andrew (1747–1791), Salem, 1769. Height: 13″. *Courtesy, The First Church, Salem, Mass.; photograph by Richard Merrill*

[144] Scroll bells or Rimonim, by Myer Myers, New York, c.1765. Length: c.14".
*Courtesy, The Society of Friends of Touro Synagogue, Newport, R.I.; photograph
by John Hopf*

found their way into the church plate. An early example is the wavy-end
spoon (Fig. 140) made by Andrew Tyler of Boston in The First Church
of Marblehead. Occasionally these had pierced bowls, such as the
example made by Abraham Dubois of Philadelphia for Christ Church.
At the Essex Institute there is an early nineteenth-century ladle with a
pierced bowl; history has it that the ladle was used to remove flies from
the communion wine at the Branch Church in Salem.

Minority religions account for a few unusual objects in American
church silver. Myer Myers, America's outstanding Jewish silversmith,
made elaborate scroll bells or Crowns of the Torah (Fig. 144) for the
synagogues in Newport, New York, and Philadelphia. Called *Rimonim*,
these decorative objects were used to embellish the ends of the wooden
scroll to which the parchment copy of the Five Books of Moses was
attached. When the Torah was read, a long silver pointer shaped on
the end with a hand and a pointing finger was used. The unmarked
example in the Touro Synagogue was probably also made by Myers.

Evidently most of the silver used in Catholic churches in this country
was of foreign manufacture. Few examples by American silversmiths
are known, but a chalice made about 1830 by R. & W. Wilson survives
at St. Joseph's Roman Catholic Church in Philadelphia.

CHAPTER SEVEN

Official Silver

OFFICIAL silver can be designated as that made for official use by a government or organization, and that which is emblematic of office or membership. There are not as many examples of official silver in America as there are in England or on the Continent, due to our being a colonial country and then a democracy. A permanent hierarchy and a resultant attachment of greater significance to outward signs of power are necessary to produce much official silver.

In England, silver and gold chains, collars, and badges of office were made to be worn by such officials as mayors, sheriffs, and waits of a city. Many towns in England also had a civic mace, developed from the medieval weapon or the military mace, as a symbol of authority. While no examples are known in American silver, there is a civic mace in Williamsburg, Virginia, which was made in England. As far as is known, this is one of the few maces which continued the civic tradition in the new country.

However, two oar maces of Admiralty have survived in American silver. Fashioned in the shape of an oar, these maces were used as emblems of the authority of the British High Court of Admiralty and were carried in procession when the President of the Admiralty Court entered the room. While he presided "in Admiralty," the oar rested in a bracket before him on the bench. In America, Vice Admiralty Courts were established in New York, Philadelphia, Boston, and Rhode Island. In Boston, an account of the execution of Quelch the pirate in 1704

159

noted that the condemned man was "allowed to walk on Foot through the Town . . . the Silver Oar being carried before them . . ." [58]

The silver oar of the Boston Vice Admiralty Court which survives was not made until the second quarter of the eighteenth century by Jacob Hurd (Fig. 145). It is engraved on one side of the paddle end with the royal arms and the cypher of George Rex, and on the other side with an anchor. Very similar to it is the silver oar made by Charles Le Roux about the same time, and presented by the British Crown to the New York Vice Admiralty Court. The New York Court had been established since 1678 and the Boston Court since about 1694. Both were dissolved at the beginning of the Revolution and the oars, being considered the property of the Marshals of the Court, were taken home by these officers and inherited by their descendants. Oars in English Courts of Admiralty range in size from four and a quarter inches to forty-five inches, so that by comparison, the American oars are of medium length, both being about twenty-three inches long.

One of the most important pieces of American silver used for official purposes is the inkstand (Fig. 146) made by Philip Syng of Philadelphia. Commissioned in 1752 by order of the Assembly of Pennsylvania, the standish originally cost £25/16/–, and achieved historical immortality when it held the quill pens, the ink, and the sand used by the members of the Second Continental Congress at Independence Hall for the signing of the Declaration of Independence.[59]

In the case of the Declaration of Independence, the signing of the names was sufficient, but in more ordinary circumstances it was customary for governments and organizations to have a silver seal which could impress in wax the official signature of the body. Early in the eighteenth century, Marbletown, New York, had a seal (Fig. 147) cut with its arms and motto by Jacob Boelen. Paul Revere cut the seal for Phillips Academy in Andover (Fig. 189), with the design of industrious

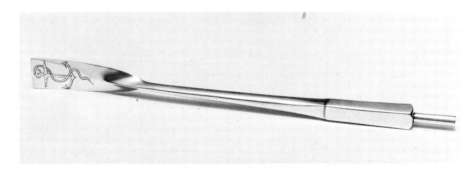

[145] Admiralty oar, by Jacob Hurd, Boston, c.1740. Length: 23½". *Courtesy, Massachusetts Historical Society*

[146] Inkstand, by Philip Syng, Jr. (1703–1789), Philadelphia, 1752. Commissioned by the Assembly of Pennsylvania for £25/16, and used for the signing of Declaration of Independence and Constitution. Length: 10¼". *Courtesy, Independence Hall Collection; photograph, courtesy, Philadelphia Museum of Art*

[147a, left] Notary Public seal used in Boston by Samuel Cooper, who was notary public from about 1796 to 1806. Possibly cut by Joseph Callender (1751–1821), Boston, die-sinker for the Massachusetts Mint. Diameter: 1¾". *Courtesy, The Bostonian Society.* [147b, right] Seal, by Jacob Boelen (1657–1729), New York, c. 1700. Used as official seal of Marbletown, New York. Diameter: 2⅞". *Courtesy, The Metropolitan Museum of Art, Bequest of A. T. Clearwater, 1933*

bees. Some men specialized in seal-cutting, and "Office and Company Seals, Dies, &c. with any device" were advertised by Samuel Brooks in the *Federal Gazette* on June 10, 1793.

Seals were cut by American silversmiths for individuals as well. Andrew Belcher of Milton, Massachusetts, had among his possessions in 1771:

> 4 Family Seals with handles
> 1 Gold Watch with one Seal & Locket
> 1 Silver Watch with three Seals
> 1 Triangular Seal set in Gold.[60]

These seals could be used for signing such official documents as a will or a deed, and in fact we know much more about the design of these seals from the wax impressions made from them on surviving manuscripts than from the surviving seals. Individual designs for seals ranged from the family coat of arms, to initials, a figure, or simple heraldic devices.

Charles Oliver Bruff of New York advertised in *The New-York Gazette & Weekly Mercury* on July 18, 1774, that he had a stone-seal engraver who could provide his customer with "arms, crests, cyphers, figures, heads and fancies." Among the heads he had to offer were

Shakespear, Milton, Newton, Pope, Homer, Socrates, Hannible, Mark Anthony, Caesar, Plato, Jupiter, Apollo, Neptune, Mars, Cleopatria, Diana, Flora, Venus,

[148] Phi Beta Kappa medals, obverse and reverse, owned by Zechariah Howard (left) and Benjamin Pickman (right), Harvard Class of 1784. Width: 1". *Courtesy, Harvard University*

Marcellany, with the figures of most of the above, and others too tedious to mention.

Individuals also bought from silversmiths and jewelers the emblems which signified their official membership in certain organizations. Phi Beta Kappa medals (Fig. 148) and the Eagles of the Society of the Cincinnati (Fig. 149) were purchased by the members of these elite groups. When the Phi Beta Kappa Society was organized at William and Mary on December 5, 1776, it was specified:

And for the better establishment and sanctitude of our unanimity, a square silver medal was agreed on and instituted, engraved on the one side with SP, the initials of the Latin (Societas Philosophiae) and on the other, agreeable to the former, with the Greek initials of Φ . . . B . . . K . . . and an index imparting a philosophical design, extended to the three stars, a part of the planetary orb, distinguished.[61]

Two medals and two charters were brought by Elisha Parmele to New England for the establishment of branches of the Phi Beta Kappa

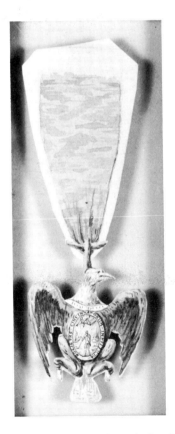

[149] Watercolor sketch for the eagle badge of the Society of the Cincinnati, drawn by Major Pierre Charles L'Enfant, when the society was founded in 1783. *Courtesy, W. Stephen Thomas, Rochester, N.Y.; photograph, courtesy, Rochester Museum of Arts and Sciences*

Society at Yale in 1780 and at Harvard on September 5, 1781. In this way "a medal of the same form and kind with that herewith transmitted to you, without any alteration whatever" could be provided to the members of Alpha of Massachusetts (Fig. 148). The medals were usually made of silver, and occasionally of gold or even brass. These medals, or keys, as they became, were supplied to members of the chapters by the local silversmiths and jewelers. Franklin Richmond and George W. Babcock of Providence were employed to make the keys for the Brown University chapter after its establishment in 1830.

When the Society of the Cincinnati was formed in 1783 by the officers of the Continental Army, they resolved:

> The Society shall have an Order, by which its members shall be known and distinguished, which shall be a medal of gold, of a proper size to receive the emblems, and suspended by a deep blue ribbon, two inches wide, edged with white, descriptive of the Union of America and France.[62]

Major Pierre Charles L'Enfant, who was himself a member of the newly founded Society, was charged with preparing the design of an eagle with a medallion on its breast showing Cincinnatus being presented with the sword by the Roman senators. Once the design was accepted, L'Enfant made water-color sketches of the Eagle for each of the State Societies (Fig. 149). The first Eagles of the Cincinnati were procured in France. George Washington, President-General of the organization, was presented by the officers of the French Navy with a most elaborate and beautiful version, lavishly set with diamonds, rubies, and emeralds around the delicately enameled emblem.

Shortly thereafter, Jeremiah Andrew, a jeweler in Philadelphia, advertised in the Baltimore newspaper on December 17, 1784, that he had completed a number of medals for the Society of Cincinnati, "allowed by many of the Society to be preferable to those imported." Two months later he called on Washington and showed him the Eagle medal which he had made. Washington had three Eagles when he died in 1799, two gold Eagles in addition to the diamond one. John Cooke of New York also advertised making the emblems for members of the Cincinnati in 1802.[63]

Members of the Masonic order also had silversmiths provide them with the devices of Freemasonry. These varied from simple small medallions engraved with the many Masonic symbols (Fig. 190) to fancy parts of the Master's regalia designed as a mason's square or a compass and arc containing an imported jewel.

The Grand Lodge of Massachusetts commissioned Paul Revere to make a gold urn (Fig. 150), which became a part of the official ritual at the first installation of each Grand Master. It was designed to contain a lock of George Washington's hair which the Lodge had requested and received from his widow at the time of his death in 1799. When the lid of the urn is removed, this remembrance of the most famous of all American Masons can be seen preserved beneath a thin flat piece of crystal or isinglass. When it is not being carried in the procession at installations, the urn is placed inside its mahogany veneered, inlaid pedestal, protected by a lining of robin's-egg-blue velvet.

While limited in number, these silver and gold emblems of office represent a select group of objects that provide pictorial evidence of the developing institutional history of America.

[150] Gold urn, by Paul Revere, Boston, 1800, made to hold a lock of George Washington's hair presented to the Grand Lodge of Massachusetts by his widow. Height (urn): 3¾". *Courtesy, Grand Lodge of Massachusetts*

[150a] Urn, by Harvey Lewis, Philadelphia, 1822. Stylized swans form the handles, and on one side is a relief view of the Fairmount Water Works. The urn was designed for presentation to Frederick Graff (1774–1847), who was Chief Engineer for the Philadelphia Water Works. Height: 13⅜″. *Courtesy, The Historical Society of Pennsylvania*

CHAPTER EIGHT

Presentation Silver

BECAUSE of its beauty and durability, silver has always been considered foremost among the materials selected for presentation pieces. Since these objects can commemorate diversified happenings, from births to funerals, sporting events to battles, and naval engagements to Indian peace treaties, presentation silver has great historical interest and many fascinating stories to tell.

Among the earliest presentation pieces made in this country are funeral rings (Fig. 151), usually made of gold, which were presented at funerals to the closest friends, relatives, and minister of the deceased. Often decorated with a skull or some other symbol of death, and engraved inside with the deceased's initials and date of demise, these rings were given in such numbers that the Massachusetts General Court soon passed an act restraining such costs for funerals.

Judge Samuel Sewall made careful note in his diary of the rings he received and, if he were unable to attend a funeral, even mentioned the gift he missed. One Salem minister, Dr. Samuel Buxton, received so many tokens of remembrance in the course of performing his services to parishioners that when he died he left a quart tankard full of mourning rings. Apothecary Thomas Barton of the same town in 1751 left his wife "all my gold rings had at funerals, save what may be made use of for my own funeral." Such tokens were treasured by those who received them. The Reverend William Bentley remarked that when Mary Pickman died in 1817, her husband gave him "a rich mourning

[151] Gold New England funeral rings. Left column (top to bottom), by David Northee, 1752; Jacob Hurd, 1740; Richard Conyers, 1707; John Coney, 1694. Right column, rings made in 1767, 1738, and lower two made for same funeral of William Pickman, Salem, 1735. *Courtesy, Essex Institute, Salem, Mass.; photograph by Richard Merrill*

[152] Ceremonial spoons, by Cornelius Vander Burch, New York, made for the funerals of Olof Stevense Van Cortlandt in 1684 (left) and of seven-year-old Henricus Van Deursen in 1692 (right). Length: 6⁵/₁₆". *Courtesy, Yale University Art Gallery, Mable Brady Garvan Collection*

ring which has the highest value in my esteem & is among the richest of my cabinet." [64]

In New York, spoons were sometimes made for use and presentation at funerals. Their separate cast handles might have an owl's head, monkey's head, or some other appropriate terminal design. Two examples in the Garvan collection were made by Cornelius Vander Burch, one (Fig. 152) when Olof Stevense Van Cortlandt died in 1684 and the other when H. V. Deursen died in 1692. This same form of spoon, with cast handle but lacking the death symbols, was also made in New York for other ceremonial occasions, such as christenings and marriages. The New-York Historical Society has an example, made by Jesse Kip, of one piece of silver with a trifid handle ending, which was given to Cornelia Duycken by her uncle and godfather at the time of her first birthday.[65]

Another favorite gift to children was the presentation of a silver or gold rattle. Called coral-and-bells or whistle-and-bells in the eighteenth century, these objects (Fig. 102) were designed to delight. The bells could be rattled, the whistle could be blown, and the coral was polished to facilitate teething. A ring at the whistle end made it possible to suspend the rattle by a ribbon or silver chain around the toddler's neck so that it would stay within easy grasp. Alexander Pope, in the *Rape of the Lock* indicated that these were frequently the gift of a grandmother:

> Her infant grandame's coral next it grew
> The bells she jingled and the whistle blew.

As early as 1675, a "whissle silver chaine and childe's bell" was listed in the Boston inventory of Captain John Freake.[66] In New England, these children's rattles were usually made of silver, but in New York a few gold rattles were made by such local goldsmiths as Nicholas Roosevelt.

Weddings provided another occasion for silver gift-giving. William Jefferey described this custom in his journal in 1673. "Mistress Vaughan, the grandmother of the bridegroom, came. . . . She giveth but one present at the marriage of each grandchild, always a silver cup, to be for the first born great-grandchild. She hath had inscribed on one side of this, the Latham arms, and desiring mine own on the other, as now joined in this marriage, it hath been done." [67] Often the piece of silver was marked with the arms of the bride's family (Fig. 153).

[153] Teapot, sugar caster, and cream pot, by John Coburn (1725–1803), Boston, c.1753. Given by Thomas Welles of Glastonbury, Conn., to his daughter Mary when she married David Hale in 1753. Height (teapot): 6½". *Courtesy, Heritage Foundation, Deerfield, Mass.*

[154] Coffeepot and sugar bowl, by Joseph Richardson (1711–1784), Philadelphia, 1754. Made for the wedding of Sarah Shoemaker and Edward Pennington on November 26, 1754, and engraved with her cypher. Height (coffeepot): 11″. *Courtesy, The Historical Society of Pennsylvania*

Thomas Welles of Glastonbury, Connecticut, presented each of his daughters, at the time of their marriage, with a set of silver consisting of a teapot engraved with the Welles arms, a sugar caster, and a creamer. Two of these sets made by John Coburn of Boston have survived.

In Philadelphia, a coffeepot and sugar bowl (Fig. 154) were made by Joseph Richardson for the wedding of Sarah Shoemaker and Edward Pennington in 1754. Richardson's account books indicate that he was also called upon to make silver for wedding anniversaries, particularly twentieth or twenty-fifth wedding anniversaries. Often the piece of silver was made so that the number of ounces it weighed corresponded to the number of years of the marriage.

At Harvard University, a few of the tutors were honored by the presentation of silver suitably inscribed *Ex dono pupillorum*. Both Nicholas Sever and Henry Flynt were recipients of gifts from students

[155] Pair of candlesticks, by John Coney, Boston, 1716. Presented to tutor Henry Flynt by his Harvard students, and engraved "Ex dono Pupillorum 1716." Height: 7½". *Courtesy, Heritage Foundation, Deerfield, Mass.*

(Fig. 155). Harvard University itself was given a handsome covered cup (Fig. 39) by the Honorable William Stoughton at the time of his death in 1701.

Silver and even golden trophies were presented to the winners of horse races and lotteries in the eighteenth century. In 1727, an announcement appeared in the *American Weekly Mercury* on March 23rd explaining what the prize would be for the lottery to be drawn in Perth Amboy:

£501 of Silver and Gold work, wrought by *Simeon Soumain* of *New York*, Gold-Smith, all of the newest Fashion. The highest Prize consists of an Eight square Tea-Pot, six Tea-Spoons, Skimmer and Tongues, Valued at £18 3s. 6d. . . .

A set of gold teaspoons and a strainer spoon (Fig. 55) by Simeon Soumain survive today.

Organizations made use of silver to honor men of note in their society. About 1800, this custom became widespread. The Massachusetts Humane Society awarded Dr. Samuel Brown of Boston a silver

[156] Tray, by John Myers (w. c.1785–1804), Philadelphia, 1798. Presented by the Board of Managers of Philadelphia Hospitals to Dr. Benjamin Rush for his services during the epidemic. *Courtesy, Mr. and Mrs. Benjamin Rush; photograph, courtesy, Philadelphia Museum of Art*

mug made by Joseph Loring in 1803 for "his ingenious Treatise on the Yellow Fever." Dr. Benjamin Rush had already received a large tray in 1798 (Fig. 156) for his "disinterested, benevolent and important services" during the epidemic in Philadelphia that year. Agricultural societies as well as local humane societies made awards of tea sets and medals and cups to outstanding members of their community.

One of the popular forms of such presentations at the time was the pitcher now known by the name of Paul Revere. He made one in 1804 for the parishioners of the First Congregational Church in Milton, Massachusetts, to present to their minister Joseph McKean when he gave up his duties there. In 1806, he made another (Fig. 129) for presentation by the Mechanic Association to Samuel Gilbert, who had ingratiated himself to the society by collecting unpaid dues during his office as secretary. The same organization several decades later honored Uriel Crocker for his services as treasurer (Fig. 34).

Perhaps the largest category of presentation silver is that made to honor the captains of ships who performed daring or heroic deeds at sea. The earliest of these is the large covered cup at Yale, made by Jacob Hurd for Commander Edward Tyng of the *Prince of Orange*, a snow or warship built at the expense of the Massachusetts Bay Colony for the express purpose of protecting her fisheries. Tyng and his ship took the first French privateer on this coast on June 24, 1744. An identical cup (Fig. 19) was made by Hurd for presentation in December

[157] Tankard and pair of canns, by Benjamin Burt, Boston, 1779. Presented to Jonathan Harraden, Captain of the ship *Pickering*. Height (tankard): 9¼". *Courtesy, The Peabody Museum of Salem*

of the same year to Richard Spry, Commander of the *Comet Bomb*, for taking a French privateer "from Cape Breton, which had for some Time infested our Coast," according to the local newspaper.

It became the custom also for the owners or the underwriters of the ship to reward the captain if he was able to save the ship from disaster or bring home in her hold especially valuable cargo. Jonathan Harraden of Salem was given a tankard and a pair of canns (Fig. 157) made by Benjamin Burt and neatly engraved with portraits of his sixteen-gun ship *Pickering*, which under his command had made a particularly successful trip to the Spanish coast in 1779. When the ship *Industry* was attacked by four French privateers in the Straights of Gibralter on July 8, 1800, her captain, Gamaliel Bradford, put up a gallant defense. As a result, Samuel Parkman commissioned Paul Revere to make an elegant coffee urn (Fig. 158) for presentation to Bradford.

It was the insurance companies which had an interest in the safety of the schooner *Tatler*. When Captain Nathaniel Garland was able to defend his vessel from the "piratical assault of the crew" on September 17, 1823, both the Salem Commercial Insurance Company and the Marine Insurance Company of Salem had J. B. Jones make silver toddy pots (Fig. 90) as a reward for his efforts.

Undoubtedly it was the War of 1812, with its successful American naval engagements and resultant silver presentations, which gave great impetus to similar presentations for lesser feats. During that war, many American heroes were rewarded for their bravery in action. The city of Albany presented Captain Isaac Hull with a covered pitcher (Fig. 159) engraved with the city arms on one side and on the other, a fiery representation of his ship the *Constitution* sinking the British *Guerriere* on August 19, 1812. A similar pitcher was presented in 1814 to Captain Thomas Macdonough by the citizens of Lansingburgh.

As patriotism and victories mounted, whole silver services were given to the heroes. The citizens of Baltimore had a service (Fig. 137) made by Fletcher and Gardiner for Commodore John Rogers after his defense of their city on September 12–13, 1814. In all, there were fifty-two pieces and the cost was an impressive four thousand dollars. Commodore Stephen Decatur was even more handsomely rewarded two years later, when he received very handsome gifts from both the citizens of Philadelphia (Fig. 32) and the citizens of Baltimore (Fig. 71).

One of the most interesting presentations for a naval victory is the pitcher (Fig. 160) presented to Captain Samuel C. Reid by the citizens of New York. Engraved on one side is a complete pictorial account of Captain Reid's defense of the brig *General Armstrong* off Fayal in the Azores on September 26, 1814.[68]

After the War of 1812 was over, the tradition of presenting the captain of the ship with a piece of silver was continued by the passengers of transatlantic vessels. Perhaps at first it was in gratitude for bringing them safely through a rough crossing. However, Captain Thomas Bennett of the *Packet Ship,* sailing from New York to England, seems to have been given such a present by his passengers so frequently that one suspects it had become tradition with every crossing on his ship (Fig. 84).

It was not just naval heroes who were recognized by the gift of a piece of silver. The most historic piece of American silver is the bowl made by Paul Revere (Fig. 161) to celebrate the heroic action of the ninety-two members of the House of Representatives in Massachusetts who stood firm in their protest to George III on June 30, 1768, even though they knew that it meant the dissolution of their assembly. Engraved around the sides with patriotic devices, including a reference to Wilkes's article in issue number forty-five of *The North Briton,* in which Wilkes championed the cause of the American colonists, the bowl was designed by Revere to weigh exactly forty-five ounces, and from it, on the night of the presentation, forty-five loyal toasts were drunk.[69]

Very similar in design is the bowl made five years earlier by William Homes for presentation to Thomas Dawes by his officers and captains

[158] Urn, by Paul Revere, Boston, 1800. Presented to Captain Gamaliel Bradford for his defense of the ship *Industry*. Height: 19″. *Courtesy, Massachusetts Historical Society; photograph, courtesy, Museum of Fine Arts, Boston*

[159] Covered pitcher, by Robert Shepherd and William Boyd, Albany, 1812. Presented by the city of Albany to Captain Isaac Hull for the victory of the *Constitution* over the *Guerrière* on August 19, 1812. Height: 15⅜″. *Courtesy, Wadsworth Atheneum, Hartford, Conn.*

[160] Pitcher, by William Thompson (w.1809–1845), New York, 1814. Presented by the citizens of New York to Capt. Samuel C. Reid for his defense of the brig *General Armstrong* in the Azores on September 26, 1814. Height: 8¾″. *Courtesy, The Museum of the City of New York*

[161] Liberty bowl, by Paul Revere, Boston, 1768. Made to commemorate the action of the Massachusetts Bay House of Representatives on June 30, 1768. Diameter: 11″ *Courtesy, Museum of Fine Arts, Boston*

[162] Tankard, by Thomas Dane, Boston, 1757. Presented to Joseph Frye by his officers on April 20, 1757. Finial missing. Height: 8¼″. *Courtesy, Maine Historical Society; photograph by Mason Philip Smith*

[163] Map case, by Louis Boudo (w.1809–1827), Charleston, S.C., 1825. Presented to Lafayette by the State of South Carolina during his tour of the United States in 1824–1825. Height: 9⅞″. *Courtesy, The Metropolitan Museum of Art, Bequest of A. T. Clearwater, 1933*

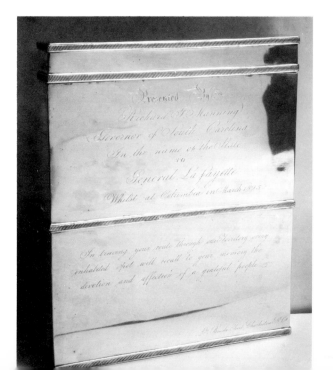

in the regiment which he served as Adjutant. Earlier during the French and Indian wars, silver was presented to heroes of the Battle of Louisburg. William Swan, following the design of Jacob Hurd's presentation cups, made the piece of plate (Fig. 202) which the Province of Massachusetts Bay gave to Benjamin Pickman, Jr., for his services in connection with the Cape Breton campaign. In 1757, a tankard (Fig. 162) was presented to Colonel Joseph Frye (for whom Fryeburg, Maine, was later named) by the officers who served with him in Nova Scotia. It was not only his care and conduct of the troops which they wished to commemorate but also, with a bit of humor, their "proper Resentment of his Paternal Regard for them Since their Return to New England."

General Lafayette, who did so much for the American cause during the Revolution, was honored everywhere, particularly at the time of his return tour to this country in 1825. The State of South Carolina presented him with a silver map case (Fig. 163) made by Louis Boudo of Charleston. The case contained a map so that "In tracing your route through our Territory every inhabited spot will recall to your memory the devotion and affection of a grateful people."

Lafayette had been given a gold box by the City of New York in 1784; other recipients were Governor Clinton, George Washington, John Jay, and Baron Steuben. Engraved with the arms of the city, these gold boxes were presented with the freedom of the city. A similar box (Fig. 164) had been presented by the city as early as 1735 to Andrew Hamilton for his defense of John Peter Zenger, which resulted in the first major victory for freedom of the press. New York, in fact, made a tradition of presenting gold boxes, in much the same way that Dublin did. One was given to Major General Jacob Brown for his defeat of the British at Chippewa and Bridgewater in July 1814, and much later one was given to Cyrus W. Field for his success in laying the first transatlantic cable in 1858.

Such feats of engineering were recognized by other forms in New York. In 1773, Captain Thomas Sowers, an engineer attached to the British army, was given a large salver (Fig. 165) by the General Assembly and Governor Tryon for repairing the Battery. The salver is handsomely engraved with the New York arms and a trophy of military and engineering emblems. In Boston in 1786 the engineering of the lengthy Charles River Bridge, 1,503 feet long and the first bridge in America to be erected over a broad river, was commemorated by the presentation of silver to two directors (Fig. 166). Made by Benjamin Burt and Zachariah Brigden, respectively, a tankard and a teapot were presented to Richard Devens and Captain David Wood, and were engraved with a vignette containing a view of the bridge.

[164] Gold freedom box, by Charles Le Roux, New York, 1735. Presented by the City of New York to Andrew Hamilton for his successful defense of John Peter Zenger. Length: 3¾". *Courtesy, The Historical Society of Pennsylvania*

[165] Salver, by Lewis Fueter (1746–1785), New York, 1773. Presented by Governor Tryon and the General Assembly to Captain Thomas Sowers, Engineer, for repairing the Battery on March 13, 1773. Diameter: 21¾". *Courtesy of The New-York Historical Society, New York City*

[166] Tankard by Benjamin Burt, Boston, 1786. Presented by the Proprietors of the Charles River Bridge to Richard Devens, Special Director. Height: 9⅛". *Courtesy, Museum of Fine Arts, Boston; gift of Maxim Karolik*

Boston citizens also recognized the skill of Edmund Hartt, "constructor" of the frigate *Boston*, which was launched at his yard on June 12, 1799. They presented him with a tea set (Fig. 83) consisting of a teapot and stand, sugar urn, and creamer, all made by Paul Revere and engraved with Hartt's monogram.

It was bravery which prompted the presentation of a covered barrel-shaped pitcher (Fig. 167) to Isaac Harris in 1810, when he saved the Old South Church from burning. His heroic actions are vividly depicted in the engraving on the side of the pitcher.

Primary achievements were also cause for the awarding of silver. The first ship to navigate the Western Canal and Hudson River, traveling from Seneca Lake to New York City, was honored by the presentation of a covered pitcher to the owners of the ship. A panoramic view of the ship, the *Mary & Hannah*, on the river, together with the dam and a mill (signifying the importance of this first voyage to the manufacturers of flour in New York), is engraved on the side (Fig. 231).

Another large group of American presentation silver was that made to be given as tokens of peace to the Indians. This custom had started

[167] Covered pitcher, by Ebenezer Moulton, Boston, 1810. Presented to Isaac Harris for saving the Old South Church from burning. Height: 10½". *Courtesy, Museum of Fine Arts, Boston*

at an early date. Gorgets, protective throat plates, and the last vestiges of full suits of armor were among the earliest desirable ornaments presented to Indians. Early in the 1730s, Koenraet Ten Eyck, a silversmith in Albany, recorded an impressive number of silver breast plates in his account books. Barent Ten Eyck, his son, made a silver gorget (Fig. 168) dated 1755 which was found in an Indian grave at Franklin, North Carolina, where a battle with northern Indians had taken place in 1760.

Joseph Richardson of Philadelphia also made gorgets for the Indians. In fact, he was employed to make thousands of objects, such as earrings, crosses, and hair plates, by a Quaker organization with the elaborate name of "The Friendly Association of Regaining and Preserving Peace with the Indians by Pacific Measures." Their first venture into the business of silver gifts to Indians had been a medal (Fig. 169a) cut by Edward Duffield and struck by Joseph Richardson in 1757. Daniel Christian Fueter of New York was the maker of two sets of medals

(Fig. 169c) presented by Sir William Johnson to the hierarchy of Indian chiefs among the Six Nations.

After American independence had been won, conflict with the Indians continued to be one of President Washington's most trying problems. The United States government therefore continued to commission silversmiths to make ornamental objects for presentation to the Indians. Joseph Richardson, Jr., made hundreds of wristbands and armbands (Fig. 170) for the government to give to Indian chiefs. An advertisement in the *Charleston City Gazette*, August 12, 1794, refers to one of these armbands:

Lost on Thursday night last, by the [Chief] Humming Bird, a broad silver arm band, presented him as an ornament by the secretary of war, in Philadelphia; as the band can be of no particular use in its present form, to any person but an Indian, it is hoped whoever may be in possession of it will return it, and receive a handsome reward from Silas Dinsmore.

Oval medals were also made in quantity, engraved with the United States eagle, the newly adopted seal of our nation, on one side, and on the other side with an agricultural scene in the background and Washington and an Indian passing the proverbial peace pipe in the foreground (Fig. 171).

Of greater rarity is the silver peace pipe (Fig. 172) presented to the Delaware Indians by General William Henry Harrison in 1814 when the second Treaty of Greenville had been concluded. Even earlier, in

[168] Gorget, by Barent Ten Eyck (1714–1795), Albany, 1755. Found in an Indian grave in Macon County, North Carolina. Width: 6″. *Courtesy, Museum of the American Indian, Heye Foundation*

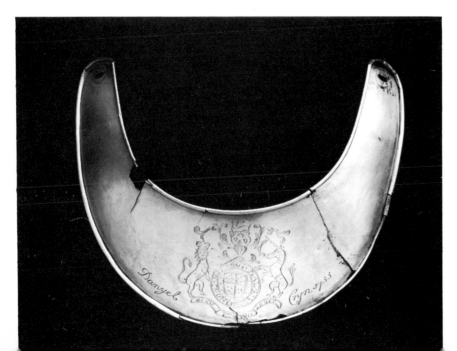

[169a, 169b] Medal, obverse and reverse, cut by Edward Duffield and struck by Joseph Richardson, Philadelphia, 1757. Presented by the Quakers to Indians in order to promote peace. [169c, 169d] "Happy While United" medal, by Daniel Christian Fueter, 1766. *Courtesy, American Numismatic Society*

[170] Wrist band, by Joseph Richardson, Jr., Philadelphia, c.1795. Engraved with United States Seal. Width: 1½". *Courtesy, Henry Francis du Pont Winterthur Museum*

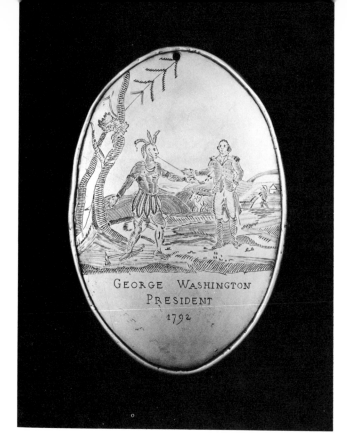

[171] Oval medal, by Joseph Richardson, Jr., Philadelphia, 1792. Height: 5⅛".
Courtesy, Museum of the American Indian, Heye Foundation

[172] Tobacco pipe, American, 1814. Presented to the Delaware Tribe by Major
General William Henry Harrison at Greenville, Ohio, in July 1814. Length: 21".
Courtesy, Smithsonian Institution

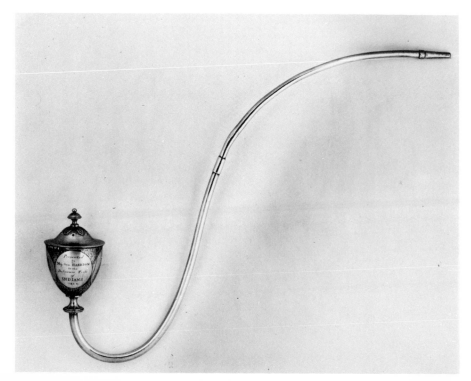

1762, Nathaniel Hurd had Paul Revere make "a Silver Indian Pipe." Since silver is not very well suited to a pipe because of its ready transference of heat, it is surprising to read in William Bentley's diary for June 1809, "Happy Boyce is said to have received a Silver pipe from being often smoking." [70]

These are only a few of the many examples of early American presentation silver. Some are of national interest and some are highly personal, but all represent chapters in our country's history worth noting and remembering.

[172a] Watercolor drawing, by Charles Fevret de Saint-Memin (1770–1852), c. 1795, of an Osage Indian wearing a silver armband presented by the United States Government. *Courtesy, The Henry Francis du Pont Winterthur Museum*

III

THE ROLE OF
THE AMERICAN
SILVERSMITH

[173] Portrait of Paul Revere, painted by John Singleton Copley, c.1765, when Revere was about thirty. *Courtesy, Museum of Fine Arts, Boston, gift of Joseph W. Revere, William B. Revere, and Edward H. R. Revere*

CHAPTER NINE

The Men and Their Training

THE variety and beauty of early American silver inevitably incites interest in the men who were able to create such objects. Curiosity is aroused about what manner of men the silversmiths were, where they came from, where they got their training, and how they actually carried on their work.

Lured by false hopes of gold and silver in the new land, silversmiths were among the first to take ships bound for Virginia. Captain John Smith reported with regret, "The lust of gold was apparent in sending out refiners and goldsmiths, who never had occasion to exercise their craft; as also the jeweller for there were no precious stones nor jewels, save only such few pearls as might be found in the oysters, of which there are plenty." [71]

By 1634, John Mansfield had come to Charlestown, Massachusetts, and Richard Storer, who had served almost six years as an apprentice to the London goldsmith James Fearne, arrived in Massachusetts the following year. The first decades of colonization, however, required the basic work of hammering out a habitable situation rather than the hammering out of luxurious silver vessels. As a result, many of the first silversmiths to arrive in this country soon became discouraged and, like Richard Storer, went back home again.

Before returning to England, however, Storer had made a contribution to the encouragement of his craft in the new country. His half-brother John Hull, who had also come from England in 1635, recorded in his diary, "After a little keeping at school I was taken to help my father plant corn, which I attended to for several years together; and then by God's good hand I fell to learning by help of my brother [Storer] and to practice the trade of goldsmith, . . . and obtained that ability in it as I was able to get my living by it." [72]

Normally a young boy began to learn the trade of a goldsmith when he was about fourteen. Hull was born in 1624 and so began his apprenticeship with Storer about 1638. Since the term of apprenticeship in those days was seven years, John Hull should have continued in training with his master until 1645, when he had reached the majority age of twenty-one. John Hull soon formed a partnership with Robert Sanderson, another Englishman, who was sixteen years his elder and who had served his full apprenticeship with the London goldsmith William Rawlins. Together, Hull and Sanderson produced the first pieces of American silver known today.

New Amsterdam was next to be settled by silversmiths. One of the first to practice this craft was Jurian Blanck, who was called a "Goutsmidt" when he was married in the Reformed Dutch Church of New Amsterdam in 1643. No work by him has been identified, but the work of his son Jurian Blanck, Jr., who came of age in 1667, survives in a pair of beakers made in 1684 for the Church in Brooklyn and a covered cup made for the marriage of Eve Philipse and Jacobus Van Cortlandt in 1691.

Jacob Boelen, who was born in Amsterdam, Holland, in 1657 and was brought by his parents to New Amsterdam two years later, is another of the early New York silversmiths. Ahasuerus Hendricks was one of several silversmiths who signed the "Oath of Allegiance" to the English monarch in 1675, and Cornelius Vander Burch and Jacobus Vander Spiegel were among the first native-born New Yorkers to learn this trade.

As the names suggest, most of the early silversmiths in New York were of Dutch ancestry, even after the British had taken New Amsterdam. Toward the end of the seventeenth century, there was an influx of French emigrés, and a number of them were silversmiths. This was due in large part to the Revocation of the Edict of Nantes in 1685, and a decree by Louis XIV three years later that all plate should be melted down and no new plate manufactured. Bartholomew Le Roux was one of the first of the Huguenot emigrés to come to New York, where he became a Freeman of the city in 1687.

It was at this time that Philadelphia began to be settled. Caesar Ghiselin, also a French Huguenot, and John Pearse were listed as silversmiths among the passengers on the ship *Bristol Factor*, arriving in Pennsylvania in 1681. Johan Nys and the Quaker Francis Richardson were both being patronized by William Penn by 1700.

Charleston, South Carolina, also received Huguenot silversmiths before the end of the seventeenth century. Both Nicolas De Longuemare and Solomon Legare were working there before 1700, but no examples of their work are known today. The patronage for silversmiths was not so great in the southern colonies. The economy was such that most of the people who could afford objects of silver ordered them from London in exchange for their plantation produce.

Maryland and Virginia, although they had silversmiths practicing their trade before 1700, had none whose work survives today. It was not until the eighteenth century that the centers of silversmithing moved out beyond the three major cities of Boston, New York, and Philadelphia, into surrounding towns and newly settled areas. Job Prince and later John Potwine moved from Boston to Connecticut, and Cornelius Kierstede moved from New York to New Haven. Both New York and Pennsylvania provided silversmiths for New Jersey. Pennsylvania also supplied silversmiths to Delaware, Maryland, and the Carolinas. Soon all the colonies on the Atlantic seaboard had men practicing this craft.

The number of silversmiths began to increase just as the progeny of families increased. As soon as a silversmith became established, he looked for a young man who could assist him with some of the more time-consuming and boring parts of his trade that did not require much skill. At the same time, the lad could begin to learn the business of a silversmith, and as he grew older and began to take on more difficult tasks, another young boy could be taken into the shop. Sometimes Negroes were trained in the shop. "A likely young negro fellow, by trade a Silver-smith, Jeweller and Lapidary" was offered for sale by William Faris of Annapolis in 1778 with the recommendation that "there is very few if any, better workman in America." [73]

By the time he retired, a successful silversmith might have trained half a dozen or more men, who then practiced their trade, training other young men in turn. Hull and Sanderson, for instance, trained Jeremiah Dummer, Samuel Paddy, Timothy Dwight, Samuel Clark, and probably William Rouse and John Coney. Jeremiah Dummer, who is generally considered America's first native-born and native-trained silversmith, in turn trained Kiliaen Van Rennselaer of New York, Edward Winslow, John Edwards, John Noyes, Daniel Gookin, and William Cowell.

It is of little wonder that the silversmiths in America proliferated to the point that by the middle of the eighteenth century, there were dozens of silver shops in every important city, and usually at least one silversmith in every town of any size in the northern colonies. In the southern areas, there were at least one or two good silversmiths in the major cities and towns. By this time, too, men of more diverse nationalities sought refuge and work in the New World. Daniel Christian Fueter, a political exile from Switzerland, went to London first and then settled in New York until it was safe for him to return to his native land.

After the Revolution, this trend continued and many Swiss, German, Irish, and French silversmiths came to this country. These craftsmen, in addition to the large numbers of native silversmiths, found patronage here. Not only had the population at large increased tremendously in the young republic, but prosperity and the numbers of potential patrons had risen rapidly.

The market and the development of industry were such that by the early years of the nineteenth century silver firms had begun to develop. These large establishments employed many craftsmen and were quick to take up any new time-saving machinery which could be invented. As a result, the silver-producing companies began to swallow up the individual silversmiths. The handcraft tradition and "the art or mystery" of the silversmith began to lose ground as men were trained in factories to produce the wares that once had been made in small shops under vastly different circumstances.

Previously, the training of silversmiths had been a much more personal matter. Based on the medieval guild system, a young boy was bound over to a master for his education. In many cases, legal indentures were drawn up which specified exactly what their responsibilities were to each other. The apprentice was to serve his master for seven years obediently, stay out of ale houses and away from cards, and avoid matrimony. The master in return guaranteed to instruct him in the best manner possible in the art of a goldsmith, providing him with bed, board, and proper schooling.

A typical indenture is that by which Jacob Ten Eyck was bound to Charles Le Roux in the summer of 1719 in New York:

This Indenture Wittnesseth that Jacob Ten Eyck aged about fifteen years hath put himself and by these Presents doth Voluntarily and of his own free Will and Accord by and with Consent of Coenraet Ten Eyck his father put himself apprentice to Charles LeRoux of the City of New York Goldsmith with him to live and (after the Manner of an Apprentice) to serve from the fifteenth day of July Anno Dom. One thousand seven hundred and Nineteen till the full Term of seven years be Compleat and Ended. During all which Term the said Apprentice his said Master Charles LeRoux faithfully shall serve his Secretts keep his lawful Commands gladly Every where Obey: he shall do no damage to his said Master nor see to be done by Others without letting or giving Notice to his said Master. he shall not waste his said Masters Goods nor lend them unlawfully to any, he shall not Commit Fornication nor Contract Matrimony within the said Term, at Cards

Dice or any Other unlawfull Game he shall not play whereby his said Master may have damage, with his own Goods nor the Goods of others during the said Term without Lycense from his said Master he shall neither buy nor sell. he shall not absent himself day nor night from his Masters Service without his leave nor haunt Alehouses Taverns or Playhouses but in all things as a faithfull Apprentice he shall behave himself toward his Master and all his during the said Term. and the said Master during the said Term shall by the best Means or Method that he can Teach or Cause the said Apprentice to be taught the Art or Mystery of a Goldsmith. shall find or provide unto the said Apprentice sufficient Meat Drink and Washing in winter time fitting for an apprentice and his said father to find him Apparell Lodging and washing in summer time and his said Master to suffer his said Apprentice to go to the winter Evening School at the Charge of his father. for the true performance of all and Every the said Covenants and Agreements Either of said parties bind themselves unto the Other by these presents.[74]

In 1694, the Common Council in New York had decreed that no merchant or "handy Craft Tradesman" should take an apprentice unless there was a formal indenture and that the term of apprenticeship could not be less than four years. Boston, too, in 1660 had decreed that no one could open a shop who was not twenty-one and who had not served his full seven years as an apprentice. Since there were no guild halls in this country to supervise directly such matters as the length of term, some silversmiths did not fulfill the entire seven years. By 1768, William Young advertised in Philadelphia for "an Apprentice of a reputable Family, and an ingenuous Turn, . . . to serve not less than five Years." [75] Previously, the only time it was legal to begin working as a silversmith without having finished the full number of years was when the master died in the last years of the term and it was necessary for the apprentice to take over his business for the support of the family.

Often, after the actual term of apprenticeship was finished, a young silversmith might continue on with his master, serving as a journeyman and receiving a daily wage or serving as a shopworker and being paid by the work done. Once he had the means to set up his own shop, he did so. Partnerships were not so frequently formed in the Colonial period, although a few, such as John Allen and John Edwards, found it practical for a while. More often they just did business with each other when it was convenient, buying supplies and even wrought silver from each other when it suited. After the Revolution, and particularly in the nineteenth century, however, partnerships became commonplace.

There were a few attempts in the eighteenth century for silversmiths to band together into some sort of guild. A single notice appeared in Portsmouth, New Hampshire, in 1762 for a meeting of "The Honourable Society of Goldsmiths," and a notice appeared in the New York City directory of 1786 announcing that the Gold and Silver Smith's Society met on Wednesdays in a private house. It listed the names of nine members in addition to chairman Myer Myers.[76]

In 1788, in many of the major cities, there were parades celebrating the accepting of the new Constitution. The marchers were organized according to their business, and this brought about an organization of the silversmiths in each of those cities. In Philadelphia, the goldsmiths, silversmiths, and jewelers were led by their senior member, William Ball, who carried an urn. Behind him, Joseph Gee and John Germon carried a white silk banner with the silversmith's arms on one side and the motto "Justitia virtutum regina." On the other side, the genius of America was depicted holding in her hand a silver urn with the motto "The purity, brightness, and solidity of this metal is emblematical of that liberty which we expect from the New Constitution." Behind these banners marched the masters, journeymen, and apprentices, who totaled thirty-five members.[77]

It was at the end of the eighteenth century that craftsmen in general began organizing local Mechanics Societies. The New York Mechanic Society used as its insignia a raised hand wielding a hammer, with the motto "By hammer and hand all Arts do stand." John Burger used the same motto to decorate the top of his fancy trade card, engraved for him by Cornelius Tiebout, also of New York. In New England, Paul Revere became the first President of the Massachusetts Charitable Mechanics Association (Figs. 34, 129). In many ways, these Mechanics Societies functioned as the Old World guilds had done by improving the standards of craftsmen and encouraging good workmanship and design.

Throughout the first two centuries, the silversmiths occupied an important position in American society. Because of their association with precious metals and the fact that their patrons were the people of means in the community, they enjoyed the same stature that lawyers and bankers and doctors enjoy in twentieth-century society. Many of the early silversmiths held important civic positions and took an active part in the formation of the new government. Paul Revere had his counterparts throughout the Colonies.

Many ultimately became wealthy merchants, either in combination with their silver business, or by turning to merchandising when industrialization advanced in the nineteenth century. There were, of course, some who fell by the wayside. Silversmiths as a group were not exempt from having the opportunists, the fleecers, the counterfeiters, and the failures that any similar group would produce. For the most part, however, they were honorable men and a vital part of the backbone of the American society in its formative years.

CHAPTER TEN

The Shops, Equipment, and Methods

UNTIL the nineteenth century, the silversmith usually had his shop at his own home in the center of town. He was conveniently located for his customers and friends. Otherwise he would have had to apologize, as Williamsburg's James Geddy did, for the ". . . Objection of his Shop's being too high up Town, . . . the Walk may be thought rather an Amusement than a Fatigue." [78]

In the big cities, where there were many houses and more than one silversmith, the shops were usually marked with some sort of decorative sign. Many chose the sign of the Golden Cup, which was the chief emblem of the goldsmith's guild in England; others chose one of the objects which they made, such as the sign of the Tankard or the Tea Kettle and Lamp. A favorite sign for those who made jewelry was that of the Ring and Pearl. Charles Oliver Bruff's sign was the target of thievery in 1779, possibly because of his Tory sympathies, and he pleaded with the citizens of New York to "inform him where his Sign of the Tea-Pot and Tankard may be had that was taken away a few nights ago." He even offered a reward if it were returned in good order. [79]

Sometimes the silversmiths also attracted the attention of passers-by with displays of their wares in the front windows. Once inside the shop, the potential customer could see other objects displayed in small showcases. In many instances, the workshop and the showroom may have been in two different areas. Records show that American silversmiths frequently had the workshop in a separate building or room at the back of the house. One, at least, had his workshop down in the cellar. One

REMOVAL.

BENJAMIN WOOD,
COMB MANUFACTURER,

HAS JUST RECEIVED

In 'addition to his former assortment, a handsome selection of FANCY ARTICLES ; consisting of

Tortoise-shell, Mock, And Ivory } COMBS.

ALSO,

LOOKING GLASSES,

In gilt, curled maple, & mahogany frames; cloth and hair brushes, fancy baskets, &c.
may 29   2w

WILL'M A. WILLIAMS,
GOLD & SILVER-SMITH,
Clock & Watch Maker.

Has removed his shop to King-street, between Royal and Fairfax-streets, (south side,) where he is prepared to execute all orders in the above lines in the best and most expeditious manner, and on the most reasonable terms.   He has on hand and intends keeping, a handsome assortment of

Jewelry, Silver and Plated Ware, &c. &c.

ALSO, 1 case elegant

BRITTANNIA WARE.
may 29   2w

[174] Silversmith's shop of William A. Williams (1787–1846), advertised in the *Alexandria [Virginia] Gazette and Advertiser,* June 10, 1823. *Courtesy, American Antiquarian Society*

obvious reason for removing the shop somewhat from the house was the fire danger inherent because of the forge. Otto de Parisien of New York was one of many silversmiths whose shops "took Fire by Means of his Furnace." Often the workshop was crudely built, and when it had served its usefulness or needed extensive repairs, it was simply pulled down and a new building constructed. Robert Fairchild, a silversmith in Stratford, Connecticut, was able to arrange, when he sold his house in 1768, to have an option on removing his shop from the premises.[80]

While a good view of the exterior of William A. Williams' shop appeared in the *Alexandria Gazette and Advertiser* in 1823 (Fig. 174), no contemporary views of the interior of an early American silversmith's shop are known, nor have any actual shops survived with enough original features to give a very accurate picture of what they looked like inside. In recent years, a number of silversmith's shops have been reconstructed, based on research and especially on the pictorial evidence of London and Continental shops. It must be admitted that the delineation of these engraved views of shops was not done with any thought of the needs of future scholars. Also, they undoubtedly depicted the finer shops and not the most ordinary ones. Nevertheless, the American silversmith probably followed the same general scheme shown in these views, especially in the larger cities.

Most of these views (Fig. 175) show some sort of counter with glass showcases, either on top of the counter or against the wall behind. Often scales and weights were kept on the counter. The views also include on occasion the work which took place in the background. The open forge with its huge bellows dominated the scene. A shop worker invariably stood with his arm upraised to strike a piece of silver he was forging at an anvil set in a tree-trunk base. Hung on the walls in readiness were the tools of the trade.

The only known early American representation of a silversmith at work is the woodcut (see end paper) which appeared in the advertisement of Thomas You, who worked at the sign of the Golden Cup in Charleston, South Carolina, in 1766. Shown in typical posture, wielding a hammer over the anvil, the silversmith, his sleeves rolled up, wears a protective leather apron over his breeches. At Colonial Williamsburg, in the reconstructed shop of James Geddy, the scene comes to life with modern silversmiths hammering and filing at their work (Fig. 176). The tools they use are those used by eighteenth-century silversmiths, and the anvil is one believed actually to have been used by Paul Revere.

At Old Salem, North Carolina, the early nineteenth-century workshop of John Vogler has been restored, and displays many of his tools and the watches, clocks, and silver on which he worked. Among these tools

[175] Trade card of London goldsmith Peter de la Fontaine, engraved by William Hogarth, c.1740, depicting the interior of an English shop. *Courtesy, British Museum*

[176] Restored silversmith shop of James Geddy, Jr., Williamsburg, Virginia, with modern silversmiths using old tools and methods to make silver. *Courtesy, Colonial Williamsburg*

[177] Iron heads and stakes used by John Vogler to form silver objects, c.1803–1827. *Courtesy, Old Salem, Inc., Winston-Salem, N.C.*

[178a, 178b] Swage used by John Vogler to form relief design of a bird with a bough in its beak on the back of spoon bowls, c. 1803–1827. *Courtesy, Old Salem, Inc., Winston-Salem, N.C.*

[178c] Fork, by Thomas Harland (1735–1807), Norwich, Conn., c. 1805, with swage decoration of profile bust of Washington within a laurel border. Length: 8⅜". *Courtesy, The Henry Francis du Pont Winterthur Museum*

are the iron heads and stakes (Fig. 177) which he used in forming the silver. One of these is shaped in the form of a bowl for a tablespoon. Another (Fig. 178a) is a swage cut with the design of a bird with a peace bough in his beak. This Vogler used to decorate the backs of the shaped spoon bowls and to form the drop at the base of the bowl (Fig. 178b).

Every silversmith was equipped to make spoons and probably made more of them than any other form. Contrary to public opinion, the early spoons were almost always fashioned in one piece. The silversmith took a slot of silver; by hammering it in one direction, he could lengthen it at one end to form the handle, and by hammering it in the opposite direction he could widen the other end to form the bowl. When he was learning to make spoons, Daniel Burnap of Connecticut made notes in a little book which give the precise directions. He even noted the weight and drew the length of the slot of silver to be used at the start.[81]

In another place in his notebook, Daniel Burnap recorded the receipt for making gold beads, another standard item that any silversmith would know how to make. His directions were to take a very thin, flat

Drawn by Edward Mayo from the original directions for making silver spoons, recorded by Daniel Burnap (1760–1838), Coventry and East Windsor, Conn., c.1780. *Courtesy, Connecticut Historical Society* strip of clean gold and

Then cut it out & punch out the centers, and then half hollow them, and then anneal them and hollow them up, & rub them down, and then cramp them, and then charge them, & then solder them, & then boil them out, & then file them up, & then polish them, & then anneal them, & then color them, & then boil them out in clean water, & then burnish them, and then open the holes to a suitable bigness & they are compleated . . .

The tools which Burnap used to accomplish this process survive, and include the stamp to cut out the little circles of gold, simultaneously marking the center where the punch was to be made. It was much easier to put the hole in the center of the bead at the beginning, when it was still flat. Also included are the tools used to shape the flat pieces of gold into half-rounds which were then soldered together circumferentially to form the hollow beads.

The old sand cushion which Burnap used to hold a piece of silver while he worked on it is also at the Connecticut Historical Society. The same type of cushion is shown under the hand of Paul Revere in the portrait which Copley painted of him (Fig. 173). Copley arranged a few other engraving tools on the table beside Revere; they show us what early American silversmiths' tools looked like.

John Staniford's tools are preserved at Old Deerfield, a few of the Moulton tools at the Towle Company, and the Northey tools at the Essex Institute, but for the most part our knowledge of what tools the American silversmith might have had in his shop comes from a study of the plates of silversmiths' tools in Diderot's *Encyclopédie* and of the surviving inventories of the estates of individual silversmiths. Perhaps one of the most representative listings is that taken of the shop of Nathaniel Helme in 1789. His shop shows a greater supply of tools than those of other silversmiths in the town of South Kingstown, Rhode Island, but fewer than the larger city shops would have had:

40½ Pewter Patterns
29 Spoon Leads & other Lead
 9 pr. brass flasks or Goldsmiths Cast'g forms
 1 pr. wooded Cas'g Screws 1 Lamp & 2 blow Pipes [for soldering]
 1 Box with Handle on the Top Containing a Number of Clock and Watch Tools
 1 Wood Stand or rack with a Number of Old Files & Engravers
 1 Gold Smiths Skillet & 2 Ingot Moulds
10 Gold smiths Hammer 1 Soup Spoon punch & 1 Square bottom Tumbler punch
 1 Tin Gold Pan
 1 Box Containing Spoon & button punches
 1 Button Stamp
 2 Drawing Irons [for use at the drawing bench]
    some large plate Tools

3   pr Gold Smith Tongs
      Old Steel Chaps & Tongues [for buckles]
1   black Lead pot & abt 1 Doz crucibles
1   round Box of Buckle Tools
1   pr Gold Smiths Bellows & Frame for d[itt]o
1   Gold smiths Forging Anvil
1   Book Cyphers
1   Hand Laith & Blocks
1   old Tin Box Jewellers & Beed Tools.[82]

The list of equipment in the shop of Richard Conyers of Boston in 1709 is three times as long and includes two glass showcases, a ring swage, a clasp stamp, a tankard swage, and snarling irons for adding repoussé decoration or fluting to a piece. As early as 1733, Caesar Ghiselin had a flatting mill at the time of his death in Philadelphia. This he had used to flatten pieces of silver by passing them between rollers, a much easier and smoother method than that of hammering the silver on flat anvils. John Coney of Boston, according to his inventory of 1722, had "112 Hammers for Raising Pibling Swolling Hollowing Creasing Planishing etc.," as well as thimble stamps, caster punches and candlestick molds. In 1740, George Hanners, also of Boston, had a fork stake, and a "Death's head stamp" for funeral rings. Francis Richardson of Philadelphia had a porringer anvil and touchstones among his shop equipment in 1729.[83]

From such listings as these, a composite picture can be drawn, not only of what the American silversmith could make, but also of how he made these things. The first step for any silversmith was to melt down and refine, in crucibles or boiling pans at the forge, the metal he was going to use. Antimony, saltpeter, borax, lead, and sulfur were the materials most often used for refining gold and silver. These elements combined with the impurities so that the pure silver could be poured off. Daniel Burnap described the process:

Melt the silver in a crucible in a moderate fire. As soon as the silver is melted, fling into it a plenty of fine saltpetre. Then pour the metal off almost as soon as the saltpetre is put in, & the alloy will stick to the flux & the silver left pure.

After the refined metal had been alloyed with the proper amount of copper, the silversmith poured it into an ingot mold or a flat skillet. When it had cooled, he could hammer it into a sheet on a large forging anvil until it was the proper thickness. If he were making a vessel such as a tankard, he might use his shears to cut out a circular piece of metal, or else he could have cast the molten metal directly into a flat skillet of the dimension and depth he desired. In either case, he then determined the exact center of the disk, and marked it with a small punch. Using this point, he inscribed a series of concentric circles on the silver with a compass to direct the blows of his hammer.

Since hammering makes silver brittle, the silversmith had to reheat the metal constantly in the charcoal forge, which he operated with hand bellows, a process called annealing. In handling the silver, he used his "nealing" tongs. The metal was forged, first on a wooden block with a shallow circular depression in it, and then on the anvil and with stakes of various shapes, until the sides of the tankard were formed.

It was essential for the silversmith to keep the strokes of his hammer even in order to keep the thickness of the silver uniform. As each complete course of hammering was done, the silversmith could thicken the top edge of the piece by hammering at right angles to the edge, a process called caulking. During the forging, he used calipers to measure from the center punch to the outer edges to make certain that the piece was raising up evenly and did not list to one side.

Once the body of the tankard was formed properly, the silversmith began with other pieces of silver to form the lid, the base, and the handle. Any strengthening and decorative moldings to be added were made by pulling silver strips through shaped openings in a steel plate on the drawing bench. Some of the smaller parts, such as finials for tankards or handles for porringers, were cast in flasks, as the molds were called, previously filled with sand and impressed with the pattern. As it was formed, each part had to be cleaned up and filed so that the roughnesses were smoothed off, and pittings left in castings by the sand had to be filled with solder if they were too large to be removed by polishing.

In order to remove the hammer marks, each of the forged parts had to be planished with a flat-faced hammer against an anvil which would not change the shape of the piece. This could take as long as the actual forging had taken, but finally an entirely smooth surface was achieved. At this point any gadrooning or repoussé decoration was added, the silversmith employing a snarling iron and hammers. The snarling iron was an elongated Z-shaped instrument, one end of which could be inserted into the body of an object; the other end could be struck with the hammer. In this way, the silver could be stretched in spots so that it could be hammered or chased into the desired relief decoration. While the repoussé work was being done, the silver was filled with pitch, or, if it was small enough, it was embedded in pitch, to hold it in place and also to put something behind the metal which was resilient enough to allow the decoration to be formed without letting the chasing tools punch holes in the metal.

Sometimes the body of the object or the rims were to be pierced. In this event, the silversmith marked the pattern on the metal, drilled an opening in the center of each of the intended interstices so that his saw blade could be let through the hole, and sawed out the desired piercings. The rough edges would then have to be filed and smoothed off. If cut-card work was to be added, the patterns had to be cut out of flattened silver, and the edges filed smooth.

When all the basic parts had been formed and finished, they were assembled and, piece by piece, crimped together with wire, or held in a vise, and soldered together. For this part of the process, the silver and the solder had to be heated to the correct temperature by means of a small lamp fanned by a blowpipe. The silversmith had to be able to inhale and exhale steadily in order to keep the heat uniform.

Inevitably, there was excess solder which had to be filed off or, in the case of round bases, removed by turning on a lathe. Thumbpieces had to be hinged onto a tankard, and finials often were attached with a bolt-and-wing nut. Gilding might be added to certain parts. If engraved decoration were to be added, the silversmith traced the pattern on the metal and then with his graver cut the initials, coat of arms, or border into the surface. Finally, the maker's mark could be struck into the piece.

The basic work of making a piece of silver was now complete, and the process of finishing could be begun. The object would be given a final emersion in the pickle solution to clean its surface. Scratch brushes would then be used to remove the dull finish. Burnishing and careful polishing would bring the object to a high luster. Occasionally, a compound of sulphur would be used to oxidize certain areas of the design prior to the final polishing.

A number of changes in the mechanics of making silver were introduced at the end of the eighteenth century and the beginning of the nineteenth, all of which heralded the beginning of mass-production. One of the most important of these was the greater use of thinly rolled silver. By 1790, sheet silver could be obtained from refineries in various thicknesses, thus eliminating many of the tedious preparatory steps. Newell Harding was one of the first silversmiths in the nineteenth century to seize upon the advantages of applying power to the rolling of silver. In many cases, the silversmith still raised his vessels up from a single piece, but more and more the tendency was to cut out flat pieces of silver and seam them together.

In raising, the silversmith cut from the thin sheet of silver a large disk equal in diameter to the average diameter plus the average height of the object to be formed. He then hammered the disk just beyond the edge of his anvil, forcing the metal around the outer part of the disk to shape in as it was being raised.

Because of the greater thinness of rolled silver, certain forms, such as spoons, could also be made in a different way. A template of the spoon form could be used to cut out the shape of the spoon. The bowl and the handle could be shaped with much less difficulty than was encountered in forging them from a thick slot of metal. Machinery was being developed which could exert greater pressure, and in 1801, Thomas Bruff of Chestertown, Maryland, was able to advertise in New York such a machine which he had developed for manufacturing spoons:

> News to Silversmiths! Thomas Bruff of Chestertown, Maryland, has constructed and patented a machine for manufacturing silver spoons, which with one impression and one hand to work it, will turn out from a flat bar a spoon in a minute, ready for the punch, with the heel and name impressed upon it. This machine is capable of receiving three impressions to advantage, requiring than [sic] two hands to work it; but as the work is done in the same space of time, the product will be three in a minute, or 180 in an hour, which is as many as 40 hands can finish. This machine must certainly be an object to silversmiths, as it not only saves labor but subjects the workman to little loss of metal.[84]

Decoration for silver, which had begun to be mass-produced in the eighteenth century with the casting of borders or motifs, became almost completely mass-produced in the nineteenth century. Milling machines turned out yards and yards of stamped silver edgings which could readily be soldered onto finished pieces. New hand tools were developed so that in place of the graver, a tool with a rotating wheel at the end could be used to roll on a wiggle-work border or a beaded edge.

In the nineteenth century, machinery was also developed which could stamp out large parts as well as small. Spinning metal against a wooden form and shaping it also became more common. Soon the industrialization of silver manufacturing was complete, and the silversmith no longer worked in his own home. Instead, he went to a factory filled with new machinery and was paid a regular wage. This, together with the development first of Sheffield plated wares in the eighteenth century and then electroplated wares in the mid-nineteenth century, effected the end of the era of hand-made silver.

It is only by being aware of what actually went on in the individual shop, and the many processes which were involved in making a single object by hand, that we can fully appreciate the abilities and the artistry of the early American silversmiths.

Business Procedures

JUST as it is helpful to understand the processes by which a piece of silver is formed into a beautiful object, so it is also enlightening to understand how the silversmith handled other aspects of his business. Fortunately, a number of account books and miscellaneous papers of silversmiths have survived and tell the everyday procedures of their shops.

Many craftsmen also kept small notebooks in which they could write down such things as how to make solder, how to refine silver, or what prices to charge for certain items. Not many of these notebooks have survived, but Daniel Burnap's at the Connecticut Historical Society and Joseph Richardson's at the Winterthur Museum are particularly illuminating.

In addition to recording what materials he gave his apprentices to work with, Joseph Richardson also used his book to make note of any pieces of silver that had been lost or stolen in Philadelphia, the name of a good clockmaker or silversmith in London (Fig. 179), and the objects he had on display in his glass showcase. Other silversmiths used their day books or account books to make such notes. Paul Revere's account books at the Massachusetts Historical Society show that it was here he did his figuring and made sketches of a finial or a pair of tongs, in addition to entering debits and credits. Edward Lang's account book at the Essex Institute had the additional notation that he served his apprenticeship with a relative, David Griffeth of Portsmouth, rather than with his father, Jeffrey Lang.

[179] Page from commonplace book of Joseph Richardson, Philadelphia, c.1752. *Courtesy, Henry Francis du Pont Winterthur Museum*

Such account books are especially helpful because they record the objects made by a silversmith, how much the objects weighed and cost, often whether they were engraved with initials or arms, who bought them, and how the customer paid for them. From this information, the individual silversmith's abilities can be ascertained. When the accounts had been paid, a large X was marked through the entry. Otherwise, the charges would be carried forward to the next ledger. Usually the accounts were figured according to the weight of the object, with the cost of the silver added to the charge for working the silver—so many shillings per ounce—plus any extra charges for engraving or for wooden handles. Occasionally, a silversmith charged a flat rate, figuring that the weight of a certain type of object did not vary much. In New York, Charles Oliver Bruff advertised his rates in 1767 as follows:

For making a silver Tankard, 3 s. per ounce. For making a silver tea-pot, £ 4. For making a sugar-pot, 35 s. For making a milk pot, 24 s. For making a soopspoon, 20 s. For making six table-spoons, 21 s. For making six tea-spoons, 10 s. For making tea-tongs, bows, or others, 10 s. For making a pair of carved silver buckles, 8 s.

The account book of Joseph Richardson, Jr., at the Historical Society of Pennsylvania shows that individual charges for the engraving on objects were later paid to engraver James Smither, Jr., who had done the work for Richardson. In the same way, the charges for wooden handles could be paid to the carver or cabinetmaker who supplied them. In the eighteenth century, Daniel Trotter of Philadelphia provided wooden handles for several silversmiths, as did Joshua Delaplaine in New York, and in Boston, Isaac Fowls advertised that he "Makes Handles for Coffee Pots Tea Pots, . . ."[85] John Fitch's New Jersey accounts show that his neighbor Samuel Axford, who was a

Drawn by Edward Mayo from the original page from day book of Paul Revere (1735–1818), Boston, 1787, showing Elias Hasket Derby's purchase of a silver waiter [Fig. 29], 12 tumblers [Fig. 122], and 2 save-alls. *Courtesy, Massachusetts Historical Society* turner by trade, was paid for turning a tankard, a "Ewer foot," and a "Cann foot" for him in 1774.[86]

The elder Joseph Richardson's account book at the Historical Society of Pennsylvania and those of Samuel Williamson are additionally helpful because they show what part the apprentices, journeymen, and shopworkers played in the making of the silver and how they were paid for their services.[87] Usually, the apprentices were charged for the silver to make an object or part of an object and then were credited with the finished piece. The journeymen, as their name implies, were paid by the day. Francis Richardson's account book at the Winterthur Museum indicates that when Robert Keeble, a master silversmith whose mark had been recorded at Goldsmiths' Hall in London in 1710, was working in his shop, Richardson also paid him by the day.

The silversmiths in these shops were called upon to do a vast amount of miscellaneous work, as is shown by the account book of Nicolas De Longuemare, Jr., at the Charleston Museum. During the first decade of the 1700s, De Longuemare frequently recorded mending watches and putting crystals in them, in addition to more important commissions, such as making a great seal for the Admiralty Court. Elias Pelletreau's accounts at the Long Island Historical Society confirm that repair work occupied a large part of the silversmith's time. The repairs ranged from hammering out the bruises on pieces, plugging up holes, and replacing a bell on a rattle or a handle on a cup, to resetting a hinge or adding a spout on holloware.

Account books often indicate that some objects sold in the shop were not necessarily made there. Occasionally, silversmiths had other silversmiths make certain objects for them, possibly things they needed in a hurry or patterns that they did not have the equipment to make. Many of the account books show such friendly relations with fellow craftsmen. Another thing which caused a silversmith to go outside his shop was assaying. Few early American silversmiths were equipped to do very precise assaying, although they could do the refining themselves. Some silversmiths even sent the metal and their shop sweepings to England during the Colonial period to be assayed. After the Revolution, however, assay offices were set up in this country and more silversmiths obtained their own equipment to do this work.

Many of the silversmiths increased their business by importing, first from London, then from Birmingham, Sheffield, and the Continent, items which could be more reasonably made in larger shops and which they did not have the equipment to make. This had the added advantage of supplying them with the latest fashions, so that their customers could more readily keep up with the Old-World Joneses.

[180] Trade card of Joseph Lownes, Philadelphia, c.1790, showing the types of silver he had for sale. *Courtesy, American Antiquarian Society*

The silversmiths placed advertisements in the newspapers (see end papers) stating which objects they had just imported and which objects they had made themselves. On rare occasions, the advertisements included a woodcut of one of the objects offered for sale or of the sign of the silversmith's shop. Frequently they took the opportunity to advertise for an apprentice or to offer a good price for old silver. There was always a need for the metal, especially when people began paying in paper currency instead of coins.

Another method of advertising, which became more common toward the end of the eighteenth century, was the distribution of engraved trade cards (Fig. 180). In addition to announcing the name and address of the silversmith, these flyers listed the products available at his shop and occasionally included pictures of silver. Sometimes these engravings were made to be used as bill heads (Fig. 181); those which survive often have a listing of objects bought and their cost following the advertising.

Both the bills and the entries in account books show how silversmiths were paid for their wares. Up to the mid-eighteenth century, the city silversmith was often paid in coins, old silver, or in services rendered by the customer. In the country, the barter system continued

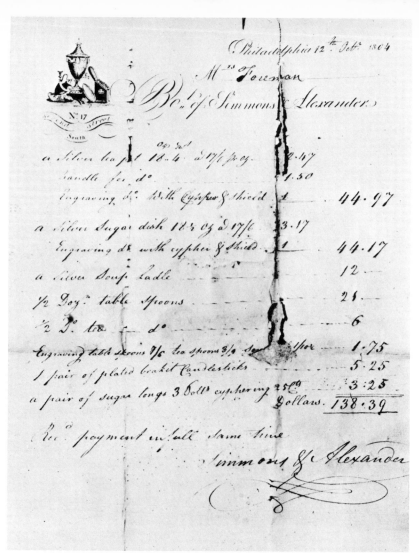

[181] Bill head of Simmons and Alexander, Philadelphia, 1804. *Photograph, courtesy, Antiques Magazine*

well into the nineteenth century, but in the cities, prior to the Revolution, payment was being made in paper as well as silver. The accounts continued to be figured in English pounds, shillings, and pence for several decades after the Revolution. After the establishment of banks in the United States in the 1790s, the dollars-and-cents system was adopted.

Silversmiths had, in a sense, served as bankers in early America, dealing as they did with the basic metals of coinage and the fundamental basis of currency. They had to be cognizant of current costs and values, and they had to keep accurate accounts. It was this business acumen as much as their skill as artisans which won them their respected positions in the communities.

CHAPTER TWELVE

Allied Crafts

WHEN John Aitken advertised in Philadelphia in the 1790s as a gold- and silversmith, clockmaker, musical-instrument manufacturer, and copper-plate engraver, it was not an act of virtuosity or boastfulness. Many silversmiths combined their work in precious metals with allied crafts. This was particularly true of the men who lived in rural areas, where the patronage for gold and silver wares was not so great as in the big cities. Such a jack-of-all-trades was Abel Buell of Connecticut, who, in a single lifetime, combined careers as a silversmith, jeweler, engraver, die cutter, armorer, map maker, engineer, inventor, auctioneer, ship owner, cotton manufacturer, and type founder.

In the city of Boston, Paul Revere was as renowned for his engraving and his copper and bell manufacturing as he was for his silversmithing and his patriotic endeavors. For more typical and less adventuresome silversmiths, it was sufficient to combine only a few of these enterprises in their day-to-day operation.

ENGRAVING

In some cases there was no logical connection between the several services rendered by a single silversmith: William Cowell of Boston also ran an inn. More often, however, there was a similarity in the type of skills needed to perform the work. Some skill as an engraver was essential to the silversmith. He needed to be able, when called upon, to cut the owner's initials into the silver objects he had fashioned, or to engrave a coat of arms or special inscription on them. Moreover, he needed to be able to shape the end of a special chasing tool he wanted to use or to cut his own touchmark.

Once he knew how to cut tools and engrave heraldic designs and ornamental borders, it was a short step to producing copperplates for bookplates for the same patrons. All that was needed was to reverse the design when cutting it into the copperplate, so that when the copperplate was inked and the print was struck from it, the design would appear correctly (Fig. 182).

For the person trained in engraving silver, engraving copper is easier in a way, in that the metal is slightly softer and therefore not so resistant to cutting. It is to be expected that the best engravers of silver were often the best producers of early American engravings as well. Such men as James Turner, Nathaniel Hurd, and Paul Revere were

[182] Copperplate engraving by Paul Revere, Boston, c.1765, of a bookplate for Gardiner Chandler, showing same design of arms Revere engraved on salver and sugar bowl made about 1761 for Lucretia Chandler (Fig. 22). *Courtesy, American Antiquarian Society*

equally adept as silversmiths and engravers (Figs. 183, 184). Their engraved work varied from certificates of membership to political cartoons, maps, bill heads and trade cards for merchants, and social invitations.

By the end of the eighteenth century, there was a greater need for specialization in crafts, so that there were some silversmiths who devoted themselves entirely to engraving. Peter Maverick, like William Hogarth before him, was first trained as a silversmith but spent most of his time in copperplate engraving and the engraving of metals. He advertised in New York on July 12, 1784: "Ladies may have their tea-

[183] Masonic meeting invitation, St. Andrew's Lodge, printed from copperplate cut by Paul Revere, 1784. *Courtesy, American Antiquarian Society*

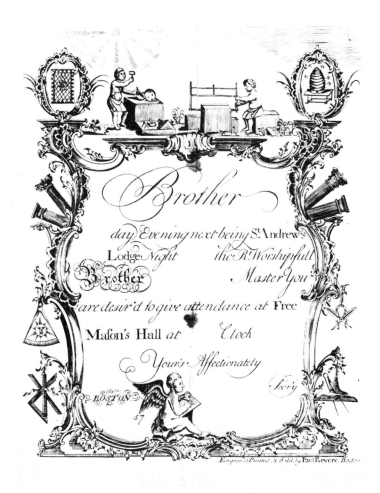

[184] Engraver at work, shown in detail of a writing certificate engraved by Abel Buell (1742–1822), New Haven, Connecticut, c.1774. *Courtesy, The Connecticut Historical Society*

[185] Tankard, by William Vilant (w. c.1725), Philadelphia, c.1725. Engraved in 1750 by Joseph Leddel of New York with scenes from Ovid and political caricatures. Height: 6¾". *Courtesy, Heritage Foundation, Deerfield, Mass.*

table plate ornamented in the newest fashion, with elegance and dispatch . . ." Other engravers such as Joseph Leddell (Figs. 185, 124), James Smither, I. Trenchard, J. D. Stout, and Francis Shallus were sufficiently self-assured to add their signature to the engraving they did on silver made by other craftsmen.

CURRENCY AND COINS

Because of his skill as an engraver, it was the silversmith who was called upon to engrave the first currencies issued in the Colonies. John Coney was employed by Massachusetts to engrave the plates for their paper money printed in 1702, and Jeremiah Dummer for Connecticut in 1709. On May 3, 1775, Paul Revere was authorized by the Provincial Congress to engrave notes for Massachusetts. The following year, John Waite and John Hallam engraved the bills of credit for Rhode Island and Connecticut respectively.

In the same way, silversmiths had been called upon to make coins. In Massachusetts in 1652, John Hull became the master of the first mint established (actually, it was without legal authority, since the colonies were not allowed to issue their own money). He and his partner Robert Sanderson minted the willow tree coins beginning in 1652, the oak tree coins in 1662, and the famous pine tree shillings and pence in 1663 (Fig. 186). According to Nathaniel Hawthorne's *Grandfather's Chair*, when John Hull's good-sized daughter Hannah married Samuel Sewall, Hull matched her weight in pine tree shillings for her dowry.

After Hull's death in 1683, Sanderson may have continued to mint the coins for a while, but in 1688 the mint was abolished. A few silversmiths used their abilities to counterfeit coins. Samuel Casey was one of the most famous; but Gerritt Onckelbag was fined in 1703 in New York for illegal coining, Edward Hunt of Philadelphia was hanged, and Obadiah Mors was pilloried in Newport and had his ears cropped for this offense.

It was not until after the Revolution that legal gold and silver coins were minted in this country. Ephraim Brasher of New York struck the rare gold "Brasher doubloon" (Fig. 187) in 1787. In 1791, Congress authorized a mint to be set up, and the following year the first coins were struck at the new mint in Philadelphia. Coinage was limited in the first years, but soon both gold and silver coins of various denominations (Fig. 188) were being issued. Joseph Richardson, Jr., was appointed by George Washington in 1795 to be Assayer of the Mint, and eventually gave up his business as a silversmith to devote his full time to this allied occupation.

[186] Group of oak and pine tree coins, minted by John Hull and Robert Sanderson, Boston, c. 1652–1683. *Courtesy, American Numismatic Society.*

[187a, 187b] Gold "Brasher Doubloon," obverse and reverse, by Ephraim Brasher, New York, 1787. *Courtesy, American Numismatic Society*

[188] Silver Liberty coin, struck by the United States Mint in Philadelphia, 1794. *Courtesy, American Numismatic Society*

SEALS AND MEDALS

There was really no difference between striking coins and striking medals, so silversmiths fulfilled this request occasionally, too. Daniel Christian Fueter and Joseph Richardson both struck medals in the Colonial period (Fig. 169), and after the Revolution, it was still the silversmiths to whom the United States government often turned when medals were needed (Fig. 171).

Cutting dies for coins and medals was the same process employed in cutting seals, another of the crafts allied to silversmithing (Fig. 189). From the earliest days, silversmiths cut the monograms, arms, or devices (Fig. 147) required by organizations, governments, and individuals. In 1693, John Coney cut a seal for Harvard College, and in 1702, Arnold Collins of Newport cut the Anchor and Hope seal for the colony of Rhode Island.

JEWELRY

Jewelry was one of the crafts most commonly allied with silversmithing. Frequently it is difficult to distinguish between the two in the work of one man. George Christopher Dowig of Philadelphia called

[189a, left] Seal of Phillips Academy, cut by Paul Revere, Boston, after the school was chartered in 1780. *Courtesy, Addison Gallery of American Art, Phillips Academy, Andover.* [189b, right] Seal of Dartmouth College attributed to Nathaniel Hurd, Boston, c. 1773. Dimensions: 2⁵/₁₆″ by 2⅝″. *Courtesy, Dartmouth College*

himself by both names when he advertised the sorts of jewelry he had for sale in the *Pennsylvania Gazette* on August 1, 1765:

Wedding, Mourning and other Gold Rings, particularly a Sort of Rings out of which Water springs, most curious Wedding-rings of an entire new Invention, Earrings of a new Fashion, all Sorts of Stone and Gold Lockets for Ladies, Stone Stock, Shoe and Knee Buckles, . . . He also sells various Stones, viz. Garnets, Crystals, etc. and Paste.

Crystal, stone, and paste jewelry was most frequently advertised, but occasionally imported precious stones were mentioned, such as the "great Variety of Rings, set knot Fashion, Entourage, Cluster, &c. Viz. Brilliant Diamonds and Rose Diamonds of all Sizes, Rubies, Topazes, Emeralds, Saphirs," Daniel Fueter offered in New York in 1763. Abel Buell perfected a machine for cutting and polishing crystals and precious stones and in 1767 referred to himself as a "Jeweller and Lapidar." [88]

No jewelry set with precious stones is known today with marks of early American silversmiths, and in fact very little marked jewelry of any sort has survived. It is through advertisements that we know who did this sort of work and what the jewelry was like. One of the largest categories extant of early American jewelry is that of mourning rings (Fig. 151). At first rather plain bands of gold carved with a skull or some other device of death, by the mid-eighteenth century they came to

[190] Gold beads and clasp, by Samuel Casey, South Kingstown, Rhode Island, c. 1765. Owned by Prudence Williams (born in 1742). Length: 17¼". Clasp, by Joseph Richardson, Philadelphia, c. 1765. Cuff links, by James Butler (1713–1776), c. 1760. Diameter: ½". Silver gilt Masonic medal, by William Hollingshead (w. 1754–1785), Philadelphia, c. 1780. Teaspoon, by Daniel Van Voorhis (1751–1824), New York and New Jersey, c. 1800. School medal, by Francis Shallus (1773–1821), Philadelphia, c. 1807. *Courtesy, Henry Francis du Pont Winterthur Museum*

be decorated with white and black enameling or were set with stones. Sometimes a full-length skeleton printed on a tiny piece of paper would be set in under the crystal stone.

By the end of the century, the mourning ring was larger, containing a plait of the deceased's hair under the crystal, which might be encircled with stones. In place of real garnets or other precious stones, a piece of foil the proper color could be set under a plain, clear crystal. In the nineteenth century, jet stones were widely used for mourning rings and brooches. Hairwork reached a height of popularity: it was woven into bands, to be set into rings or to be made into earrings, lockets, bracelets, and even necklaces.

In the Colonial period, the most popular types of necklaces supplied by the silversmith-jewelers were coral beads or hollow gold beads fastened with a small engraved clasp or locket (Fig. 190). The coral had to be imported, but gold beads could be made by any silversmith or jeweler. Buckles, buttons, and links-of-buttons (or cufflinks) were also

J. BALDWIN'S
Store of
Clocks, Watches,
Silver Plate & Jewelry.
Sign of the Watch
SALEM
Hairwork neatly executed

[191] Trade card of Jabez Baldwin (c.1777–1819), Salem, Mass., c. 1810. *Photograph, courtesy, Mrs. Charles C. Huber*

their stock in trade. These followed the styles of the time and were engraved with the same designs used for ornamenting plate. Masonic jewels, rewards of merit, miniature frames, gold and silver lace, and watch chains were but a few of the other items which could be provided by the jeweler.

CLOCKS AND WATCHES

Watch cases were made of gold or silver, and watchmaking and clockmaking were frequently allied with silversmithing, as Jabez Baldwin's trade card indicates (Fig. 191). Clock and watch parts were often imported, particularly in the Colonial period, so that understanding the mechanisms and being able to assemble and repair the works were the primary concerns. Clockmakers and watchmakers also needed engraving skills for decorating the backplates and faces of the clocks. No one did a better job than Daniel Burnap. His own clock (Fig. 192) included

[192] Engraved clock-face of Daniel Burnap's own musical clock, c.1790. *Courtesy, Wadsworth Atheneum, Hartford*

a dial for the selection of one of the six different tunes to be played when the hours were chimed.

INSTRUMENTS

Some silversmiths made other kinds of instruments. Benjamin Clark Gilman of New Hampshire was a silversmith particularly gifted in instrument making, as was Nathan Storrs of Massachusetts. Surveying instruments, compasses, mathematical and nautical instruments were all within their ken. Spectacles in silver cases and other optical items were also sold by silversmiths, who occasionally put their maker's mark on the side arms of the silver or gold frames. Paul Revere made lancet cases and spatulas for physicians, and was able himself to perform services as a dentist. He advertised in the *Boston Gazette* in 1770 that

he still continues the Business of a Dentist, and flatters himself that from the Experience he had had these Two Years (in which Time he has fixt some Hundreds of Teeth) that he can fix them as well as any Surgeon-Dentist who ever came from London, he fixes them in such a manner that they are not only an Ornament, but a real Use in Speaking and Eating.[89]

FIREARMS AND MILITARY EQUIPMENT

Another specialized type of instrument making often allied with the silversmith's trade was that of gunsmithing. Ralph Atmar, Jr., "Goldsmith and Engraver," advertised in Charleston in 1800 that he had imported from Liverpool an assortment of gun materials and would "undertake to fit them to match any pattern in the best manner. He bushes guns with Gold, Silver, Copper or Iron. Any part of Gun-Work shall be finished, that he undertakes." He also sought an apprentice "who will be taught the Goldsmith's Business, and may gain an insight in the Mechanism of Guns." [90]

Often the stock of the gun was inlaid with engraved silver, steel, or brass. The pair of pistols presented to Commodore Thomas Macdonough in 1814 has elaborately engraved gold plates on the side which depict the whole scene of his victory over the British on Lake Champlain.

Swords were also sold by the silversmiths. Over eighty early American silversmiths are known to have made silver hilts for swords. Jacob Hurd was the maker of the small sword at Pilgrim Hall in Plymouth carried by General John Winslow, who served as second in command of the expedition against the Arcadians in 1755 and as commanding officer at Crown Point in 1756. Francis Dana's hunting sword (Fig. 193) was made by John Bailey of Fishkill, New York, who also made the "service" sword carried by George Washington during the Revolution.

The straps by which the swords were suspended were ornamented with silver, and Deodat Williams, the Connecticut silversmith, advertised in 1776 that he made "officers silver mounted hangers with either lions, eagles, painters or plain heads, etc." Other trappings of the

[193] Hunting sword hilt, by John Bailey (w. c.1760–1785), New York and Philadelphia, c.1777. Belonged to Francis Dana. *Courtesy, Massachusetts Historical Society; photograph, courtesy, Harold L. Peterson*

[194] Brass and ivory memorandum case, by Jeffrey Lang, Salem, Mass., 1746. Owned by Daniel Gott of Wenham. *Courtesy, Henry Francis du Pont Winterthur Museum*

military were offered in 1796 by Marcus Merriman in New Haven: "Epauletts, Yellow and White, from two to five Dollars, Made and Sold." The Moultons of Newburyport did a big business in military equipment and when Ebenezer Moulton died in 1824, he had on hand in his shop eighteen gilt swords worth seventy-two dollars, eight silver-mounted hangers, thirteen plated hangers, a plated scabbard, fourteen sword blades, and quantities of epaulets, tassels, and sword knots.[91]

OTHER METALS

Because of their fundamental knowledge of metals, silversmiths often worked with base metals as well as with precious metals. Munson Jarvis of Stamford, Connecticut, advertised as both a silversmith and an ironmonger. The Northeys in Essex County, Massachusetts, made objects of copper, pewter, iron, and brass, as well as silver. Jeffrey Lang used the same touchmark on a brass memorandum case (Fig. 194) he made for Daniel Gott of Wenham that he used on a silver porringer (Fig. 49) he made for Lois Orne of Salem. Paul Revere set up a brass foundry in 1788, and in 1801 established a copper mill in Canton, Massachusetts, where he produced the copper sheathing for the flagship *Constitution*.

A few men who received their first training as silversmiths later became better known as pewterers. Timothy Brigden of Albany combined both these trades, although he is considered primarily a pewterer. The teapots which Israel Trask of Beverly, Massachusetts, made in Britannia clearly show the techniques he had learned during his apprenticeship as a silversmith (Fig. 194a).

Because of their dexterity with metals, it was logical for silversmiths to be assayers or in charge of weights and measures for cities. In New York in 1672, Jurian Blanck, Jr., was appointed City Censor of Weights and Measures. Later Cornelius Vander Burch and Jacob Boelen were "Recommended for the Office for Regulation of Weights and Scales, Curr'y, Gold, and Silver" in 1694. Thomas Savage served as Sealer of Weights in Boston from 1725 to 1736, and when Baltimore established its Assay Office, Thomas H. Warner was appointed Assayer in 1814.

A few silversmiths achieved fame as inventors. John Fitch of Trenton is noted for his work on the steamboat. Jacob Perkins of Newburyport was honored by the London Society of Liberal Arts for his genius: among his inventions were counterfeit-proof currency, a machine to manufacture wire into nails, and a steam-gun which could fire a hundred shots a minute.

From inventing to innkeeping, and from engraving to assaying, American silversmiths contributed much in their extracurricular activities to the development of American enterprise.

[194a] Pewter teapot, by Israel Trask (1786–1867), Beverly, Mass., c. 1820–1830. Trask was trained as a silversmith and the oval shape of his teapots and the bright-cut decoration show the close relation to silver teapots of the early nineteenth century. Height: 8". *Courtesy, Thomas D. Williams*

IV

SPECIAL FEATURES OF AMERICAN SILVER

[194b] Trade card of William V. Beuren, New York silversmith, c. 1795. Engraved by Peter Rushton Maverick, also trained as a silversmith. The advertisement notes that the highest price is offered for gold and silver. *Courtesy, The New-York Historical Society*

CHAPTER THIRTEEN

The Metal

FOR thousands of years, silver and gold have been considered the most precious of metals. In fact, not until palladium was discovered at the beginning of the nineteenth century were any other metals so highly esteemed. It is the intrinsic characteristics of silver which make it so desirable. It has a specific gravity of 10.47 and a melting point of 962 degrees centigrade. It is highly lustrous, and yet it is durable and permanent. It is easily manipulated, and yet it has, when alloyed with a small amount of copper, great tensile strength. Add to these qualities both rarity and beauty, and it is easy to understand why silver is such a splendid metal for objects of all sorts, and why it has been sought by man throughout the world and throughout the ages.

The chief source of silver during the latter half of the Middle Ages and until the discovery of the New World was in Germany, the Rhineland, Bohemia, and Spain. With the Spanish exploration and conquest of the Central and South American countries, Mexico, Peru, and Bolivia produced enormous quantities of silver ore which were shipped as bullion to Europe and from there around the civilized world. It is little wonder that Spanish ships were preyed upon by pirate ships of other countries, and that the ports of the American colonies played their part in such activity.

The Earl of Bellomont reported to the London Board of Trade in 1698 regarding New York,

This city hath been a nest of Pirates, and I already find that several of their ships have their owners and were fitted from this Port . . . Two men in this

[195] Table of coins and weights, engraved by Nathaniel Hurd (1729–1777), Boston, c.1765. *Courtesy, Memorial Hall, Deerfield, Mass.*

town had for their share £12,000 each, which were brought from Madagascar and got their with the barter with pirates. Besides there came home to the mouth of this port 8 or 9 pirate ships since my coming to this government, which would have brought in a vast quantity of those goods, and by the confession of the merchants in the town they would have brought in a £100,000 in gold and sliver.[92]

In addition to bullion and old silver, another source of supply of the metal was in circulated coins. Minted coins from Mexico and Peru, from Spain, Portugal, France, Holland, even Arabia, and of course from Great Britain, came into the colonies and were circulated. Some of these were gold coins: guineas, moidores, pistoles, johannes and half-joes, and Spanish doubloons found their way into the hands of American goldsmiths. In 1740, Joseph Richardson of Philadelphia credited his uncle Lawrence Growden with the receipt of "a Lewdore [Louis d'or] & a pistole . . . a half Guinea . . . & a Caroline." [93]

The more common silver coins in circulation here were those listed inside the boxes of scales and weights (Fig. 195) used to check the true weight of each coin in an age of "clipping." These were Spanish dollars or eight-reales, most often presented in their subdivision as pieces of eight. British crowns, half-crowns, and shillings were other common silver coins. When George Washington ordered twelve camp cups from Edmund Milne in 1777 (Fig. 41), he supplied the silversmith with "16 silv.ʳ Doll.ˢ"[94]

Many of these coins came into the Colonies through trade. As early as 1698, Gabriel Thomas reported, concerning Pennsylvania, that ". . . they have constantly good price for their Corn, by reason of the great and quick vent into Barbadoes and other Islands; through which means Silver is become more plentiful than here in England, considering the Number of People . . ."[95]

The value of silver coins fluctuated according to the economics of a particular place at a particular time. In Boston, for instance, the value of silver was set at 7 shillings per ounce in 1700 and rose steadily to 14 shillings in 1722, 34 shillings in 1744, and 60 shillings in 1749. Such things as the issuing of Bills of Credit in various Colonies produced their effect and led to inflation and ultimate depreciation. The same situation prevails today, and in recent years the English pound has had to be devalued several times. In the United States, silver is now worth about $2.00 an ounce.

Originally the pound sterling was equal to one pound of silver. The term "sterling" itself derives from the Easterlings, who were coiners from East Germany brought over by Henry II (1133–89) of England to improve the realm's coinage. Their silver coins were called sterlings originally, and 240 of them weighed a pound. There are still 240 pennies in the British pound, even though the pennies are copper today. The pound sterling was divided into 20 parts of 12 pennies each, 12 pennies constituting a shilling. The three denominations were known by their medieval Latin names: "libra" for pound, "solidus" for shilling, and "denarus" for penny; and so their abbreviations became "£," "s." and "d."

In 1300, Edward I ordained that wrought silver must be of the same standard as the coins of the realm, thereby establishing the sterling standard. This meant that in colonial America, as in England, 925 parts out of 1000 were of pure silver. The remaining 75 parts were mostly copper, which had been found from the earliest days to be the most satisfactory alloy, giving the metal greater durability without affecting its shining gray color. Up to a fifth of copper could be added to silver without affecting its color. The result is that with a small amount of copper alloy, sterling silver is almost twice as hard as pure silver, has a tensile strength almost twice as great, and is less vulnerable to tarnish.

Silver is weighed in the United States and England according to the troy system, in which there are 12 ounces to the pound and 20 penny-weight to the ounce. Sterling standard is therefore expressed as 11 ounces 2 pennyweights pure silver to 18 pennyweights copper per troy pound. The Britannia standard was introduced briefly from 1697 to 1720, in an effort to curtail the melting down of the coinage of the realm to make plate. By this standard, the amount of pure silver was raised to 11 oz. 10 dwt. and the amount of copper lowered to 10 dwt. in a troy pound.

The metal in the American colonies followed the English standard of sterling, even though there were not the regulatory means of enforce-ment in this country. Actual tests of pieces of early American silver show that they met the sterling standard of purity. After the Revolu-tionary War, however, the United States Mint fixed the American stand-ard for coins in 1792 at 892 parts fine, and in 1837 this was raised to 900 parts pure silver to 1000, a 10% alloy. The first change was reflected in the advertisement of the Philadelphia goldsmith Joseph Cooke which appeared in the *Federal Gazette* on March 16, 1795:

[196] 1. English crown, George II (1727–1760), 1741. 2. Brazilian moidore, John V (1706–1750), 1727. 3. Mexican 8 escudos, Charles III (1759–1788), 1778. 4. Brazilian johannes, Maria I (1786–1805), 1787. 5. Mexican pistole, Ferdinand VI (1746–1759), 1749. *Courtesy, American Numismatic Society*

. . . tea sets of plate, made of silver equal to dollars, burnished, and not inferior in workmanship to any from Europe, 15 s. per oz. for silver and making; high polished do. made of British standard, 18 s. 9 . . .

The difference between the two standards led to the stamping of silver made in this country with various symbols of its purity. In Baltimore, for example, a mark of 925/1000 or one of 11 OZ was struck on silver. COIN, PURE COIN, DOLLAR, and STANDARD were other marks used to indicate the quality of the metal. Sometimes the letter C or D was used to indicate coin or dollar, and Rogers Brothers' store in Hartford in the mid-nineteenth century made a specialty of silverware made exclusively of dollars. STERLING, used occasionally before 1860, became more common as a mark after 1868, when the Gorham Company changed to the English standard and other companies began to do the same.

Because value and weight are inseparable in silver, the weightiness of a piece of plate or of the family tea service has always had a special significance and has always been regarded as a prestigious feature. Naturally, the more it weighed, the more grandfather had to pay for it. Often the original weight was scratched on the base of a piece; if its weight changed at a later date the new figure could also be added. Values of pieces of silver over the years have been ascertained by multiplying the weight times the going rate for an ounce of silver. Therefore, when silver was listed in the estate of a deceased owner, its weight was given again and multiplied by the current market value per ounce.

The weight of a piece is still a vital statistic for silver today, and in museums or in auction catalogues, it is standard cataloging procedure to include the present weight in addition to the linear measurements. The exact weight is after all the most certain form of identification of a piece of silver. Two identical forms of silver rarely weigh exactly the same amount. The set of six matching tankards (Fig. 141), for example, was listed by Paul Revere in his accounts.

Their weight in 1772:			*Their weight in 1968:*		
24 oz.	13 dwt.		24 oz.	9 dwt.	13 gr.
25	1	12 gr.	24	17	22
25	3		24	18	19
24	5	12	23	18	20½
25	1		24	15	20
24	19		24	13	12

Although these tankards look identical and their measurements overall are the same, the weights of the six pieces varied from 24 oz. 5 dwt. to 25 oz. 3 dwt. Even in the same piece of silver, the weight changes from one generation to the next because of polishing or more major repairs. As an illustration, a sugar box made about 1700 by Edward Winslow for his own use was listed in an inventory of 1770, when it weighed 19 oz. 5 dwt. In 1778, it was inventoried as weighing 19 oz., and by 1935, the weight had been reduced to 18 oz. 17 dwt.[96]

It is the weight of the metal, therefore, which makes it possible for silver to be documented in a way no other art form can be. By means of their weight, individual pieces can be correlated without doubt to original bills, account book entries, and inventory listings. Family histories can be substantiated by means of original and/or present weight. To illustrate how this is done, the pair of candlesticks (Fig. 155) marked by John Coney, by tradition the gift of Harvard students to their tutor Henry Flynt in 1716, was listed in the Flynt inventory when he died in 1760:

	oz	d	gr	
To a Candlestick N°: 1 . . .	10	10	0	[£] 26/5/0
To Ditto N°: 2	10	0	0	25/5/0 [97]

The present weights of these two candlesticks are 9 oz. 18 dwt. 18 gr. and 9 oz. 10 dwt. 6 gr. By subtraction it can be ascertained that over the years, undoubtedly through polishing, the candlesticks have lost 11 dwt. 6 gr. and 9 dwt. 18 gr. of silver. To make the subtraction, it is necessary to convert the original weight to figures which make the subtraction possible, remembering that there are 24 gr. in a dwt. and 20 dwt. in an oz.:

10 oz.	10 dwt.	0 gr.	$\rightarrow$	10 oz.	9 dwt.	24 gr.	$\rightarrow$	9 oz.	29 dwt.	24 gr.
− 9	18	18		− 9	18	18		− 9	18	18
									11 dwt.	6 gr.

Such weight losses have even greater significance if there is more loss than one would normally expect from simple polishing over the years, or if the present weight is greater than the original weight. The loss or gain may be due to some change to the piece. Perhaps a handle has been added or a spout put on, or silver may have been added in making a necessary repair.

Occasionally one finds a piece of silver listed in a document with only a monetary value attached to it and its weight not given. The weight still can be determined by finding out the value of an ounce of silver at the time and place the inventory was taken, and then dividing this into the value given the object.

There is no other material that has been valued with such care over the years and that has so many rewarding intrinsic qualities. It is this special feature of the metal which has made early American silver so highly regarded since the day it was made.

CHAPTER FOURTEEN

Engraving

ONE of the special features of silver is that the metal lends itself, above all other materials, to engraving. In return, engraving enhances silver because it breaks up the shining surface into a myriad of hairline reflections of light. The suitability of silver for engraving made it possible for objects to be decorated with a personal identification of initials, scenes, arms, or inscriptions, which could also be recognized in case the piece of silver was lost or stolen. Many advertisements in early American newspapers give descriptions of the engraving on silver. The tankard stolen from widow Susanna Campbell in Boston in 1704 was described as having "Sir Robert Robinson's Coat of Arms engraven on the forepart of it, wherein are three ships, & the motto in Latin." [98]

The simplest form of engraved identification was the owner's initials. During the seventeenth century, these were usually just pricked into the surface of the metal. Such pounced initials appeared on the earliest American silver (Fig. 51) and continued into the early eighteenth century. By the end of the seventeenth century, however, deeply cut square letters with double-lined vertical strokes (Fig. 4) had been introduced, and they were to continue for at least a hundred years.

The engraving of the letters could take the form of a single family initial, a particular person's initials, or the combined initials of a husband and wife. Where three letters were involved, it was customary in the colonial period to engrave these in a triangular arrangement. The surname initial was usually placed at the apex, the husband's first

235

initial in the lower left, and the wife's first initial in the lower right, as was done on Caesar Ghiselin's folding spoon (Fig. 51).

There are, of course, some exceptions in the arrangement of initials. The 1659 beaker engraved B^{T}C (Fig. 2) signifies The Boston Church. Albany silver, probably following Continental tradition, is more likely to have the husband's initials forming the base line of the triangle, and the wife's first initial at the apex. Such engraving was described in an advertisement in the *New-York Packet* on December 7, 1784, when some silver was stolen from Peter Degroote, "among other things . . . 7 silver tablespoons marked P^{H}DG."

The initials were usually roman capital letters with serifs, shaded, and with a dot or some other decoration in the middle. Probably derived from the ampersand, these middle motifs varied from a fleur-de-lis, or a group of dots, to an asterisk, which one patron of Joseph Richardson referred to as an "aster."[99]

While block letters continued in the eighteenth century, the use of script initials became more common. In the first part of the century, the letters were very round in shape. Pattern books were being published which provided designs for the silversmith to follow for intertwined initials or reversed, mirror-image cyphers. In the late seventeenth century, Vérien, a French designer, and Jeremiah Marlow of London had published such books of cyphers, which could be cut out and used as patterns. In 1725, while he was serving his apprenticeship, Joseph Richardson of Philadelphia ordered an "alphabet Cypher book to Engrave by" from London.[100]

The most important of these early pattern books for American silversmiths was the *Book of Cyphers,* published by Joseph Sympson in London about 1726. Silversmiths from New England to Philadelphia used this volume, copying its designs faithfully. Samuel Casey of Rhode Island turned to the pattern in Sympson for the engraving of the initials *I C* on a cream pot (Fig. 197), and Simeon Soumain of New York followed the design for *E C* when he made Elizabeth Cruger's sugar bowl (Fig. 18).

By the mid-1700s, it was common to put the script initials all on a line instead of in triangular fashion. In the last quarter of the eighteenth century, the script became elongated, more elliptical in shape, and slanted slightly to the right at the top (Fig. 198). Furthermore, the letters were often contained in an oval enclosure. Joseph Cooke of Philadelphia advertised in the *Federal Gazette* on March 16, 1795, that he would engrave "the initials of any person's name . . . from Locking-

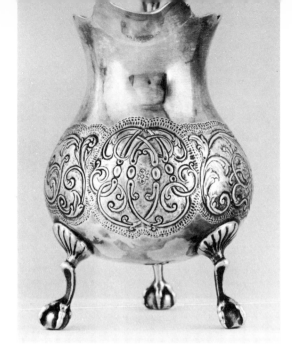

[197a] Cypher of IC on cream pot, by Samuel Casey, South Kingstown, Rhode Island, c. 1760. Patterned after Sympson's *Book of Cyphers*, 1726. Height: 4″. *Courtesy, Museum of Fine Arts, Boston, gift of Mrs. Charles Gaston Smith's Group.*
[197b] Cypher of IC from Sympson's *Book of Cyphers*, London, 1726. *Courtesy, Henry Francis du Pont Winterthur Museum*

[198] Engraved page from Lockington's London cypher book, 1777, showing combination of letter P with other letters of the alphabet. *Courtesy, The Metropolitan Museum of Art, New York; The Harris Brisbane Dick Fund, 1936*

ton's best London cypher book, . . ." He charged "one dollar each" for this service. By this time, too, a person often had more than one given name. As a result, the appearance of three initials all on a line may indicate either the initials of one person or the initials of husband and wife.

Inscriptions followed the same general development as the initial letters, with words being engraved in the style of handwriting of the period. Seventeenth-century handwriting (Fig. 3) differed markedly from that of the eighteenth century (Fig. 161), and since engraving was often added to silver by later generations, it behooves an interested person to learn to distinguish these differences. It was customary with long inscriptions to vary the style of lettering in order to set off the important name or event within the dedication (Fig. 19).

An engraved coat of arms on a piece of silver was an indication of the family prestige and bespoke the owner's rank in society. Hezekiah Usher of Boston made light of the arms on his silver in his will in 1697: "As to . . . Bridget, I do give her the tumbler with the Armes of a Spread Eagle with two heads, but I think one head for a body is enough." [101] Such flippancy should perhaps be expected in the new country, where less importance was attached to rank and where there was no Heralds' College to supervise the bearing of arms.

Americans have always been notoriously loose in their appropriating of heraldic arms. Few were entitled to them, and many simply looked up in a book of heraldry the family name and then assumed that coat of arms.

George C. Channing (in his *Early Recollections of Newport, R.I., from the Year 1793–1811* [Newport, R.I.: 1868]), remembered that about 1800 in Newport, "There was a great deal of family pride in those days; and I was never more amused than when girls ransacked books of heraldry to ascertain the 'coat of arms' said to have belonged to their ancestry."

There is even proof in American silver that if a person's own name was not to be found in a book he often picked the closest thing to it. The Sill family satisfied itself with the arms (Fig. 199) of Lady Jane Still even though they were displayed in a lozenge proper only for a widow or spinster. These arms were easily found in John Guillim's *Display of Heraldry*, the 1724 edition of which is shown in Copley's portrait of the silversmith Nathaniel Hurd (Fig. 200), one of the finest mid-eighteenth-century American engravers of arms.

The Redwood Library in Newport had a copy of Guillim's *Heraldry* by 1747 and the Providence Library in 1763 had a "large & beautiful Folio Edition" of Guillim which was to be kept in the library for the "general

[199a] Arms engraved on tankard (Fig. 133), by Cornelius Kierstede for the Sill family. [199b] Arms shown in Guillim's *Display of Heraldry*, London, 1724, for Dowager Lady Jane Still, borrowed by Kierstede for the Sill family tankard. *Courtesy, Henry Francis du Pont Winterthur Museum*

[200] Portrait of Nathaniel Hurd, by John Singleton Copley, Boston, c.1765. Large volume in foreground is Guillim's *Display of Heraldry*. *Courtesy, The Cleveland Museum of Art, John Huntington Art and Polytechnic Trust*

inspection of the members" and was "not to be taken from the library on any pretense, under the penalty of ten dollars for every offense." In New York in 1774, William Bateman gave notice that he had "a book of heraldry which contains some thousand of names, where gentlemen who want their coat of arms engraved by him, and do not know them, may search the book gratis." [102]

By the end of the eighteenth century, a great many more books on heraldry had been published. Thomas Reynolds formed a collection of such books in 1786 in New York so that he could search arms and set up a registry of them to be deposited in the city library.[103] After the Revolution and the establishment of a democracy, many Americans felt strongly against the use of arms. Initials were preferred by these people, and many enclosures on silver which were meant to contain arms were left unfilled or contained instead a patriotic device, or something innocuous, such as a flower.

While coats of arms had originally been enameled on silver to show the proper colors, by the time American silver began to be made, arms were engraved rather than enameled. Hatching was used to show the tinctures. A gold color was denoted by dots; silver or white was left plain. Red was expressed with vertical lines; blue with horizontal lines; green by diagonal lines slanting down from top left to bottom right; purple slanting from top right to bottom left; black by superimposed vertical and horizontal lines; and dark red by superimposed diagonal lines. In the American engraving of arms, however, tinctures were frequently omitted, as they were even on English silver occasionally.

The enclosures for coats of arms changed over the years. The earliest in American silver were square-topped shields such as John Coney engraved for the Addington arms in 1679 (Fig. 38). In the seventeenth century, the escutcheon was sometimes surmounted by a helmet with a crest and plumed mantling. In New York, a type of enclosure became popular about 1700 which was composed of feathery leaves crossed at the bottom and tied with a ribbon (Fig. 199). Often this was crowned with a floral marriage chaplet.

At the turn of the century, the square-shaped escutcheon was replaced by circular or shaped cartouches surrounded by elaborate foliation, scrolls, grotesques, and baroque strapwork. A superb example of this type appears on a tankard (Fig. 201) made by Benjamin Wynkoop for his own use and engraved in the center with a rebus for Wynkoop, rather than with a formal coat of arms. In Boston in the early eighteenth century, the arms as well as the strapwork and mantling were often contained within a circular border. Characteristic, too, was the filling in of the background of the framework with imbrication (Fig. 202), crossed diagonal lines, or simulated brickwork.

[201] Tankard, by Benjamin Wynkoop, New York, c.1710. Engraved with Wynkoop arms and cypher of BW for Benjamin Wynkoop, who married Femmetze Vander Heul in 1697. *Courtesy, Mr. and Mrs. Dunbar W. Bostwick; photograph, courtesy, Museum of the City of New York*

[202] Arms of Benjamin Pickman engraved on cup by William Swan, Boston, 1749. *Courtesy, Essex Institute; photograph by Richard Merrill*

By the middle of the eighteenth century, the enclosure had become asymmetrical and was composed of florid scroll-work ruffles, and shells (Fig. 120). There were delightful faces, playful cherubs, and charming vases of flowers worked into the framework. Joseph Edwards, Jr., charged Joshua Green eighteen shillings and eight pence for engraving the Green coat of arms in this type of cartouche on a pair of canns in 1765 (Fig. 203).

The asymmetrical cartouche was shortlived, and just about the time of the American Revolution, the style shifted again. This time the shape of the enclosure was a curved shield with a three-pointed top (Fig. 27). The ornament around the shield became more restrained and was made up of delicate festooning, and bell-flower swags hung by ribbons from small oval medallions. Very thin crossed laurel or palm branches were other favorite surroundings of this period.

About 1800, another type of shield made its appearance and became increasingly important. This was a square shield with a pointed base, a flat top, and straight sides which splayed out at an angle just below the top (Fig. 79). The mantling which developed with this type of enclosure was in the form of heavy drapery.

By 1840, the popular design was a Rococo Revival cartouche, so florid that it was described by one scholar as seeming to be in imminent danger of disintegration.[104] By this time, arms were less common on American silver, and often script initials were used instead to fill the mantling.

In addition to the enclosures for arms, silversmiths often engraved decorative borders around the silver to emphasize its form and add to its overall appearance. These borders also followed a development that is noticeable. The earliest engraved borders were often nothing more than scribings or a circular line. The more elaborate pieces in the late seventeenth century, however, had interlaced strapwork borders containing a meandering vine with intermittent flowers (Fig. 7). Engraved floral borders were especially popular at this time and were composed of the same flowers found in contemporary textiles and needlework, such as tulips, roses, and pinks, often appearing on a single robust serpentine vine (Fig. 96).

Early in the eighteenth century, engraved borders were not so widely used, but by 1725 they had been revived in the form of narrow, tape-like borders made up of alternating shells and flowers or cherubs' faces, on a diapered background (Fig. 17). Borders simulated the tooling in leatherwork and often arrow-shaped designs were used throughout the mid-eighteenth century. At the height of the Rococo period, however, cast ornament and gadrooning were preferred for edgings, and engraved borders were less likely to appear.

[203] Cann, by Joseph Edwards, Jr. (1737–1783), Boston, 1765. Engraved with arms of Green family described by Guillim as: "Ar. on a fesse az. betw. three pellets, each charged with a lion's head erased ar. a griffin passant, betw. two escallop-shells or. — Crest, a woodpecker picking a staff couped, raguled, and erect, all proper." *Courtesy, Museum of Fine Arts, Boston*

Mr Joshua Green to Joseph Edward, Junr Dr

April 22, 1765	To Pr Pocket Book Clasps - - - - £	0 : 7 : 2
May 11	To Pr Tea Tongs - - - - - - - - - - -	0 : 18 : 8
18.	To 2 Silver Canns - - - - - - -	11 : 18 : 10
	To 1 Silver Porrengers - - - - - -	3 : 11 : 1½
June 3.	To 2 Silver Castors - - - - - - -	4 : 1 : 7¼
7.	To 6 Do Tea Spoons - - - - - - -	1 : 5 : 8
17.	To 6 Do Table Spoons - - - - - -	5 : 9 : 8
21.	To 1 Do Punch Strainer - - - - -	2 : 5 : 6
July 5	To 2 Do Gravey Spoons - - - - -	3 : 6 : 1½
6	To 1 Do Marrow Spoon - - - -	0 : 11 : 8
	To Engraving 12 Crests - - - -	0 : 8 : —
	To Do 2 Coats of Arms - - - - £	0 : 18 : 8
	£	35 : 2 : 8¼

Drawn by Edward Mayo from the original bill from Joseph Edwards, Jr. (1737–1783), Boston, 1765, to Joshua Green for 2 canns [Fig. 203] and other silver, and for engraving 12 crests and 2 coats of arms. *Courtesy, Museum of Fine Arts, Boston*

The last quarter of the eighteenth century saw a great diversity in engraved borders. Neat borders of attenuated C-scrolls and classically delicate motifs were widely used, laurel and guilloche patterns being especially popular (Fig. 29). By 1800, trailing vines and Greek-key designs had been added to the repertoire (Fig. 83). Double and triple borders were used with delicate swags forming borders below architecturally-derived top edgings. Two new types of borders were introduced, bright-cut engraving and wiggle-work (Fig. 28), which further increased the variety of multiple borders.

The mass-production of milled borders in the early nineteenth century put an end to the superabundance of engraved borders of the preceding period. It was not until the Victorian period and the Rococo Revival that engraved borders made a reappearance, and then there was so much surface ornamentation that it was hard to distinguish between the borders and the rest of the decoration.

Occasionally, engraved scenes appeared on American silver. In the mid-eighteenth century, political cartoons found their way to the sides of a silver vessel (Fig. 125). Scenes of singular achievement, such as a man saving a burning building, and daring feats of bravery or a sketch of a naval engagement (Figs. 160, 167), were engraved on silver in the decades on either side of 1800.

Certain forms were more conducive to engraved motifs and scenes than others. Patch boxes and snuff boxes, for instance, one expects to see with engraved designs embellishing the surface (Figs. 5, 164). Medals which were not struck in a die, but were simply cut-out pieces of metal, also needed to be engraved to make them distinguished and to record the reason for their being awarded (Fig. 171).

Since engraving adds so much interest and information to a piece of silver, it is little wonder that when the surface of silver is beautifully ornamented with this form of decoration, it is much more highly prized. It is not easy to carve a free-flowing curved line into a metal surface and to give it dimension and texture. American silversmiths, fortunately, had some very skillful engravers among their ranks.

[203a] Detail of engraving on sugar bowl, by Paul Revere, Boston, 1799. Presented to Edmund Hartt (see Fig. 83). *Courtesy, Museum of Fine Arts, Boston*

CHAPTER FIFTEEN

Reading the Marks

READING the marks on silver takes more skill than one would think. It requires a more thorough education than simply being able to identify the letters of the alphabet. In some cases, the least important feature of a mark is the letters it contains. Actually, the art of reading marks is the art of reconstructing in the mind's eye the features of the die which struck the mark (Fig. 204). Each silversmith, in the course of a normal career, probably used four or five different dies to strike his mark. Unlike the American Colonies, in England, at least in the cities where there was an assay office, these marks were carefully supervised and marks indicating the town, the date, and the quality were added to the maker's mark. The die for the maker's mark or touchmark was required to be destroyed when a new mark came into usage. Apparently it was also customary in the American Colonies to destroy the die when a maker retired or died, since few such touches have survived.

It was basically the need to satisfy the customer of the purity of the metal, whether of gold or silver, that gave rise to the use of hallmarks. As early as 1238, in England there had been severe penalties inflicted upon those who did not conform to the regulations of the guild at Goldsmiths' Hall, and a piece of silver which did not meet the standard could be broken up and utterly destroyed. Over the years, from the founding of Goldsmiths' Hall in London, the sterling standard varied slightly. Usually it was 925 parts per 1000 or 11 oz. 2 dwt. troy of silver in every 12 oz. troy, the other 10 dwt. being made up largely of copper.

245

[**204a, 204b**] Die for maker's mark of John Vogler, Salem, N.C., and the mark struck by the die on a spoon, c.1815. Length of die: 2⅞". *Courtesy, Old Salem, Winston-Salem, N.C.*

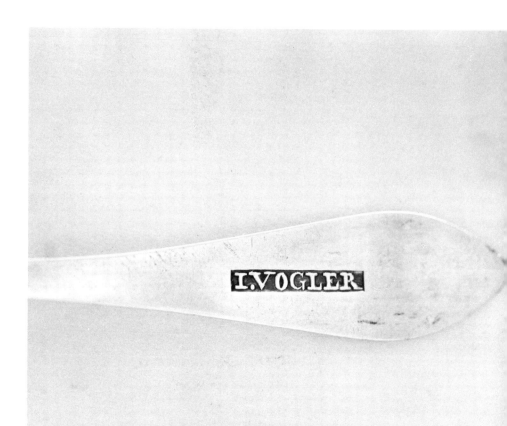

During the period when the Colonies were first being settled, a number of goldsmiths in England were marking their plate only with maker's marks, and much English silver of this date is to be found without other official hallmarks. The reason for this is that the law that applied to the goldsmiths at the time was the Elizabethan Statute of 1575, which failed to mention specifically any mark other than a maker's mark. This situation remained unchanged until 1697, by which time goldsmiths had been working in the Colonies for several generations, using only a maker's mark. In 1697, however, a statute was passed in England which raised the standard of silver from the sterling standard to what was called "the Britannia standard," that is, to 958.3 parts silver per 1000, or 11 oz. 10 dwt. per 12 oz. troy. The Statute of 1697 also made it obligatory for the Goldsmiths' Company in London to place the hallmarks of a lion's head erased, or town mark, the figure of Britannia, and a date letter on pieces of silver, in addition to the maker's mark. Even when the old sterling standard was returned by the Plate Duty Act of 1719, which came into effect on June 1, 1720, the continuation of the various hallmarks was required by all the assay offices as they became established in the major cities of England, Scotland, and Ireland. This practice has continued from the eighteenth century to the present day.[105]

There were many towns and cities in England or Great Britain with sizable populations and a number of working goldsmiths which had no assay office, and indeed no attempt was made to provide such offices in every area. As a result, there were never any assay offices set up in the American colonies under British rule. When a group of silversmiths in Philadelphia repeatedly tried to have an assay office established in that city by petitioning the Courts in 1756, 1767, and on fourteen different occasions up to 1770, their pleas were consistently rejected.[106] Consequently, there are no real hallmarks in Colonial American silver, only maker's marks.

There are, however, pseudo-hallmarks which one should learn to read. A leafy scroll mark (Fig. 205) was adopted by several of the Philadelphia silversmiths as a kind of quality indicator, and William Ball, who had come from Dublin, used a STERLING mark, as goldsmiths in a few Irish towns had done since 1710. By the mid-eighteenth century, a number of New York silversmiths added a stamp of N: YORK to their touchmarks, and throughout the Colonial period one frequently finds the maker's mark struck four times on a single piece of silver, giving the illusion of a full sequence of English hallmarks.

After the Revolutionary War, the design of an eagle's head, derived from the Great Seal of the United States, often was substituted for the

English leopard's head, a profile of George Washington for the monarch's head, and a star from the American flag (Fig. 206) instead of a lion. A few silversmiths used the symbols of their state seals. Several Essex County, Massachusetts, men added the design of an Indian with bow and arrows (Fig. 207), while in Connecticut, Merriman and Bradley of New Haven used the staff and three bunches of grapes (Fig. 208), the design which John Coney had engraved for Connecticut's Colonial currency in 1702. In Rhode Island, stars, the eagle, and a sheaf of wheat were used, as well as the anchor design of that state's shield. The hammer and arm, emblem of the Mechanics Society, was the choice of other silversmiths.

However, some American silversmiths crassly copied the English hallmarks with little or no attempt to personalize them. English pseudo-hallmarks were especially favored by the New York silversmiths who used a bust design imitating the king's head and a pseudo-date letter in the early nineteenth century. In Baltimore between 1814 and 1830, an assay office was actually set up and true hallmarks were required on silver made in that city during those years (Fig. 209).

By the early nineteenth century, too, it became more general to have the name of the city added to the maker's mark. As the population expanded, there might have been more duplication of makers' initials in cities, and indeed this is a perennial problem in reading marks, since there was always the possibility and the occasional actuality that two men working in the Colonies had the same name or at least the same initials.

It was in the nineteenth century that quality marks on American silver came into more general usage. The word COIN is frequently found on silver from about 1830 to about 1860. The silversmith was attempting to tell his customer that the silver used in his product was of the same quality as the coins even though at this time he was less likely to have made the piece directly from coins than in former days. It was now possible for him to buy sheet silver and save the trouble of melting down the coins and preparing the metal. The word STERLING was not generally stamped on silver until about 1850, and sometimes at that date one also begins to find the use of numbers to indicate the purity of the metal, as had been done earlier in Baltimore.

Date letters were not generally used in American silver outside the Baltimore assay office until the mid-nineteenth century, and then they are most frequently found in New York silver in the shape of a diamond with a number in each of the four corners, in a fashion similar to the registry marks used on English ceramics and other materials at the same time.

[205] Leafy scroll mark used by Joseph Richardson and a few Philadelphia silversmiths, c.1765. *Courtesy, Yale University Art Gallery, Mabel Brady Garvan Collection*

[206] Pseudo-hallmarks of William S. Nichols (1785–1871), Newport, R.I., c.1825. *Photograph, courtesy, Heritage Foundation, Deerfield, Mass.*

[207] Indian mark of Caleb Warner and other Essex County, Mass., silversmiths, c.1810. *Photograph, courtesy, Heritage Foundation, Deerfield, Mass.*

[208] Connecticut emblem of staff and grapes used by Merriman and Bradley of New Haven, and other Connecticut silversmiths, c.1820. *Photograph, courtesy, Heritage Foundation, Deerfield, Mass.*

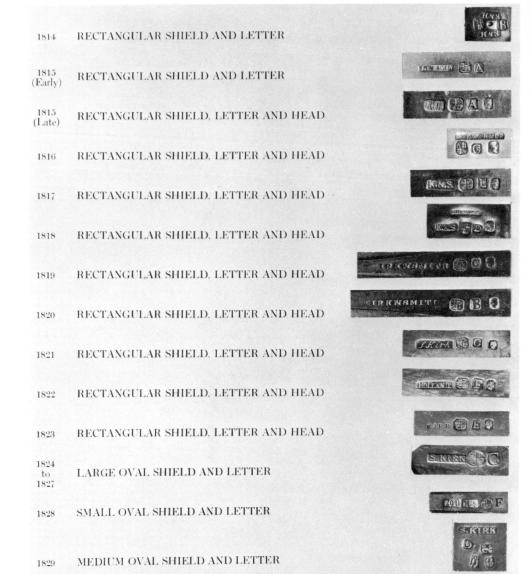

1814	RECTANGULAR SHIELD AND LETTER
1815 (Early)	RECTANGULAR SHIELD AND LETTER
1815 (Late)	RECTANGULAR SHIELD, LETTER AND HEAD
1816	RECTANGULAR SHIELD, LETTER AND HEAD
1817	RECTANGULAR SHIELD, LETTER AND HEAD
1818	RECTANGULAR SHIELD, LETTER AND HEAD
1819	RECTANGULAR SHIELD, LETTER AND HEAD
1820	RECTANGULAR SHIELD, LETTER AND HEAD
1821	RECTANGULAR SHIELD, LETTER AND HEAD
1822	RECTANGULAR SHIELD, LETTER AND HEAD
1823	RECTANGULAR SHIELD, LETTER AND HEAD
1824 to 1827	LARGE OVAL SHIELD AND LETTER
1828	SMALL OVAL SHIELD AND LETTER
1829	MEDIUM OVAL SHIELD AND LETTER
1830 (?)	MEDIUM OVAL SHIELD

[209] Baltimore Assay Office marks, 1814–1830. *Courtesy, Maryland Historical Society, and Pleasants and Sill*, Maryland Silversmiths

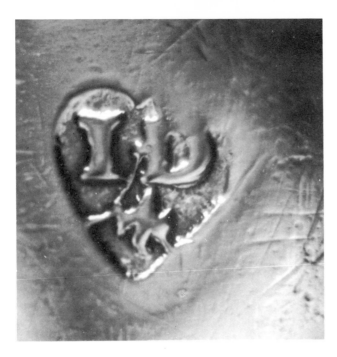

[210] Mark used by Jeremiah Dummer, Boston, c.1690. *Photograph, courtesy, Heritage Foundation, Deerfield, Mass.*

In reading marks, it is important to pay attention to many features other than just the lettering or device which appears in the mark. It is essential to figure out what sort of die stamped the mark. Evidently, a silversmith usually cut his own mark. No eighteenth-century records, either in account books or advertisements, have been noted that suggest that the die was cut by another person, although later, in 1812, Samuel Williamson of Philadelphia sent name punches to Jacob Leonard of Georgetown and John Adams of Alexandria, Virginia.[107]

There is usually a substantial relationship between the quality of a mark and the quality of the workmanship of the object on which it appears. The silversmiths who were the best engravers obviously would have had the best, most finely cut die for their mark. The design of the mark was chiseled or engraved into the end of a steel rod, and could be cut so that the design would appear in either relief or intaglio. The earliest marks, when stamped, appeared in relief, and it was not until about 1800 that the intaglio mark became more generally popular (Fig. 220). To cut a relief mark, the design is graven into the metal die. To cut an intaglio mark, the metal is cut away, leaving the design outstanding. In cutting a mark, the letters must be cut in reverse; otherwise, the mark would read backwards, like a mirror image, when it is struck.

Looking at a mark to see the die that stamped it can be very revealing, because the cutting of a mark exhibits characteristics in much the
same way as does handwriting. There can be minute errors or defects in
a die, and the shaping of the enclosure of the mark can disclose as
many features as the letters it contains. It is actually possible to see the
wear in a single maker's die as it was struck into pieces of silver over
the years. One of the marks used by Jeremiah Dummer (Fig. 210) had a
crack in the die, and this fissure became enlarged as the die was struck
into various pieces of silver. It is therefore theoretically possible that
if all the known marks of Dummer were photographed, the pictures
could be arranged chronologically by the growth of the crack in the
die, and thereby the objects could be dated more accurately.

Having established how the mark was cut and any flaws or peculiari-
ties it might have, it is next important to notice the shape of the
enclosure of the mark, for this too changed over the years. The earliest
marks were in irregular enclosures, depending upon the design of the
devices in the mark. Robert Sanderson's mark (Fig. 211) in the 1650s
accordingly was shaped in a rough square around the sides and base of
the letters RS, and then bulged out in a circle at the top to enclose the
sunburst above. Toward the end of the seventeenth century, the shield,
quartrefoil, trefoil (Fig. 212), and heart became popular enclosures for
marks, while early in the eighteenth century the oval and the circle

[211] Mark used by Robert Sanderson, Boston, c.1660. *Photograph, courtesy,
Heritage Foundation, Deerfield, Mass.*

[212] Trefoil mark used by Jacobus Vander Spiegel (1668–1708), New York, c.1700. *Courtesy, Philadelphia Museum of Art*

became more prevalent. Mid-eighteenth century enclosures were often shaped cartouches (Fig. 213) or conforming rectangles. The rectangular mark superceded all others in popularity during the second half of the eighteenth century, and by 1800 it was given a serrated or an engrailed edge. By 1825, banner-shaped marks (Fig. 214) and lunette-shaped marks are found, but increasingly in the nineteenth century, an intaglio mark without any enclosure was used.

From this it can be seen that a general dating of a mark on a piece of silver can be arrived at simply by studying the outlines of it. We can also guess the provenance of the mark in some cases because certain enclosures were more consistently used in some areas than in others. The trefoil mark (Fig. 212) is invariably an indication of New York origin, while the shaped cartouche (Fig. 213) is indicative of Massachusetts. The banner-shaped mark (Fig. 214) appears most frequently in

[213] Cartouche mark used by Jacob Hurd, Boston, c.1750. *Courtesy, Henry Francis du Pont Winterthur Museum*

[214] Banner mark of John B. Dumoutet (1761–1813), Philadelphia, c.1810. *Courtesy, Henry Francis du Pont Winterthur Museum*

Philadelphia and points south and west, while the outlined rectangle with incurved corners (Fig. 215) suggests an origin in the Rhode Island area.

After studying the enclosure, the letters and devices contained within should be scrutinized. The earliest goldsmiths' marks in England were symbols which were derived, in some cases at least, from the goldsmith's shop sign. By the seventeenth century, however, it was customary for initial letters to accompany these devices. In this country, John Coney used the initials of his first and last name above the rebus of a rabbit (or coney) for his mark (Fig. 216). Other popular devices were the fleur-de-lis, crown, star, crescent, and heart. Sometimes the initials were separated by a pellet (a raised period) or by a colon or period. This was done more frequently as the eighteenth century progressed, particularly after the Revolutionary War, and perhaps on occasion to distinguish between the work of a father and son with the same initials. Periods were infrequently used before 1800, and often only one period between the two initials sufficed. The colon was most often used to separate the initial of the first name from a full last name, so that Thomas Dane's mark in mid-eighteenth century Boston was T:DANE (Fig. 217).

[215] Outlined mark used by Pardon Miller (1797–1852), Providence, and other silversmiths in the Rhode Island area, c.1830. *Photograph, courtesy, Heritage Foundation, Deerfield, Mass.*

[216] Mark used by John Coney, Boston, c.1700, with coney or rabbit below initials. *Privately owned*

[217] Mark of Thomas Dane, Boston, c.1760, with colon between first-name initial and last full name. *Photograph, courtesy, Heritage Foundation, Deerfield, Mass.*

In England during the Britannia period (1697–1720), the maker's mark consisted of the first two letters of the last name; that is, the mark of William Gamble was Ga. Apparently, this practice was never followed in the Colonies, because no American mark of this type has yet been identified. However, by this time the multiplicity of marks had given rise to sufficient confusion to warrant the use in Boston of a full last name. In that city, Edward Webb used WEBB as his mark prior to his death in 1718. By the second quarter of the eighteenth century, Jacob Hurd and John Burt used a first initial and full last name, which in their cases amounted to a mere three additional letters over the use of two first initials. Other Boston silversmiths soon followed suit, even if their last names were as long as Greene, Edwards, Brigden, or Cowell. This was a departure from the English tradition, in which a full last name was rarely, if ever, used. Not a single full-name touchmark is to be found in the list of early London makers' marks. The use of a single letter, although relatively rare, is another departure in American marks. Samuel Minott of Boston used a single M on his silver in the mid-eighteenth century (Fig. 218b), and Theophilus Bradbury of Newburyport occasionally used a single B in the early nineteenth century. By the early 1800s, it had become necessary to use full first and last name, often with a middle initial as well. A street address was sometimes included by the second quarter of the nineteenth century.

[218a, 218b] Two marks of Samuel Minott (1732–1803), Boston, c.1765; one, a full last name and the other a single last name initial. *Photograph, courtesy, Heritage Foundation, Deerfield, Mass.*

[219] Mark of Jacob Ten Eyck (1705–1793), Albany, c. 1730. Initial I stands for J; T and E are conjoined. *Photograph, courtesy, Henry Francis du Pont Winterthur Museum*

[220] Intaglio marks of Obadiah Rich, Boston, c.1830–1845. *Privately owned; photograph by Richard Merrill*

Sometimes two initials in a mark might be conjoined when appropriate. The Ten Eycks in New York found this practical, saving both space and time in cutting the die, and so Jacob Ten Eyck's mark became I Έ (Fig. 219). Early New York makers frequently followed a Dutch tradition by using a trefoil-shaped mark, which was most convenient as their Dutch names required three initials. The earliest version used the base of the trefoil for the first two initials and the apex for the initial of the second part of the last name, so that Jacobus Vander Spiegel's mark was I^{S}V. (Fig. 212). In the eighteenth century, the order was changed by a few of the New York silversmiths who put the initial of the first half of the last name in the apex. Peter Van Dyck's mark therefore was P^{V}D. The heart was similarly suited to three initials and it, too, was occasionally used in New York.

As a number of these marks illustrate, the letter I was used instead of the letter J until about the time of the Revolutionary War. Sometimes a crossbar was added to the I. In marks where there is an I, it more often represents a J, since this is one of the most frequent first name initials to be found: John, James, Joseph, Jan, and Jacob were exceedingly popular names in this country. Almost always, the letters in silversmiths' marks were formed with serifs (Fig. 217), there being only rarely a noteworthy exception, as in the marks of Jacobus Vander Spiegel (Fig. 212) and John Brevoort, and a few others. Capitals were used in most cases but, in the mid-eighteenth century, script marks were designed, especially for use in the full-name touches. Ampersands were used, almost exclusively from the nineteenth century on, to indicate partnerships. Previously, separate maker's marks for partnerships were used, as in the case of Minott and Simpkins of Boston, whose own separate marks were stamped on the silver produced during their partnership. Earlier, about 1700, when partnerships were rare in this country, John Allen and John Edwards both put their first two initials in a quatrefoil. The use of such partners' marks as & Son(s), & Bro(s)., and & Co. is wholly nineteenth- or twentieth-century.

Once it has been determined what the letters and devices in a mark represent in terms of initials or name, possible date, and locale, it is necessary to turn to reference books to start the process of identification (see Bibliography). These books list the marks alphabetically, either by the last name of the maker, as in E. M. Currier, *Marks of Early American Silversmiths,* or according to the way the mark reads, as in S. G. C. Ensko, *American Silversmiths and Their Marks.* Facsimiles of the marks are given in these books so that it may be possible to find one similar to the mark at hand. If it is consistent with the surmised date and provenance of the piece on which the mark appears, then the next step is to look for an article or book on the silversmiths of that area or on the individual maker. In these books, there may be other examples of the maker's work for comparison and even, in the case of more recent articles and books, actual photographs of his marks. From this it is possible to compare closely to be certain that the marks are *exactly* the same. Even then, it will not be possible to be absolutely sure unless the two pieces on which the marks appear are brought together and the marks viewed in juxtaposition. The way the die is struck or the lighting used to take the photographs can change the appearance of a mark.

If the marks seem to be identical, it is then necessary to determine on what basis the mark was originally attributed to a particular maker. It would be wonderful if all the authors of books on makers' marks from the beginning had cited the source of their attribution. Unhappily, this is an unreasonable demand, and it is only within the last few years that enough specialized study of American silver has warranted a more scholarly approach.

Attributions can be made in various ways. In the case of silver, one of the firmest foundations for assigning a mark is in documentary material, such as a bill or an account book entry. Where silversmith's account books have survived, as in the case of Paul Revere, Elias Pelletreau, and the Richardsons, it is possible to tie a piece of silver directly to its maker, since the weight of the object, down to the last pennyweight or grain, was recorded and this weight would vary from piece to piece. Also, silver often has its original owner's initials on it, so that this can be an additional check between the piece and the name of the person charged in the account. Occasionally, the initials or coat of arms to be engraved on the object were also noted in the account, so often that it further confirms the identity of the piece in question. Following this method, the marks which appear on the Derby tumblers

Pere VanCortland Esqre ~*To John Heath*

To a Boole w.t 29-15 ^a.d p.ct Silver at 9/4 f.o o.z £13-17-8
To Making the Boole at 3/6 f.o o.z ———— 5-4-1
To a Sugar Box w.t 13 ^or y.est g Silver at 9/4 f.o o.z — 6-6-
To Making the Book ———— 2-0-
To Engraving a Cot Armes & a Crist -1-0-
To Mending a Cup 2 Booxis & Teapot Tankar
and Spoone   0-12-
                         £ 28-19-0

D.o C.r By 3 6-3 ^a.d 2.d & 11-16 ^a.d p.ct Silver
and Lase 11-15
        54-10.¹ Silver at 9/ f.o o.z £24-14-2
          Ballance D.o w   4-5-8
9 19 4
4. 5. 6   Rec.d the a Bove in full
1 7 10   John Heath

Drawn by Edward Mayo from the original bill of John Heath (w. c. 1760–1765) to Pierre Van Cortland, New York, c.1760, for a punch bowl [fig. 97] and a sugar box. *Courtesy, Yale University Art Gallery*

(Fig. 122) and tray (Fig. 29) and the Tracy goblets (Fig. 40) can be irrefutably identified as Paul Revere's, just as the Peel sugar bowl (Fig. 93) proves its IR mark to be definitely the touchmark of Joseph Richardson, Sr.

Occasionally, a bill has been preserved along with the piece of silver. In this way, John Heath's mark on the Van Cortland bowl (Fig. 97) is corroborated. Other contemporary records can be used, such as church records, where payment to a particular silversmith may have been noted in the minutes in return for the procured piece of plate still in the possession of the church. Town records may also provide this sort of information, as in the case of the New York City gold freedom boxes (Fig. 164). The records of other organizations and societies may document the maker of a piece. More rarely, a family letter may contain a reference to an order for silver. In all of this, the family history of the silver is important, so that pieces with original inscriptions, initials or arms are the key pieces in attributing marks. Family tradition can also be helpful, particularly in determining the provenance of a piece and in what geographical area the silversmith might have worked. This is especially true of silver made outside the biggest cities. Although city-made silver traveled widely, the products of the local silversmith in small towns usually were purchased in and remained in the neighborhood, at least until this century. To be truly acceptable, however, family traditions should be authenticated by listings in wills and inventories, or by some other documentary means, since human memory does not always conform to fact.

In a few instances, wills and inventories have been found to name the mark and/or the maker of a piece of silver. In 1726, the will of Samuel Winckley, Portsmouth, New Hampshire, listed "a silver Porringer made by Mr. Dummer, two silver Canns wth my Name on Them & made by Mr. Tyler, 2 large silver porringers & one silver Can Mark SW: & the Goldsmiths mark in Each I:R: Silver Tankard made by Mr. Greenough, six silver spoons made by Mr. Cunny [Coney], a Silver Spoone Made by Dan^{ll} Greenough." The inventories taken in Philadelphia of the Norris family silver also gave the marks on each piece, but did not go so far as to identify the makers by name.[108]

Once in a while, a maker's mark may be identified through the use of a newspaper advertisement. John Brevoort's mark, which might otherwise have been assumed to be IB, was described in an advertisement for stolen silver on October 6, 1760, in *The New-York Gazette:* "made by John Brevoort, stampt with his Stamp thus, IBV, in a Circle." In another instance, Charles Oliver Bruff advertised in 1767, "I design to put the stamp of my name, in full, on all my works . . ." As this suggests, maker's marks were often referred to as stamps in the eighteenth century, rather than as marks, while engraved initials might be referred to as being "marked" on a piece.

Full-name marks are obviously much easier to identify, particularly when they are accompanied by a town mark, as in the nineteenth century. The most difficult to identify are the simple two-first-initial marks. To compound the errors possible, a great many silversmiths had the same initials. Particularly common combinations are IB and IR. If the men worked in the same city at the same time, commensurately more thorough scholarship is required. An elliptical WC mark was for years assigned to William Cross before being correctly given over to William Cowell, who was also working in Boston early in the eighteenth century. Edward Webb and Edward Winslow in the same town and at the same time both used EW marks which have been confused. Even with the full-name mark, this confusion can occur. The mark D · ROGERS was assigned many years ago to Daniel Rogers, who was known to have worked in Newport, Rhode Island, whereas the proper owner of the mark, Daniel Rogers of Ipswich, Massachusetts, was an unknown goldsmith until recent years. And in New York City a third silversmith with the name of Daniel Rogers was discovered!

The most helpful evidence in attributing initial marks is the combination of the initial mark struck along with a full-name touch on the same piece of silver. Fortunately, this occurred in a number of instances in Colonial silver, so that some of these key pieces survive today. A silver bowl in St. John's Church, Salem, N.J., bears three different I · L rectangular marks together with I · LEACOCK in a rectangle, all of which can safely be attributed to John Leacock of Philadelphia. A punch bowl at the Boston Museum of Fine Arts, made by William Homes of Boston in 1763, bears both the HOMES in rectangle mark and the WH in rectangle mark, thereby identifying definitively at least one of the many WH marks of that period.

Even if it is not a full-name touch, but another initial mark, which is combined on a single piece, this can be helpful. The chocolate pot (Fig. 85) by John Coney has both his rectangular mark and his heart-shaped mark with fleur-de-lis below. The inkstand (Fig. 105) has the crowned IC with coney below in shield combined with the oval IC mark. Since in each case one of the marks can be documented, it automatically and logically corroborates the other mark.

In every case, a great many factors should be brought to bear on the attribution—the date of the piece of silver, its engraved decoration, regional features, history, and documentation. Church silver is particularly helpful because of this, since in many cases the silver was purchased locally and the church has kept it in its point of origin over the years. Thus, if a number of pieces in a church all have the same marks, and if there was a silversmith working in that town at the right time, it is substantial evidence that he might have been the maker. Of course, the histories must be checked to see that the silver was given by people who lived in the town at the time it was made, and was not given in recent years by someone who moved there from Peoria or, worse still, from the Channel Islands.

Marks which belonged to an Irish or a Channel Islands maker have been known to have been assigned to American makers. Such possible errors in identification must be guarded against, since the number of digits in the evaluation of a piece may largely depend upon its being American. In fact, it is always wise to check marks to see that the one in question is not an English one lacking its other hallmarks or with its hallmarks intentionally removed.

While most silversmiths had their own marks, it is possible that in a few rare instances they used the mark another man had also used. It is suspected that the patriot Paul Revere may have used his father's mark for a while, perhaps because he was not yet of age when his father died and he took over his shop. Jacob Gerritse Lansing (1681–1767) of Albany, and his grandson Jacob Gerritse Lansing (1736–1803), who came of age about the time the grandfather retired, are thought to have used the same IgL mark. Furthermore, the shopworkers who were employed by Joseph Richardson and are known to have made whole pieces of silver for him, which he in turn sold to his customers, probably used a Richardson mark rather than their own.

Special care must be taken with the marks of father and son when both had the same name or initials. Naturally, since the work of the father is earlier, and therefore probably more valuable, it is often to a person's advantage to attribute the mark to the elder silversmith. This is especially true where it makes the difference between an eighteenth-century piece of silver and a nineteenth-century one, or a Colonial piece and a post-Revolutionary example.

Marks are not always as clear as one might hope. If they are merely clogged with silver polish, that can be remedied. But if the owners of the silver have been too enthusiastic in their polishing over the years, part or even most of the mark may have been rubbed away. At present, there have been developed no techniques for bringing out such worn marks. X rays, ultra-violet lighting, and things of this sort have so far been ineffectual for silver. However, Winterthur Museum has recently reported promising progress in the use of a high-intensity sodium light for revealing marks and inscriptions on silver.

In other cases, the silversmith may not have held his tools firmly in his hands as he struck the mark, and it may be double-struck or chattered in appearance. Sometimes the overlapping of the letters which resulted may cause a misreading of the initials. If the silversmith did not have the right-shaped stake behind the piece of silver, or did not place it properly as he struck the mark, only a partial impression of the mark would take. In this event, it is necessary to try to reconstruct the remaining letters. The success of this will depend on how much is missing and what the name is. In the case of a mark showing only the last letters ". . . OLD," it probably can never be identified because of the numerous possibilities, such as T·ARNOLD and W. GRISWOLD, and the many silversmiths' marks which remain unrecorded.

Some American silver was never marked. The country clockmaker like Daniel Burnap of Norwich, who occasionally made spoons, proba-bly never bothered to provide himself with a mark. In England, certain objects were excused from marking, especially if a mark would deface the article. The exemptions included jewelry (except for mourning rings), thimbles, small cases and mounted boxes, clasps, nutmeg gra-ters, and rattles, among other things.[109] Marks are therefore not expected on these forms. But just because larger objects are unmarked does not mean that they are American, as many assume. There were goldsmiths in other colonies and in other parts of the world who did not mark their work. Assigning unmarked pieces to makers is a very risky business and should be undertaken with the utmost respect for the unknown.

Knowing where to look for the mark is important. There were no rules governing the placement of marks in this country, but in general they follow certain patterns. In the seventeenth century and early eighteenth century, the placement was apt to be in a very prominent spot, such as on the top of a tray or on the side of a chocolate pot (Fig. 86). If an object had handles on it, the mark might be placed to the left of the handle. Unlike pewter, silver was not marked inside the body, although occasionally one finds a mark inside a lid. Tankard lids were also occasionally stamped on the front of the lip. Gradually the marks were relegated to the underside of things, usually on the base, where they would not ordinarily be seen.

Because of the frequency with which marks appear on the precious metals, silver scholars have a decided advantage over those who labor in other fields. However, with the benefit comes a responsibility to overcome the natural inclination toward hasty conclusions and to read these marks with due deliberation and accuracy.

NEW-YORK, June 9th, 1755. LAST Saturday Night the House of James Mills in this City, Tavern Keeper, was broke open and rob'd by Persons unknown, of sundry Things of Value, among which were one Silver Pint Mugg, mark'd A. M. Makers Name P. V. D. one ditto English make old fashion'd; two old fashion'd Spoons, the Ends with Seals, English make; four ditto, mark'd J. M. C. Maker's Name TB. one ditto mark'd T. C. E. Maker's Name P. V. D. one ditto mark'd W. T. A. fix ditto mark'd B. T. S. Maker's Name P. V. D. one ditto mark'd W. B. S. Silver Marrow Scoup; one short Scarlet Cloak,

[220a] Advertisement noting the maker's marks on silver stolen from James Mills, tavern keeper. *The New-York Gazette or the Weekly Post-Boy*, June 9–16, 1755. *Courtesy, The New-York Historical Society*

[220b] Tankard, by Bartholomew Schaats (1670–1758), New York, c. 1720. Engraved with Willis arms and H^{W}E for original owners Hezekiah and Elizabeth Wyllys of Hartford, Connecticut. A later inscription on base states the tankard was brought from Warwickshire, England, by George Wyllys in 1638. Both the style of the tankard and the maker's mark indicate, however, that the tankard was made in the early eighteenth century in New York, a fact supported by a letter written by Samuel Belknap of New York to Hezekiah Wyllys on July 26, 1720, saying that he had sent the tankard and mentioning the coat of arms. Height: 6½". *Courtesy, Historic Deerfield, Inc.*

CHAPTER SIXTEEN

Dating American Silver

UNLIKE their British counterparts, the American gold-smiths did not have to have their work stamped with a date letter. Only in Baltimore, from 1814 to 1830, during the brief period of its assay office, was such a mark required, and it was not until the mid-nineteenth century that American silversmiths occasionally used such a stamp on their work.

In the absence of regular date letters, the scholar of American silver must resort to devious devices to establish the date of an object. Stylistic criteria can be applied with only relative security and success, because styles could linger or be revived. The only certainty that derives from a stylistic form of dating lies in the fact that an object cannot be any earlier than its latest design element, and even here care must be taken to make sure that all of the design elements are original.

Nevertheless, it is possible to arrive at an approximate date by analyzing the shape of an object, the design of its legs, lid, or handles, and the manner in which it was made. The style of its superficial ornamentation—chasing, engraving, or repoussé—can help determine a hypothetical date, as can the general style of any marks it might bear.

Knowing who the maker of the object was can be of greater help, however. Once the silversmith is known, his working dates help to narrow the time period. Since a silversmith normally came of age at twenty-one, this number can be added to the year of his birth to arrive at the earliest date one would expect him to be marking his own work. The latest date is usually determined by his death date. In the case of

Timothy Dwight, we know that his lovely engraved salver (Fig. 4) had to have been made before January, 1692, when he died at the age of thirty-eight, and we can assume that every object bearing his mark was made between 1675 and 1692.

However, not every silversmith worked himself into the grave, and pursuing biographical information can sometimes result in even closer dating. Blindness shortened Obadiah Rich's career to little more than two decades, although he lived to be seventy-nine. Switching to another business shortened Richard Humphreys' career: He practiced as a silversmith only from 1770 to 1797, when he became a china merchant, and finally died in 1832. Retirement also could fix the working dates of a silversmith to an earlier period than his death date would indicate.

If the maker of an object happens to be one of the few silversmiths whose account books survive, it may be possible to find the date the object was recorded as being sold. Usually, both the original weight and the original owners need to be known to identify an entry in the accounts. Family history can be helpful here, but even better is the engraved monogram or arms of the original owner. The sugar bowl (Fig. 93) made by Joseph Richardson and engraved O^{P}L can be dated exactly in 1736 because of the entry in Richardson's account book charging Oswel Peel for a sugar dish, since Mr. Peel's wife was named Lydia.

Occasionally, actual dates were engraved on objects when they were made. This was especially true in the case of presentation pieces or gifts such as the candlesticks (Fig. 155) given in 1716 to Henry Flynt by his Harvard students. Pieces which bear such original dates become key pieces in the dating of similar objects which have no engraving. With luck, these engraved dates can be corroborated by newspaper accounts, as in the case of the Liberty Bowl (Fig. 161), the Comet-Bomb cup (Fig. 19), and the Webster Vase (Fig. 116). Church records and the records of other organizations can be useful, too.

Often it turns out that the date of an object is slightly later than the date inscribed on the piece! In the case of the set of six Paul Revere tankards (Fig. 141) which are inscribed as presented to the church in Brookfield, Massachusetts, in 1768, it took four years for the church to fill this bequest, and it was not until 1772 that Revere entered the tankards in his account book.

This underscores the fact that engraved dates, whether contemporary or not, must be questioned. Somehow, family silver is particularly susceptible to predating by later generations who know little about silver styles and assume that all the family heirlooms had to have been brought over, if not on the Mayflower, at least by the first member of their family who came to this country (Fig. 220b).

Family and probate papers are therefore helpful. Occasionally, a reference in a letter to a piece of silver, or a bill, survives to pinpoint the date. Wills and inventories may mention a piece, or it may simply be the vital statistics of the original owners which give a clue to the date of their silver. For instance, the little dram cup (Fig. 1) by Hull and Sanderson can be dated 1651 or earlier. Its original owner was Ruth Brewster (her initials RB are engraved on the side), who married in 1651, changing her name to Mrs. John Pickett and therefore her initials to RP. The tiny patch box (Fig. 5) by William Rouse, which is engraved LF on the base, was owned by Lydia Foster, who died in 1681, thereby placing the date of the box to a period prior to that year.

With joint initials of husband and wife, their marriage date fixes the earliest possible date, assuming that the initials are original to the piece. The death date of either one of the partners fixes the latest possible date. However, because the value of objects often is determined by their degree of antiquity, a common fallacy is to date a piece as early as possible, that is, to the year of the marriage. In fact, it was often several years later before the husband had achieved sufficient business success to permit his investment in silver. Furthermore, there are enough instances known of the purchase of silver for twenty-fifth or even twentieth wedding anniversaries to suspect that this custom dates from an early period and is not just a phenomenon of the past hundred years.

There is one group of objects which were invariably dated. These are gold mourning rings or the pieces of jewelry presented at funerals to the minister and close friends of the deceased (Fig. 151). These mourning tokens were engraved or enameled with the deceased's name or initials, the date of his death, and sometimes his age. As a result, it is the one category which can be more precisely dated.

In dating American silver, one should not depend on any single bit of evidence, such as an owner's death date, but on all possible factors. The Humphreys urn presented to Charles Thomson by the Continental Congress (Fig. 26) is a good example of how many avenues may be followed to establish an exact date. Even though it is engraved with the date 1774, it is designed in high Neo-Classical style, which some might doubt could be as early as 1774. But by determining the maker's working dates, when the urn's original owner died, when the engraver of the urn, James Smither, was working in Philadelphia, and what the original records of the Continental Congress revealed, the date of 1774 is finally established as certain.

In trying to date a piece of American silver accurately, a great deal more should be learned about it than just its date.

[220c] Pair of coasters, by Myer Myers, New York, c. 1765. Engraved with the Schuyler crest. Diameter. 4⅞″. *Courtesy, The New-York Historical Society*

[220d] Caudle cup, by John Coney, Boston, c. 1690. Engraved I^{M}M on base for John and Mary (Brattle) Mico who were married in 1689. Inherited by Oliver Wendell Holmes who was inspired by it to write "On Lending a Punch Bowl." Height: 5⅝″. *Courtesy, Museum of Fine Arts, Boston*

SPECIAL

AIDS

[220e] Cruet stand, formerly attributed to Godfrey Shiving, Philadelphia, c. 1790, but attributed by Crosby Forbes to Cumshing, one of the earliest of the Chinese silversmiths of Canton to provide silver for the American market. Height: 10¼″. *Courtesy, Philadelphia Museum of Art*

 **CHAPTER SEVENTEEN**

Cautions

WHAT TO LOOK FOR

Instinctively, when a person looks at a piece of silver, or at any object for that matter, he begins to decide whether it is something he likes or not, and whether it is something worth looking at again. With inherited family silver, it may be a question of whether he should keep it or dispose of it. With museum collections, it may be a decision for the curator as to whether to display it or put it in a study-storage area. For a collector, it is usually a matter of whether to acquire it or pass it by.

No matter what prompts the judgment, there are a number of factors which should be considered in evaluating silver objects. Each of these factors should be given a weight proportionate to its proper importance, so that the wisest appraisal can be made.

Authenticity is one of the most important aspects to be ascertained. Is the piece what it purports to be? Is the standard of the metal what it should be? Are its marks genuine and are its other features original? Can its history be corroborated or documented? If there are doubts in any one of these areas, the evaluating process may be abandoned altogether and the object forgotten.

If, however, the piece of silver seems to be authentic, a number of other factors should be considered. Its aesthetic quality is of prime importance. The object should be pleasing to the beholder's eye. It should measure up to the same standards of artistic quality that are

271

applied to other arts, such as quality of workmanship, good proportions, beauty of design, appropriate ornamentation, and suitability to function. These things can be determined by comparing this particular piece of silver to others made about the same time and in the same style.

It is important to be aware, while studying the object, of what its present condition is compared to what its original condition was. Tarnish, bruises, exposed firescale, and copper showing through on plated wares are annoying to the eye but in most cases are not irreparable. Unless such conditions seem overwhelming, they should not be given as much weight as whether a spout has been added or whether the basic form has been changed or reornamented. Often with antique silver it is reassuring to see some minor signs of wear. One looks for and expects to find a dent on the handle of a tankard at exactly the point where the thumbpiece strikes when the lid is opened up completely. Compatible wear should be apparent on the thumbpiece as well (Fig. 13). Frequently, the bottom of a handle will push in the side of a vessel after years of generous quaffing. There should be wear on the base caused by a piece being picked up, put down, and moved, and there should not be wear in an area which could not touch anything, which would not be seen, and consequently was rarely polished.

If a piece of silver can be documented in some way, it will naturally be of greater value and interest. This means that if it has marks and these can be identified, it is to everyone's advantage—so much so that there is hardly an area of evaluation so badly abused. The determination of the marks on silver should be done with the greatest restraint and objectivity (see pp. 245–263). It is very tempting to see the maker's initials of PR on a piece, and conclude with relish that the silver object had to have been made by Paul Revere! Such wishful thinking, unless proven beyond a sliver of a doubt, is of only temporary satisfaction.

If the silver was owned at one time by an important person, a local dignitary, or simply a member of the family, this has significance, too. The silver with known histories is of greater importance than the anonymous examples. Pedigrees are as important to silver as they have been to people in establishing preeminence. If the objects are associated with some historical event or some interesting social custom, they also will be of more distinction.

Finally, the question of rarity always enters the picture. If the piece of silver is unique or represents the best possible example of its kind, or is the greatest piece produced by a particular maker, an apotheosis occurs and these select examples are transported into the rarefied atmosphere of enormous esteem and consequently astronomical prices.

This can only occur after a sort of final judgment day has taken place and all the factors have been placed in the balance—even a unique piece of silver, if it is ugly or has been irreparably damaged, cannot attain immortality or the highest price on the auction block.

Over-enthusiasm and gullibility are perhaps the greatest pitfalls in evaluating silver, but there are also other dangers which can be avoided. Common among these is the misleading inscription. It is important to be able to recognize whether or not an inscription is original to a piece of silver. Fortunately, this can be achieved by becoming familiar with the stylistic changes which took place in the continuing art of the engraver (see pp. 235–244) and by recognizing how engraved surfaces age. This is helpful because occasionally one finds a piece of silver with a date engraved on it which is much earlier than the object could possibly be. The unknowing might leap to the conclusion that the date inscribed is the date of the silver.

For example, silver made for presentation on a twenty-fifth or fiftieth anniversary may be inscribed with the date the marriage took place and so may be off by a quarter or half a century. Faulty memories on the part of family members have also contributed their share of misleading inscriptions to American silver. And occasionally an old piece of silver has been melted down and remade into a new form, with the date of the previous piece or of its bequest added to recall the event. In the case of church silver, it is not uncommon to find a piece with the date of the bequest engraved on it, and then to discover that it took the church thirty years to fulfill the legacy (Fig. 143).

The apparent style of a piece can also be misleading. Even though objects made of silver were usually in the latest style, occasional anachronisms occur. In Albany, New York, for instance, an archaic form of baluster-top spoon, which generally passed out of style at the end of the seventeenth century, occasionally was made in the eighteenth century as a traditional commemorative presentation piece. The porringer, although not a very useful object today, continues to be made in its eighteenth-century form with rarely any change in its design.

Even in the early years of the nineteenth century, there were revivals of earlier styles, and a number of items were made in the "Colonial" style, so that it is desirable to be able to distinguish between contemporary expressions of certain forms and decorations and the later interpretations of them. Happily, few craftsmen are content to mimic the earlier pieces exactly, so that little tell-tale innovations and details give away the true date of the objects. The Rococo Revival which took place about 1830 not only caused silver to be made in the eighteenth century style, but also caused many pieces of various dates of manufacture to be newly embossed with rococo repoussé ornamentation. Even in 1763, the New York goldsmith Otto de Parisien advertised: "Likewise undertakes chasing any Piece of old Plate . . ." [110]

REPAIRS

The ability to detect such early changes in silver is something that comes slowly and is achieved only with a great deal of experience, but knowing what types of changes were most frequently made can be a help. Handles represent one of the most often repaired and changed parts in old silver. Unless they were well designed and soldered to the body, they were easily damaged through use. If the handle was hollow, it could be easily dented. If solid and cast, the handle would be heavy and could pull out at the top or push in at the base.

Sometimes handles were removed or put on other vessels to make them more serviceable to a later generation. This, in fact, is what happened to a beaker (Fig. 221) in The First Church, Salem, made about 1670 by Jeremiah Dummer, which originally was a handleless beaker like the one made by his masters Hull and Sanderson (Fig. 2). A double switch occurred in the silver of the First Parish Unitarian Church, Beverly, Massachusetts. A 1729 cup which originally had two handles had one removed from it; the handle was then added to a handleless cup made in 1718 by John Coney. This change-about can not only be seen with the eye, but can also be documented by a letter written by Abiel Abbot:

> Dear Sir, As it has been thought advisable to alter some of the communion plate, shifting a handle from a cup, which had two, to a vessel which had none, I should think it very proper, if you will take the trouble, to call upon the goldsmith for his bill, & charge it among the expences of the table.

The goldsmith whose bill was called for was Israel Trask of Beverly, who charged the church $1.75 on November 29, 1809, for making the change.[111]

Handles on teapots were changed occasionally after 1800, from the earlier wooden handles to the less practical silver handles with ivory insulating rings at top and bottom. The old wooden handles wore out easily, and with a heavy load of tea could pull right out of their pinned sockets, so it is no wonder that many are not original.

Lids, too, often snapped their hinges and were broken, or they became a nuisance, and so were repaired or removed. When a tankard made in the mid-eighteenth century by Joseph Richardson had its lid

[221] Beaker, by Jeremiah Dummer, Boston, c.1670, Given to The First Church, Salem, by Francis Skerry. Handles added later in the eighteenth century. *Courtesy, The First Church, Salem, Mass.*

replaced by Henry Peterson about 1785, Mr. Peterson was kind enough to stamp the lid with his own mark to let future generations know what change had been effected. More often, no record was made. Then it is necessary to check to see that the lid is in the same style as the body of the tankard, that it is consistent with others by the same maker, and that the wear on both parts seems uniform. Also, the wear-spot where the thumbpiece hits the handle should show if the same lid has always been attached to the tankard in question. If, however, the new lid has been in use for several hundred years, it may be more difficult. An advertisement in the *New-York Gazette* calls attention to a change that had occurred to a tankard lid in 1732: "Stolen last Wednesday a Silver Tankard, containing a Quart, the Tankard hath a new Lid lately put on . . ." If this tankard survives today, it would undoubtedly be more difficult to see that the lid is not original than would be the case if the lid were put on in the last decade.[112]

Spouts often have been changed on pieces; they have been both added and removed. Many were added during the Victorian period, when individual communion cups came into church use, eliminating the passing of the communal tankard, and old tankards were converted into pitchers by the addition of a spout. Most added spouts are easily discernible because they interfere with the design of the piece and were cut into the body of the piece in a way that would not have been done if the spout had been part of its original manufacture.

Changes that required soldering for their execution can be detected by the minute air holes which never can be entirely prevented in soldering. Usually, the outline of the soldered area can be spotted by holding a piece of white paper at right angles to the surface of the metal, or else by blowing on the piece so that the condensation of the vapor of the breath shows up the difference between solder and purer silver. Later soldering usually is of a slightly different coloration, because of the difference in composition, and if a piece of silver has been so unfortunate as to be subjected to lead soldering, it is immediately apparent.

FAKES

Spotting solder outlines and changes in a piece of silver can sometimes lead to the detection of a forgery. Unfortunately, some changes have been made to silver for the express purpose of deceiving. One common trick is to remove lesser or later marks and solder in a new fake mark. Where the marks have been cut out completely, one should be able to see the outline of the solder used in filling in the gap. Marrow spoons, for instance, could have their hallmarks cut out of the central shaft and the two ends soldered back together. They can be left without marks, or fake marks can be stamped in, to make them seem to be American and therefore more rare than an English marrow spoon would be. In addition to the solder line, two clues to the deception will remain, however. One is that the shaft will be foreshortened to such an extent that comparison with other eighteenth-century marrow spoons will make it plain that it could not have been designed that way. The other clue is that if new marks have been stamped into the marrow spoon, the wear will stop at the edge of the mark and will not appear along the top of the mark, where it should be.

This latter point can be clearly seen by looking at the added TH mark on the base of a perfectly good Georgian inkstand (Fig. 222b). The lines of wear seem to stop at the edges of the mark instead of continuing over the surface. In this instance, a whole new base, which was simply one flat rectangle of silver, was set into the inkstand after being properly distressed to simulate wear, and the TH marks added to enable the inkstand to be sold as the work of a desirable New York silversmith, Thomas Hammersly.

Very little has been put into print about the faking of American

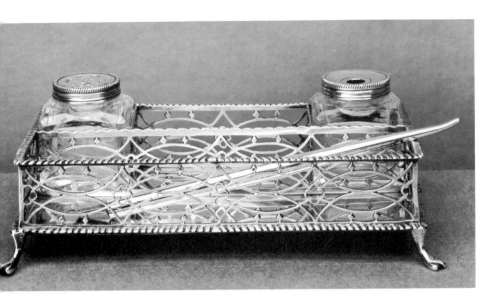

[222a, 222b] Georgian inkstand, c.1765. English hallmarks have been removed, and marks falsely attributed to Thomas Hammersley (1727–1781), New York, were added. *Courtesy, Henry Francis du Pont Winterthur Museum*

silver. Fakes are hard to prove, and many are offended by the knowledge that what they thought was genuine is not. However, the faking of American silver has been going on almost as long as the collecting of it, and at least one known forgery was exhibited as genuine at the very beginning of this century. By 1938, John Marshall Phillips had seen enough spurious silver to list, in *Antique Fakes and Reproductions*, nineteen different American silversmiths whose marks had been most frequently forged. These were Pygan Adams, Thauvet Besly, John Brevoort, Benjamin and John Burt, John Coney, John Dixwell, John Edwards, Jacob Hurd, Knight Leverett, Myer Myers, John Noyes, Gerrit Onckelbag, Paul Revere, Joseph Richardson, George Rideout, Simeon

Soumain, Philip Syng, and Koenradt Ten Eyck. Numerous other names could be added to the ranks thirty years later.[113]

Mr. Phillips also published in this discussion the first picture exposing a fake in American silver. It was a tall seventeenth-century type of New York beaker, obviously copied from the kind made by Vander Burch and the Boelens. But the engraving was so far inferior to the aspirations of the design, and the workmanship so crude, that it could not be authentic. In the past, this has been one of the biggest mistakes of would-be forgers. The fabricators would have us believe that because these objects were made long ago, they were not well made. Nothing could be further from the truth. Because of the precious nature of the metal itself, there are very few examples of early American silver that are not nicely made. There is no such thing as primitive American silver, as there is primitive furniture or painting. Some silver may be simple or plain, but it is not crude. As a result, if one looks at a spurious Indian medal (Fig. 223) supposed to have been made by Joseph Richardson, Jr., and compares it with a genuine one (Fig. 171), it quickly becomes apparent that the forgery is not well designed, that it is crudely put together, and that the engraving is rigid, stiffly executed, and in a manner that is entirely inconsistent with engraving of the 1790s.

Herein lies the greatest salvation and protection against fakes. There are virtually no people today who have all the skills as well as all the knowledge needed to produce a perfect forgery in American silver. The goldsmith's art was a combination of many skills, and it behooves the serious student to become familiar with all the techniques of the craft.

Because of the many processes involved in making silver, forgers will, on occasion, collaborate. Some years ago, a syndicate was operating in Philadelphia. One of the their prime objectives was to supply family silver to an unsuspecting member of an old Philadelphia family who was trying to reassemble his ancestors' silver. One member of the group was a die-cutter and made the stamps for the makers' marks. He did not realize, however, that eighteenth-century initials had serifs. Hence, some of the marks he fabricated had singularly straight and unembellished letters. Nor did he know that every goldsmith probably cut his own touchmark and that there would be individual differences between the marks of different makers. All his dies looked alike, whether they were supposed to be of a Philadelphia silversmith or of a New York maker.

The engraver of the group made similar mistakes. All the owners' initials he engraved on these pieces had very tall, stiff letters, even though they were put onto pieces supposed to be by different makers.

The shading of engraved letters in the eighteenth century was not understood by him, and so it was incorrectly done.

The man who made the actual silver used a variety of techniques worth noting. In some cases, he simply removed the hallmarks from English silver; in others, he took previously unmarked silver and added fake American marks. Occasionally, the object used was in a style that did not come into fashion until after the alleged American maker had died. For a sauceboat meant to be by Joseph Richardson, he took the cast handle and feet either from an authentic example or else cast them from a mold impressed by authentic ones. These were then soldered onto a newly-formed body. The error lay in the use of a modern sheet of rolled silver for the body. The metal naturally shows the striations or graining of having been flattened under great pressure, which could have been accomplished only by modern equipment. Joseph Richardson, working in the mid-eighteenth century, would not have had the machinery to produce such a uniformly thin piece of silver.[114]

Cast parts or cast pieces of silver are harder to detect when they are faked, because it is difficult to tell newly cast silver from eighteenth-century cast silver. As a result, cast candlesticks have frequently been

[223] Spurious oval Indian medal (left) given false mark of Joseph Richardson, Jr., Philadelphia, who made the authentic medal on the right. *Photograph privately owned.*

[224] Fake mark of Jacobus Vander Spiegel, New York, added to a spoon. *Courtesy, Henry Francis du Pont Winterthur Museum, Study Collection*

forged. The best indication of age is in the way the objects are finished off on the bottom, and in the evidences of wear. Wear should be fairly general rather than spotty, and not look induced with rather large and uniform cuts or knicks.

Most fakes are given false marks to make their worth greater. These should always be detectible, since it is impossible to reproduce a mark exactly. Comparison with a genuine mark of the same date will always reveal some differences under a strong glass. An early attempt to reproduce the mark of Jacobus Vander Spiegel shows such differences (Fig. 212). The authentic die used by Vander Spiegel got a crack in it sometime during its usage, and this fissure in the die can be clearly seen on the silver he made and stamped. The forger, in order to simulate this crack in the mark, cut a crude line into his faked mark, which is quite obvious when compared with the original (Fig. 224).

Attempts have been made to create identical punch marks by a process of casting from plaster molds taken from genuine marks. This can be detected because the new mark has a soft, less distinct, less crisp appearance than the original mark. A whole piece such as a spoon, its mark included, has sometimes been completely cast for purposes of fraud, but then the pits left by the casting sand will show that it has not been handwrought or stamped. Also, the marks will appear in identical positions on every new casting from the same mold, a coincidence altogether unlikely in old silver, where each mark would have been handstruck.

Fakers, realizing how difficult it is to recreate a certain maker's mark, have been known to make up an entirely fictional goldsmith as well as his mark. Then there is nothing with which to compare the false mark. George Guest, a person about whom little was known other than the fact that he was living Philadelphia about 1705, was turned into a goldsmith and given a mark. Fortunately, his authors struck the mark on later pieces of silver, with which George Guest never would have been familiar during his lifetime, so that the deception was soon uncovered.

Paul Revere, because of his famous name, has probably suffered more indignities at the hands of forgers than any other American silversmith, and for a longer period of time. Naturally, the rarer the object or the maker, the greater the rewards for the deceiver. Even an old buckle (Fig. 225), if it can be given the name and fame of Paul Revere, will be worth the effort of fabrication.

A common method of deception, and one that involves less liability for its perpetrator, is the false identification of authentic marks on a piece of silver. If the fraud is discovered, it can always be excused on the grounds of human fallibility or ignorance. As a result, Irish marks have been assigned to New York makers, and a particular PA mark of a Channel Islands maker has been called the mark of Pygan Adams of Connecticut. It is, therefore, very helpful to be familiar with the marks of other countries, and especially those of provincial Great Britain (Fig. 220e).

REPRODUCTIONS

Another quick and easy method of fraud is to take a perfectly legitimate modern reproduction and doctor it. Such a deception can be illustrated by comparing the same area on the back of two spoons from a set (Fig. 226), one of which retains remnants of its original and proper marks, as REVERE GORHAM STERLING and an MMA RE-PRODUCTION, while the other one has only a reproduced REVERE mark remaining.

Because of such unscrupulous use of honest reproductions, it is well

[225a] Pair of buckles given the counterfeited mark [225b] of Paul Revere, Boston. *Privately owned*

to be acquainted with the reproductions that have been made over the years, and to learn how to tell the original from its imitation. Firms such as J. E. Caldwell & Co. in Philadelphia and Shreve Crump & Low Company in Boston, manufacturers such as Gorham and the Towle Company, and individual silver shops such as Gebelein in Boston or The Golden Ball in Williamsburg have produced honestly marked and excellent reproductions, often of museum objects.

It is by becoming completely familiar with the original that it is possible to distinguish the reproduction or the fake. Lately, there have been developed certain additional aids. One of these involves microphotography, that is, the photographing of marks under very high magnification so that every detail of the mark can be seen and compared with every detail of a substantiated mark.

Another of the new techniques involves spectrographic analysis. Here, the content of the metal is analyzed down to the least element. Certain elements should be found in early American silver and would not be expected in modern silver. This method is also useful in testing whether, for instance, a lid or a handle is of the same metallic content as the body of a piece, and therefore presumably original.

With increased interest in American silver, and with the increased publication of information about it, the curator and collector alike have become more discerning and less easily betrayed. It is essential to be aware of the norm and to look for the exception. It is with the unknown or the object unlike any other that one takes the biggest risk —either it is the greatest treasure or the greatest mistake. Only by knowing what to look for can we be assured of recognizing the best in American silver.

[226] Marks on legitimate museum reproductions of a Revere spoon with some of the marks removed on one to make it appear to be the authentic work of Paul Revere. *Photograph, courtesy, Heritage Foundation, Deerfield, Mass.*

John-Paul Grimke

Has just imported in the Lyttelton, *capt.* Brown, *from* London.

MOURNING swords, buckles, necklaces, rings with or without diamonds, and other articles used on such occasions. Likewise, some jeweller's and silver-smith's work, all made strong and in the newest fashion; some very rich diamond earings and rings, bracelets of *Pruffian* patterns, very neat pocket-books with silver locks, fine metzotinto prints and views of various sorts, with many other things too tedious to enumerate here.

Those gentlemen and ladies who have favoured him with their orders, may send for the articles they desired him to write for, the ensuing week; which he hopes will prove to their entire satisfaction, and engage the continuance of their favours, as he shall always take all possible care that such orders he exactly complied with.

Having now some good workmen, he again does all kinds of jewellery and gold and silverfmith's work, faithfully, neat and cheap; chasing, and motto rings made as usual.

His customers, by sending to his shop, may at all times have their jewels brushed clean, *gratis*. And as he left his boy in the small-pox, who used to go to their houses to clean their plate, he takes this method to acquaint them of an easy way, by which their own servants may clean the same, without spoiling the chased work, *viz*. Wash your plate in warm water with a little soap dissolved therein; wipe it dry with a clear towel; then brush it with whiting dissolved in rum or any other spirits; which will restore to it its former beauty and brightness again.

N. B. He has brushes enough to sell.

James Povas

[227] Advertisement of John Paul Grimke (1713–1791), *South Carolina Gazette,* December 23–30, 1760, giving instructions for cleaning silver. *Courtesy, Charleston Library Society*

CHAPTER EIGHTEEN

Care of Silver

ONE of the greatest concerns to anyone interested in silver is how to care for it properly. In the case of early American silver, it is not only a concern but a responsibility to see that these historical objects are passed on to future generations with as little change as possible. Before turning to the recommended methods of cleaning and repairing, it is necessary to examine the effect of environment on silver, since we ourselves cause much of the deterioration and difficulty through improper use and display.

The best method of caring for silver is to avoid the situations which will cause changes to it. For this, we need to have a thorough understanding of the properties of the metal (see pp. 229–234). We need to know that silver will melt if subjected to a heat of 960 degrees centigrade. We need to know that because silver is usually found in mineral form as silver sulfide or silver chloride, ordinary city air with its pollutions will tarnish silver with the formation of a thin surface of silver sulfide. Salt, being a chloride, and therefore salt air in coastal areas, will have an equally unfavorable effect upon silver. Flue gases and even less obvious conditions such as vulcanized-rubber floor coverings, rubber-base paints, and even paper and textiles which have been treated with sulfur, all have a deleterious effect on silver and should be recognized and avoided.

By being aware of the specific nature of silver, we know why silver wrapped in inert plastic bags or put in closets will not tarnish so readily, why eggs and mustard darken the surface of silver so dread-

285

fully, why sets of spoons should never be held together by a rubber band, and why people who wish to display silver in cases should be careful of the paint or materials used on the shelves and sides.

One of the most alarming sights for the silver collector and the housewife alike is to open a drawer to get out a spoon, lift back the special silver cloth, and see those awful black spots, the measles of the silver world, commonly called "salt disease." The same ugly blemishes show up in salt dishes if the salt is not carefully cleaned out after every use, unless the surface has been specially gilded or treated, or unless a glass liner is used. But any chloride base can cause this dread disease, even the undiscernible perspiration on the hands of the person who has tenderly washed and dried the silver or the person who puts it away. This is why gloves are worn by cautious museum curators who handle silver. Fortunately, salt disease is not communicable and is caused only by direct contact. It cannot be transferred from one piece of silver to another in a drawer or case. Once the damage has been done, however, it is hard to correct satisfactorily.

The big underlying problem is that, whether it is salt disease or tarnish, the solution lies in the removal of a certain amount of silver. In the case of salt disease, each salt spot must be dug out, and a much wider area is always affected than just the little black central core which is apparent to our eyes. Depending upon the amount of contamination, that is, the amount of chloride deposited on the silver, the reaction will travel as deep and as wide as necessary until all the chloride molecules have found enough silver molecules to join with them in their natural configuration. This can mean that an ugly gaping hole is the alternative to a tiny black spot.

Every grain of silver we remove is a crime against a limited number of objects which represent our heritage and are irreplaceable. From the mid-eighteenth century to the present day, the ordinary weight loss that occurs to silver objects is normally about 5 to 8 dwt. It is, therefore, horrifying to find that in households where silver is automatically polished by unsuspecting servants every Thursday, whether it needs it or not, and even in museums, the weight loss has proven to be much greater, running an average of 13 to 15 dwt. of lost silver in some cases.

For Sheffield or plated ware, such repeated abrasions are disastrous, as eventually the thin layer of silver is totally worn away, exposing the base metal of copper. While to some eyes this may give the object a warm and mellow look, it is certainly an appearance that the object was never intended to have, and one which definitely causes the value of the piece to deteriorate. The Gordian question then arises of whether or not to replate the surface. This is rarely a very satisfactory solution. Silver plating today invariably reduces the object's value and generally results in a thicker surface of silver, so that the color is not the same and areas of decoration are made less sharp or in some cases are totally obliterated.

Even for solid antique silver, repeated abrasion changes the appearance by wearing away the engraving and the maker's marks. Furthermore, constant polishing eventually exposes the fire-scale which lies dormant under the surface. This fire-scale, caused by the very process of manufacturing, is the result of annealing. Actually, it is a layer of oxidized silver which was concealed by putting the object into an acid bath, boiling it, and thereby removing the oxidation only from the outermost layer of the metal. Cleaning over the years wears away this pure layer of silver and discloses the black scale beneath. Many people, seeing this darkness surfacing on their silver and not understanding it, polish it all the harder, only to make the matter worse.

By far the best solution to all these problems is to prevent them in the first place. We can prevent tarnish and protect the metal from its natural enemies, such as salt, citrus fruits, vinegar, and latex paint, by protecting the surface of the silver from any contact with these elements. This can be done by wrapping cleaned silver in Pacific cloth or in several layers of high-grade soft tissue paper with an outer layer of paper or cloth containing tarnish inhibitors. Modern products such as polyethylene bags, Saran Wrap, and aluminum foil are useful in shutting out atmospheric enemies. However, as with the impregnated cloth and paper, they should not be placed in direct contact with the silver, which should be protected first by a layer of tissue paper. Cheap wood-pulp tissues with a high percentage of sulfite should be avoided.

For silver which is not kept in storage, less effective solutions must be employed. There are a number of new products which can be used to slow down the tarnishing processes. One of the best of these is Minnesota Mining and Manufacturing Company's Tarnishield, which retards tarnishing of silver in open air for several months. It is not harmful and can be removed with silver polish. Other similar products of varying effectiveness are on the market, but it should be remembered that one of the difficulties in recommending a specific product is that its formula can be changed without a simultaneous change in name, so that it is wise to test all products before using them.

If the silver can be displayed in a dust-free case, so much the better. Anti-tarnish paper can again be helpful here, and a small cake of refined camphor placed inside the case also helps to retard tarnish. A particularly useful technique, proven at the Nordic Museum in Stockholm, is the use of treated silk lining for the case. Shantung silk is treated in a 10 percent solution of lead acetate containing 2 percent glycerol and about 1 percent ammonia, then dried and ironed. This material, used as lining for cases, retards tarnishing remarkably.

Where atmospheric conditions are especially incompatible and old silver must suffer exposure to them without benefit of a case, lacquer is a possible solution if it is carefully applied. While certain brand names of lacquer, such as Silvershield and Agateen, have been used with some success, the perfect invisible lacquer for silver at a reasonable cost has yet to be developed. Any methacrylate- or polyvinylacetate-based spirit varnishes can be used as lacquers without permanent injury to the silver, but even with the most careful application, the appearance of the silver is changed somewhat. In some cases, there may also be a problem in removing the lacquer when it begins to deteriorate and lose its effectiveness.

One way to prevent tarnish from building up on the surface of silver is to wash it frequently with soap and water. In areas where the water is full of minerals, distilled water should be used. Detergents, either for dishwashers or for washing dishes by hand, are not recommended because many contain phosphorous or sulfur compounds which can cause unsightly staining.

Another less satisfactory method of cleaning which does not remove any silver involves an electrolytic bath. This can be done by using a chemical dip or more simply by placing the silver in an aluminum pan with a teaspoon of soda. Neither is advisable for silver with any sort of decoration because the bath removes tarnish from the recessed and patterned areas of the design, which often were originally darkened to create the desired contrast. Furthermore, the chemical action leaves a white film over the surface of the metal which then needs to be rubbed off.

When an abrasive is needed to remove the tarnish, it is always advisable to use as mild a substance as possible. Only polishes specifically recommended for silver should be used. One of the best modern products along these lines is Hagerty's Silver Foam, which is a light paste applied with a soft sponge. It rinses away easily and does not clog in the interstices of the designs.

Basically, the formula for good silver polish has changed little over the years, and usually involves some sort of abrasive chalk dissolved in an alcoholic solution. In 1760, goldsmith John Paul Grimke of Charleston recommended that the silver be washed in warm water with a little soap dissolved in it, wiped dry with a clean towel, and then brushed with whiting dissolved in rum or some other form of spirits. Naturally, the coarser the abrasive, the greater the polishing will be, but the more damaging it will be as well. Advertisers of all ages have emphasized the effectiveness of their polishes accordingly. New York silversmith Alexander S. Gordon in 1801 was no exception. He advertised a type of silver powder, at a "trifling expense," which was wholesome to the silver, would eradicate the scratches, and produce a superb and durable luster. He was quick to point out that it was not like a competitor's product, which was a mercurial preparation that gave an instant gloss but ultimately corroded and destroyed the silver.[115]

If a piece of silver has been so badly tarnished over the years that such over-rated panaceas seem tempting, it may be necessary to use something as strong as jeweler's rouge on a chamois, or even to burnish the object. This must be done with great care. Buffing is to be avoided at all costs because it removes and alters the whole outer surface of the silver, and destroys the natural patina.

At this point, the question is no longer one of preservation but one of restoration. For badly tarnished silver, the solutions amount to the same thing as refinishing a piece of furniture, and are to be avoided if they mean undue loss of silver, loss of patina, or exposure of fire-scale. Before any restoration is undertaken, a careful appraisal of the situation should be made. The object should be studied to ascertain its present condition, to note whether any previous restoration has occurred which might be adversely affected in the present treatment. Changes made to the piece over the years should be analyzed, as should the way restoration will affect the value of the object.

It is a wise person who can distinguish what he should undertake himself and what he should leave for the expert to handle. The collector should do little more than basic cleaning. It is obvious that replating or electrolytic treatment should be carried out only by experienced conservators. But it is equally important that bruises and dents should be hammered out by a craftsman skilled and knowledgeable in how much stress the metal can take. This holds true for repairs such as straightening out bent handles, soldering holes in the metal, removing spouts or handles which are not original, or anything which may cause a change to the structure of the metal.

The purpose the object is to serve should be considered. If it is to be exhibited in an art museum and its aesthetic appearance is damaged by a later spout or later engraving, probably these appendages should be removed by an expert. If, on the other hand, it is to be preserved by a local historical society or simply by succeeding generations of the family of the original owner, then it is more logical to preserve subsequent changes to the object as part of its own history. For salt-diseased silver in ordinary household use, it is probably better to leave the piece as it is, or have the black holes covered with a dot of solder, than to have the corroded spots dug out and filled with solder.

For silver which has been polished so hard that the fire-scale is exposed, it may be best to leave it, since it is not very noticeable unless it is placed under bright lights and seriously scrutinized. In the eighteenth century, silversmiths apparently were faced with correcting exposed fire-scale and their solution was to repeat the final process of finishing a piece of silver. Joseph Richardson in 1737 took two second-hand salvers which belonged to his Aunt Grace Lloyd and charged her for "Boyling them & Burnishing them" to restore a pure layer of silver to the surface and cover the fire-scale.

Caution needs to be taken in effecting this solution to make sure that the weak sulfuric-acid solution used in the boiling is not allowed to act too long on the silver since it will erode the areas which have been soldered or any previous repairs. Areas of decoration on the silver which were purposely darkened by the maker to enhance the design will be removed and will have to be restored. Finally, the piece must be thoroughly washed and neutralized in a solution of washing soda to make sure that the reparative action has been stopped. When perfected, this means of dealing with fire-scale will obviously be preferable to the present harmful solutions of buffing and replating.

In the end, the major concern of anyone who likes silver is to keep it as much like it originally was as possible. This concern is a two-tined effort of preservation and restoration. Future generations will be grateful that we have not diminished their legacy.

[228] Sauce boat, by Thomas Fletcher (1787–1866), Boston and Philadelphia, c. 1830. Length: 11″ (tray). Height: 8½″ (sauce boat). *Privately owned*

Notes

1. Captain John Smith, *The Travels, Adventures and Observations of Captain John Smith*, from the London edition of 1629 (Richmond, Va., 1819), I, 169.

2. Cited by C. Louise Avery, *Early American Silver* (New York, 1930), p. 199 and Kathryn C. Buhler, *Masterpieces of American Silver* (Richmond, Va., 1960), p. 8.

3. Bernard Cuzner, *A Silversmith's Manual* (London, 1949), p. 187.

4. Mrs. Russel Hastings, "The Sanders-Garvan Beaker by Cornelis Vander Burch," *Antiques*, XXVII (February 1935), 52–55.

5. Edward J. Nygren, "Edward Winslow's Sugar Boxes: Colonial Echoes of Courtly Love," *Yale University Art Gallery Bulletin*, XXXIII, No. 2 (Autumn 1971), 38–52.

6. *New-York Gazette*, April 3–10, 1727 and *American Weekly Mercury*, March 23, 1727.

7. William Hogarth, *Analysis of Beauty* (London, 1753).

8. William Shakespeare, *Hamlet*, III, ii, 20.

9. Martha G. Fales, "Philadelphia Silver Exhibition," *The Art Quarterly* (Spring 1957), 45–47. *Journals of the Continental Congress 1774–1789*, (Washington, 1904), I, 14, 104.

10. Kathryn C. Buhler, *Mount Vernon Silver* (Mount Vernon, Va., 1967), pp. 35–36.

11. Alexander Hamilton, *Gentleman's Progress: The Itinerarium of Dr. Alexander Hamilton, 1744*, ed. Carl Bridenbaugh (Chapel Hill, N.C., 1948), p. 186.

12. *The Diary of William Bentley, D.D.* (Salem, Mass., 1905), I, 147.

13. *Pennsylvania Journal*, December 15, 1763.

14. *Pennsylvania Packet*, October 18, 1783.

15. *South Carolina & American General Gazette*, June 27, 1769. Mrs. Buhler notes that Paul Revere specifically recorded "scalloped tureen ladles."

16. Cited by Kathryn C. Buhler, "Silver 1640–1820," *The Concise Encyclopedia of American Antiques* (New York, 1958), I, 93.

17. *Ibid.*, I, 85. Mrs. Buhler has pointed out that this same basket, now at the Museum of Fine Arts, Boston, was listed in John Hancock's inventory in 1793 as a bread basket.

18. *Pennsylvania Journal*, December 15, 1763.

19. John N. Pearce, "The Stephen Decatur House and Furnishings," *The Washington Antiques Show* (Washington, D.C., 1968), pp. 31–38. Mrs. Buhler notes that James Lloyd owned "3 trencher plates" in 1693 and Edward Jackson had a pair of butter plates in 1757.

20. Cited by Buhler, "Silver 1640–1820," I, 92.

21. Rita Susswein Gottesman, *The Arts and Crafts in New York 1800–1804* (New York, 1965), p. 105.

22. Advertisement of William Whetcroft in *Maryland Gazette*, May 13, 1773.

23. Cited by Judith Banister, *Old English Silver* (New York, 1965), p. 99.

24. Kathryn C. Buhler, "The Nine Colonial Sugar Boxes," *Antiques*, LXXXV (January 1964), 88–91.

25. Cited by John Marshall Phillips, *American Silver* (New York, 1949), p. 53.

26. Cited by Kathryn C. Buhler, "Technical Notes" in Jeanette W. Rosenbaum, *Myer Myers, Goldsmith* (Philadelphia, 1954), p. 108.

27. Edward Lang, Account Book, MS, Library, Essex Institute. *Memoirs of Samuel Davis of Plymouth, Mass., 1765–1829*, ed. Ruth Gardner Steinway (Plymouth, Mass., 1960). Advertisement of William Grigg in the *New-York Gazette*, August 2, 1779, lists imported "boatswain's calls with chains."

28. Hermann Frederick Clarke, *John Coney, Silversmith* (Boston, 1932), between pp. 12 and 13. See also pp. 43–44 and checklist nos. 11–12.

29. William Faris, Design Book, MS, Maryland Historical Society. J. Hall Pleasants and Howard Sill, *Maryland Silversmiths 1715–1830* (Baltimore, 1930), Plates XLVIII–LXVII, between pp. 258 and 259.

30. Joseph Richardson, Letter Book, MS, The Joseph Downs Manuscript and Microfilm Collection, The Henry Francis du Pont Winterthur Museum, hereafter cited as DMMC, Winterthur.

31. Berry B. Tracy, "Late Classical Styles in American Silver, 1810–1830," *Antiques*, LXXXVI (December 1964), 702–706. Elizabeth Ingerman Wood, "Thomas Fletcher," *Winterthur Portfolio* (Winterthur, Del., 1967), III, 159–164.

32. Martha G. Fales, "Three Eighteenth Century Salem Coffee Pots," Essex Institute *Historical Collections*, XCVIII (October 1962), 283–286.

33. *Federal Gazette*, September 13, 1792.

34. Kathryn C. Buhler, "Samuel Casey's Apprenticeship," *Bulletin of the Museum of Fine Arts*, XXXVIII (Boston, 1940), 33–35.

35. John Marshall Phillips, "Regional Characteristics in Early American

Silver," *Antiques*, LVI (August 1949), 115. C. Louise Avery, *Early American Silver* (New York, 1930), pp. 11–208.

36. John N. Pearce, "New York's Two-handled Paneled Silver Bowls," *Antiques*, LXXX (October 1961), 341–345 and "Further Comments on the Lobate Bowl Form," *Antiques*, XC (October 1966), 524–525.

37. John D. Davis, "The Evolution of the Early American Silver Spoon c.1650–c.1850," (Master's dissertation, University of Delaware, 1962).

38. Thomas J. Wertenbaker, *The First Americans* (New York, 1927), p. 284 cites Captain Nathaniel Butler's *Unmasked Face of Virginia* published in 1622. Captain Edward Johnson, *Wonder-Working Providence of Sion's Saviour in New-England, London, 1654* with historical introduction and index by William Frederick Poole (Andover, Mass., 1867), pp. 174–175.

39. William Clark, 1647, Essex County Probate Court, Salem, Mass.

40. Nathaniel Rogers, 1655, Essex County Probate Court, Salem, Mass. The Steenwyck inventory cited by C. Louise Avery, *An Exhibition of Early New York Silver* (New York, 1931), p. 3. Phipps inventory cited by Phillips, *American Silver*, p. 26.

41. R. W. Symonds, "The English Export Trade in Furniture to Colonial America," *Antiques*, XXVIII (October 1935), 156.

42. David Neal, *The History of New England* (London, 1720), cited by R. T. H. Halsey and Charles O. Cornelius, *A Handbook of the American Wing*, 3rd edition (New York, 1926), pp. 50–51.

43. *Maryland Gazette*, March 11, 1728.

44. Col. de Peyster inventory, cited by Avery, *op. cit.*, p. 4.

45. Cited by Phillips, *American Silver*, pp. 63–64.

46. Joseph Richardson, MS Account Book, Historical Society of Pennsylvania.

47. *Boston Evening Post*, January 4, 1773.

48. Joseph Richardson, MS Day Book, Library, Historical Society of Pennsylvania. The present location of the service bought by Lydia Spencer is unknown.

49. Franklin D. Scott, ed. and trans., *Baron Klinkowstrom's America, 1818–1820* (Evanston, Ill., 1952), p. 130.

50. Cited by Phillips, *American Silver*, p. 115.

51. Kenneth and Anna M. Roberts, eds., *Moreau de St. Mery's American Journey* (New York, 1947), p. 266.

52. John F. Watson, *Annals of Philadelphia and Pennsylvania* (Philadelphia, 1868), pp. 580–581.

53. Kathryn C. Buhler, *Mount Vernon Silver* (Mount Vernon, Va., 1957), pp. 49–56.

54. "An American Rarity," *Antiques*, LXXX (October 1961), p. 340.

55. Elias Hasket Derby, 1799, Essex County Probate Court, Salem, Mass.

56. E. Alfred Jones, *The Old Silver of American Churches* (Letchworth, England, 1913). All cited material in this chapter is derived from this source unless otherwise indicated.

57. Charles James Jackson, *An Illustrated History of English Plate* (London, 1911), I, 386.

58. National Maritime Museum, *Oar Maces of Admiralty* (London, 1966), pp. 7, 11.

59. Frank M. Etting, *An Historical Account of the Old State House of Pennsylvania* (Boston, 1876), pp. 24, 168–170.

60. Abbott Lowell Cummings, *Rural Household Inventories* (Boston, 1964), p. 242.

61. William T. Hastings, *The Insignia of Phi Beta Kappa* (Washington, 1964, 2nd printing 1968), pp. 5–17.

62. Major Edgar Erskine Hume, "General George Washington's Eagle of the Society of the Cincinnati," *The Numismatist*, XLVI (December 1933), 749–759.

63. Buhler, *Mount Vernon Silver*, pp. 46, 49; Gottesman (1965), p. 96.

64. *The Diary of William Bentley, D.D.* (Salem, Mass., 1914), IV, 593. For preceding citations see Martha G. Fales, "The Early American Way of Death," Essex Institute *Historical Collections*, C (April 1964), 75–84.

65. John Marshall Phillips, "Dutch–New York Spoons," *Bulletin of the Associates in Fine Arts at Yale University*, VIII (June 1937), 11–13. Carolyn Scoon, "Cornelia Duyckinck's Birthday Spoon," *The New-York Historical Society Quarterly*, XXXIV (October 1950), 315–317.

66. Capt. Freake reference cited by Phillips, *American Silver*, p. 26. The Joseph Blackburn painting of Isaac Winslow and his family portrays the granddaughter of silversmith Edward Winslow holding a gold rattle possibly made by him.

67. Cited by Phillips, *American Silver*, pp. 44, 47.

68. Wallace C. Baker, "Exploit at Fayal," *American Heritage*, X (June 1959), 60–64.

69. Benjamin F. Stevens, "The Silver Punch Bowl Made by Paul Revere" (Boston, 1895). Reproduced from the *Boston Sunday Herald*, January 20, 1895.

70. Paul Revere, MS Day Book, Library, Massachusetts Historical Society. *The Diary of William Bentley*, D.D. (Salem, Mass., 1911), III, 438.

71. Cited by Phillips, *American Silver*, p. 24.

72. John Hull Diary, *American Antiquarian Society Library and Transactions of the Society*, III, 142.

73. *Maryland Journal*, November 9, 1778.

74. Cited by Avery, *An Exhibition*, pp. 13–14.

75. *Pennsylvania Gazette*, June 30, 1768.

76. Notice in the *New Hampshire Gazette*, November 5, 1762; notice in the *New York City Directory*, 1786, illustrated in Rosenbaum, *Myer Myers, Goldsmith* (New York, 1954), p. 47.

77. *Francis Hopkinson's Account of the Grand Federal Procession in Philadelphia, 1788*, ed. Whitfield J. Bell, Jr., Old South Leaflets, Nos. 230–231 (Boston, 1962).

78. Cited by Stephen G. C. Ensko *American Silversmiths and Their Marks III* (New York, 1948), p. 59.

79. *New-York Gazette and the Weekly Mercury,* March 22, 1779, cited by Gottesman (1954), p. 64.

80. Survey records of the Philadelphia Contributionship, Microfilm roll no. 36, survey no. 877, DMMC, Winterthur. *New-York Gazette and the Weekly Mercury,* April 25, 1774. George M. Curtis, *Early Silver of Connecticut and Its Makers* (Meriden, Conn., 1913), p. 21.

81. Penrose R. Hoopes, *Shop Records of Daniel Burnap, Clockmaker* (The Connecticut Historical Society, 1958), pp. 120–121. Subsequent references to Burnap will be found in the same source, pp. 117, 147–166.

82. William Davis Miller, *The Silversmiths of Little Rest* (Kingston, R.I., 1928), pp. 30–31.

83. Inventory of Richard Conyers in Phillips, *American Silver,* pp. 14–16; Caesar Ghiselin, 1734, Philadelphia County Probate Court, Philadelphia, Pa.; Coney inventory illustrated in H. F. Clarke, *op. cit.,* between pp. 12 and 13; George Hanners, 1740 Suffolk County Probate Court, Boston, Mass.: Francis Richardson, 1729, Philadelphia County Probate Court, Philadelphia, Pa.

84. *American Citizen and General Advertiser,* October 3, 1801, cited by Gottesman (1965), p. 94.

85. Daniel Trotter, Receipt Book, MS, owned by Theodore T. Newbold. J. Stewart Johnson, "New York Cabinetmaking Prior to the Revolution," (Master's dissertation, University of Delaware, 1964). Isaac Fowls advertisement in *Boston Chronicle,* August 1–8, 1768.

86. Carl M. Williams, *Silversmiths of New Jersey* (Philadelphia, 1949), p. 134.

87. Ellen Beasley, "Samuel Williamson, Philadelphia Silversmith, 1794–1813" (Master's dissertation, University of Delaware, 1964).

88. *The New-York Gazette or the Weekly Post-Boy,* March 10, 1763, cited by Gottesman (1938), p. 42. *Boston Gazette,* December 7, 1767, cited by Lawrence C. Wroth, *Abel Buell of Connecticut* (Middletown, Conn., 1958), pp. 33–34.

89. *The Boston Gazette and Country Journal,* August 20, 1770.

90. *City Gazette and Daily Advertiser,* October 23, 1800, cited by Henry J. Kauffman, *Early American Gunsmiths* (Harrisburg, Pa., 1952), p. 5.

91. Ebenezer Moulton, docket number 19011, Essex County Probate Court, Salem, Mass.

92. Cited by Phillips, *American Silver,* p. 37.

93. Joseph Richardson, MS Account Book, Historical Society of Pennsylvania.

94. Cited by Buhler, *Mount Vernon Silver,* p. 34.

95. Gabriel Thomas, *An Historical and Geographical Account of the Province of Pensilvania and of West-New-Jersey in America* (London, 1698), p. 31.

96. John Marshall Phillips, "The Winslow Sugar Box," *Bulletin of the Associates in Fine Arts at Yale University,* VI (June 1935), 45–46.

97. Henry Flynt, docket number 8000, Middlesex County Probate Court, Cambridge, Mass.

98. *Boston News-Letter,* November 6–13, 1704, cited by George Francis Dow, *The Arts & Crafts in New England, 1704–1775* (Topsfield, Mass., 1927), p. 58.

99. Letter from Grace Lloyd to Joseph Richardson, MS, DMMC, Winterthur.

100. Powell Papers, Invoice Book, DMMC, Winterthur.

101. Jones, *The Old Silver of American Churches,* p. 48.

102. *Rules for governing the Proprietors of, and Institutions for rendering useful the Books belonging to the Providence Library* (Providence, R.I., 1763). *The New-York Gazette and the Weekly Mercury,* November 7, 1774, cited by Gottesman (1938), pp. 65–66.

103. *New-York Daily Advertiser,* January 2, 1786, cited by Gottesman (1954), pp. 82–83.

104. Charles Oman, *English Domestic Silver,* 4th edition (London, 1959), p. 230.

105. Board of Trade, *Report of the Departmental Committee on Hallmarking* (London, 1959).

106. *Pennsylvania Archives,* Series 8, VII, 5964, 5975, 5982–5983, 5985–5986.

107. Beasley, "Samuel Williamson."

108. Winckley will cited by Phillips *American Silver,* p. 20. Smith MSS VI, 103–104, 1762–1765, The Library Company of Philadelphia. David Stockwell, "A 1757 Inventory of Silver," *Antiques,* LVIX (January 1956), 58.

109. Rolt, *A New Dictionary of Trade and Commerce* (London, 1761).

110. *The New-York Gazette,* March 14, 1763, cited by Gottesman (1938), p. 55.

111. Letter from Abiel Abbot to T. Davis, MS 13,483 and Bill from Israel Trask to The First Church in Beverly, Massachusetts, November 29, 1809, Beverly Historical Society.

112. *The New-York Gazette,* February 8–15, 1732, cited by Gottesman (1938), p. 29.

113. John Marshall Phillips, "Faked American Silver," Chapter XII in Ruth Webb Lee, *Antique Fakes and Reproductions* (Northborough, Mass., 1950), pp. 244–252.

114. Martha G. Fales, "Some Forged Richardson Silver," *Antiques,* LXXVII (May 1961), 466–469.

115. *American Citizen and General Advertiser,* April 21 and September 18, 1801, cited by Gottesman (1965), pp. 97–98.

[229] Spearhead for flagstaff, by Amable Brasier, Philadelphia, c. 1800. *Courtesy, Philadelphia Museum of Art*

Glossary

The words selected for definition are those which are commonly used in a discussion of silver. The names of various forms of silver have not been included since they are discussed at length in Chapter I and may be referred to through the index.

acanthus. The leaf of a Mediterranean plant popular as a decorative pattern for architectural and artistic designs, characterized conventionally by a large spine and irregular edges

ajouré. A French term used to describe pierced and open work in metal objects. See *reticulated* and *pierced work*

alloy. The mixture of more than one metal or substance; the combination of the base metal copper with a more valuable metal, silver, to produce a metal of greater hardness and better malleability and durability

annealing. The process of softening metal by reheating and gradually cooling it between courses of hammering to maintain malleability, to prevent the molecular structure from becoming brittle, and to keep the metal from cracking under the blows of the hammer

anthemion. A stylized motif derived from the classical Greek honeysuckle or palmette design

anvil. The heavy iron or steel block with a polished smooth face on which metals are hammered and shaped

apprentice. A person bound by indenture or legal agreement to serve a master goldsmith for a certain length of time, usually about seven years, in order to learn the art and business of working in precious metals. The apprentice followed the master's instruction and the master provided for his maintenance and education

297

arabesque. An ornamental composition in which foliage, natural motifs, vases, and figures are combined in a fanciful pattern

assay. The test of purity applied to metals to determine the quality and the amount of base metal they contain, ascertained by use of a touchstone, heat, or cupellation

bail. A type of semi-circular rotating handle attached on two sides of a vessel with hinges

Baroque. A bold, contrasting artistic style of design or decoration featuring massive, moving, curvilinear lines and florid details, expressed in silver with embossing, fluting, and gadrooning

beading. Bead-like ornamental edging or decoration consisting of contiguous half-spheres. Sometimes called pearling in the eighteenth century

bezel. A rim added inside the top of a vessel to make the lid fit more securely

boss. A roundish ornamental protuberance

bright-cut. A type of ornamental edging cut into silver to form facets, especially on spoon handles

Britannia standard. The higher standard for silver, required in England from March 1697 to June 1720, i.e., 958 parts of silver per 1000 or 11 oz. dwt. per 12 oz., an increase of 8 dwt. pure silver per pound over sterling standard

bobeche. The flat, saucer-like addition on candlesticks to catch the wax dripping from burning candles

buffing. The removal of the entire outer surface of metal with an abrasive rotating wheel in order to polish it to a high finish or to remove outer impurities and flaws (as well as the natural patina)

burnishing. Light polishing of the surface of metals to increase the luster, accomplished with a hard, smooth, curved tool

cabriole. Term descriptive of the S-curved and tapering legs supporting objects

carat. A measurement of the weight and purity of gold meaning the twenty-fourth part by weight of the whole; pure gold is 24 carats

cartouche. The enclosure for ornamental designs, inscriptions, heraldic devices, initials, or names, often very elaborate

casting. Process of forming silver by pouring the molten metal into a mold consisting of an iron frame containing casting sand, into which a pattern has been impressed and removed

chaplet. A garland or wreath, particularly in heraldry

chasing. The process of modeling the surface of metal by hammering a punch and embossing the metal with a design without removing any of the metal. The indentations of the design can often be seen on the reverse side

chinoiserie. Adaptations of Oriental designs, in vogue in Europe and America particularly at the end of the seventeenth century, in the mid-eighteenth century, and again about 1820

Classical. Descriptive of an artistic style derived from Roman and Greek art characterized by simplicity and correctness, symmetry, and proper proportion; expressed in silver in oval and urn forms with fluting, beading, reticulation, bright cutting, and delicate engraving of swags and bellflowers

coin. A term applied to silver to indicate the purity of the metal. Originally, many objects were made from melted coins, and their purity was the same as the standard of the country's coinage. By 1830, American silversmiths were making objects from sheet metal purchased by them from suppliers, and so they began to stamp silver COIN, C, or D (dollar) to indicate that the objects were of the same standard as coinage, at that time 900 parts silver to 100 parts copper in a total of 1000

course. A complete round of hammering on a piece of silver, spiralling from the center around and around to the outside edge

crenate. Descriptive of edges cut into rounded scallops, as on the edge of a leaf, found particularly in silver on the rims of tankard lids or sauce boats and on bands of applied ornamentation

cusped. Designed with two curved tangential parts, generally referring in silver to a type of double-lobed thumbpiece on tankards

cut-card. A type of relief decoration in which a pattern is cut from a thin sheet of metal and applied by soldering to the surface of another piece of silver. Especially favored by Huguenot silversmiths at the end of the seventeenth century for Baroque designs

cypher. A combination of initials in a single design or monogram, frequently with a mirror image of the letters to balance the design

date-letter. The letter of the alphabet stamped on silver to indicate the year in which it was made or assayed. Required by the Assay Office in London but not used in America until the nineteenth century and then only sporadically

diaper. A type of pattern of contiguous diamonds

die. The metal stamp struck by a hammer to impress a particular device or maker's mark into metal objects

drawplate. The flat steel plate in the end of the draw bench, with a series of graduated holes through which wire is pulled to make it progressively narrower or of a molded shape

dwt. See *pennyweight*

engrailed. Edged with a series of curved indentations; the opposite of scalloped

engraving. The process of cutting designs and letters into the surface of metals with a scorper, removing metal in the process

escutcheon. The shield or shield-shaped area in which heraldic devices and coats of arms are depicted or engraved. Also, the area immediately surrounding a keyhole

feather edge. An engraved edge consisting of a single slanted line of wedge-shaped facets

finial. The uppermost ornamentation or termination

fire-scale. The layer of oxidized metal which occurs on silver when it is annealed. Also called fire-stain

flange. The projecting rim or edge of an object

flask. The iron frame containing sand in which metals are cast. Also, the lidded container for carrying liquids

flatware. The name generally given to knives, forks, and spoons collectively, or to flat vessels such as plates

fluted. Ornamented with a series of vertical, parallel, half-round channels or grooving; the opposite of reeding

flux. Any material used to protect the surface of metal from oxidation when being heated, or used to aid in melting or purifying metals

foliated. Ornamented with leafy decoration

forging. The shaping up of a piece of metal by hammering it against various polished steel anvils or stakes and reheating it. Also, the fabricating of an imitation of a genuine object with the intention of deceiving

gadrooning. An ornamental border of lobing either curved and convex or both convex and concave, placed vertically at an angle or spiralling from the edge

gilding. The process of coating the surface of metal with gold by painting on a mixture of mercury and gold and then heating to evaporate the mercury; more recently accomplished by electrolysis. Parcel-gilding is partial gilding by covering parts not to be gilded with a resistant

goldsmith. A metal-worker qualified to make objects of gold and silver. Although most work was with the less precious metal of silver, these men were known as goldsmiths until about the mid-eighteenth century, when the term silversmith came into more general use

Goldsmiths' Company. The craft guild of goldsmiths and silversmiths in existence in London at least since 1180 and incorporated in 1327, it established standards of workmanship by assaying and marking wrought gold and silver and by educational programs

grain. A measurement of troy weight, $\frac{1}{24}$ of a pennyweight

guilloche. An ornament consisting of two or more bands or strings twisting over each other to repeat the same figure in a continued series

hallmark. The official mark stamped into gold and silver wares by the Assay Offices of the English Goldsmiths' Company to verify quality and genuineness, to show where and when the objects were made, and sometimes to indicate if a duty had been paid

imbrication. A pattern of overlapping rounded or pointed edges, resembling tiles or shingles

ingot. A bar or cast block of silver or other metal

knop. A small knob or finial used as decoration or a termination of an object

limmel. Derived from *lemail*, the remaining scraps, filings, or sweepings of silver or gold

maker's mark. The particular mark or device of an individual craftsman, indicating that he was responsible for the quality and making of a gold or silver object

malleability. The capacity of a metal to be extended and shaped by hammering or by pressure from rollers

mask. Decorative motif of the head of a human or animal, frequently grotesque or fanciful and in relief, interwoven with foliage or scrolls

mantling. Heraldic term describing the flowing scrollwork on either side of the helmet above the shield

matting. The process of creating a contrasting roughened texture and dullness to the surface of metals with chasing or dotting punches struck closely together

molding. A shaped strip or member added to an object to increase strength or add decoration, often formed in silver by means of a drawing bench and plates

mount. Additional decorative sections of silver soldered onto an object

Onslow. A pattern fashionable in English flatware about 1760–70, featuring a handle ending turned back in a scroll. Probably named for Arthur Onslow, speaker of the House of Commons under George II

oxidizing. A process of darkening certain areas of silverwork to dramatize the design by the application of a sulfur compound to tarnish the surface

parcel gilt. See *gilding*

patera. Classical design, derived from the base of a type of urn used for sacrificial libations; a stylized petaled pattern in an oval or circular shape

patina. The appearance of the surface of an object acquired over the years by use and wear, particularly the soft luster of tiny scratches caused by polishing silver

pearling. See *beading*

pennyweight (dwt.). A unit in troy weight equal to twenty-four grains or one-twentieth of an ounce

pibling (pebbling). The process by which the surface of silver is granulated, achieved with hammers and chasing tools

pickle. The mild sulfuric acid solution in which silver is immersed to remove the surface oxidation from the metal

pierced work. A patterned decorative process whereby the metal is pierced and cut away in small sections

planishing. The process of flattening and smoothing the surface of silver through the use of a broad-faced hammer, removing the marks of the hammer blows caused in shaping the metal so that the shape of the piece is not changed but the thickness is made more uniform

plate. Wrought solid silver and gold objects, from the Spanish *plata*, meaning silver, and not to be confused with *plated* wares such as Sheffield and electroplated nickel silver

plated. See *Sheffield plate*

posey. The engraved inscription inside rings, often a short poem

pounce(d) work. An overall punched decoration like matting but with more widely spaced punches

pricked work. A type of decoration formed by a series of tiny dots, used for initials and other devices, particularly in early silver

purchase. The thumbpiece of a tankard, also called billet

raising. The process of shaping a flat disk of silver by hammering in concentric circles. When a curved shape has been formed, the hammering and shaping is continued from the other side

rat-tail. A spiny ridge used as reinforcement or decoration where two parts of silver join together, especially where the handle of a spoon meets the back of the bowl

reeding. Ornament consisting of narrow parallel convex half-round reeds vertically placed. The reverse of fluting

repoussé. A type of ornamentation formed in relief in metal by hammering up from the reverse or inner side

reticulated. Pierced patterns or designs that are netted in appearance

rinceau. A scroll pattern or ornament resembling a series of cresting waves

rococo. A word derived from the French *rocailles* and *coquilles* (rocks and shells), meaning a light, delicately poised artistic style of design and decoration combining shells, scrolls, naturalistic floral motifs, and curved lines in an asymmetrical arrangement, especially popular in the mid-eighteenth century; expressed in silver with curvilinear forms, repoussé decoration, elaborate engraving, cast shells and flowers

scorper. A small hard chisel, graver, or burin used to engrave metal

serif. One of the fine lines of a letter, especially a fine cross stroke at the ends

serrated. Descriptive of a type of border or edge composed of saw-toothed notches, especially used to describe an enclosure for maker's marks

Sheffield plate. Plated silver made by fusing, at a very high heat, a silver coating to one or both sides of a thick sheet of copper, and then rolling the composite metal down to an appropriate thickness. The process was invented by Thomas Bolsover about 1743 and first developed in Sheffield, England. By the mid-nineteenth century, it had been superceded by electroplated wares

silversmith. Synonymous with *goldsmith*

stake. A small anvil used by silversmiths in forming metal into objects

sterling. The minimum standard of purity of fineness of English silver; i.e., 925 parts pure silver to 1000 parts or 11 oz. 2 dwt. silver per 12 oz., decreed in 1300 and legal ever since, except during the Britannia period, from 1697 to 1720. The same standard was set by the United States Government in 1906 in the Stamping Act

strapwork. A type of applied decoration consisting of interlaced bands and scrollwork, or pierced scroll and ribbon patterns, often enclosing floral motifs and other devices

swage. A tool used by silversmiths for shaping or decorating objects, which are then struck with a hammer or sledge

swags. Dependant festoons or garlands of fruit, flowers, and leaves found in silver, particularly as cast ornamentation on handles or as engraved ornamentation around cartouches

thumbpiece. The pivotal part above the hinge on a covered vessel, used to open the lid easily with the thumb while grasping the handle

tincture. A term used in heraldry to express color

touch or touch mark. The test or attestation of quality, a hallmark or maker's mark, sometimes ascertained with silver and gold by means of a *touchstone* (a black siliceous stone) on which the metals can be rubbed and compared for color with rubbings of metals of known quality

trifid. Three-part forked or lobed designs, such as appeared on handles of spoons about 1700 and on cast feet about 1700 to 1750

troy weight. The system of weights commonly used in England and the United States for gold and silver (from Troyes in France), in which 1 pound equals 12 ounces, 1 ounce equals 20 pennyweights (dwt.) and 1 pennyweight equals 24 grains (gr.)

vermeil. The French process for gilding silver developed in the mid-eighteenth century but outlawed in the nineteenth century because the use of mercury in the process was harmful to the workers

water leaf. Conventionalized design of a large, broad, unribbed leaf with rounded tapering edges, especially popular as decoration on silver at the end of the eighteenth and beginning of the nineteenth century

[230] Rare covered skillet with knopped cover, by William Rouse, Boston, c. 1690–1705. Engraved with the Foster arms. Height: 4⅝″. *Courtesy, Yale University Art Gallery, lent by Mr. and Mrs. Donald W. Henry*

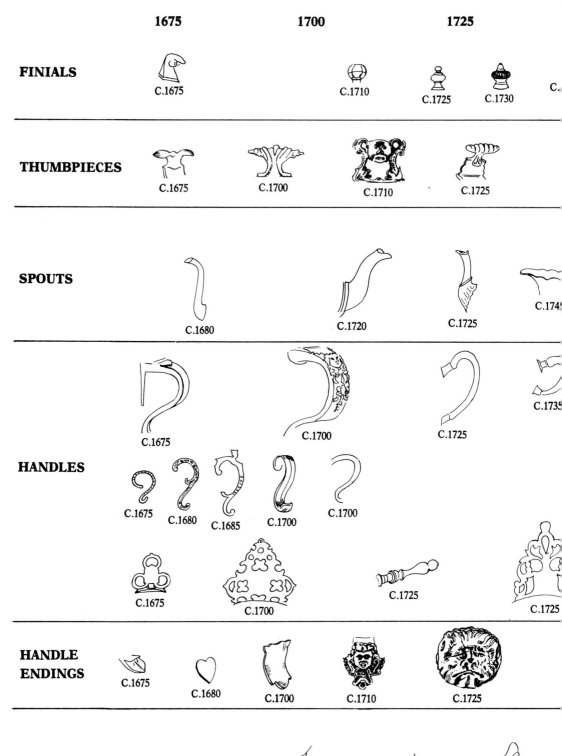

	1675	**1700**	**1725**	
FINIALS	C.1675	C.1710	C.1725 C.1730	C.
THUMBPIECES	C.1675	C.1700	C.1710	C.1725
SPOUTS	C.1680	C.1720	C.1725	C.174
HANDLES	C.1675 C.1675 C.1680 C.1685 C.1675	C.1700 C.1700 C.1700 C.1700	C.1725 C.1725	C.173 C.1725
HANDLE ENDINGS	C.1675 C.1680	C.1700	C.1710	C.1725
FEET	C.1675 C.1690	C.1710	C.1725	C.1735 C

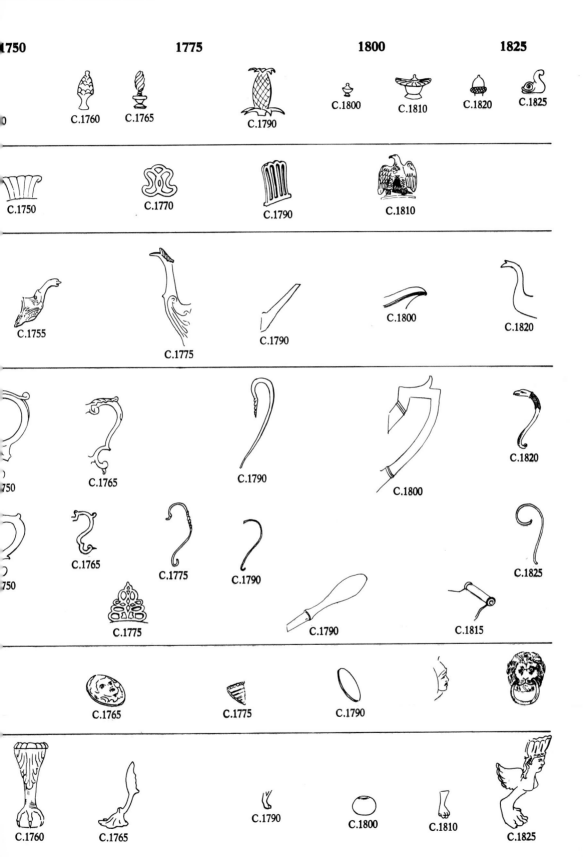

1750   1775   1800   1825

C.1760   C.1765   C.1790   C.1800   C.1810   C.1820   C.1825

C.1750   C.1770   C.1790   C.1810

C.1755   C.1775   C.1790   C.1800   C.1820

C.1765   C.1790   C.1800   C.1820

C.1765   C.1775   C.1790   C.1825

C.1775   C.1790   C.1815

C.1765   C.1775   C.1790

C.1760   C.1765   C.1790   C.1800   C.1810   C.1825

1675 **1700** **1725**

LIDS

C.1675

C.1710

C.1725

C.1740

BODIES

C.1675

C.1700

C.1720

C.1740

C.1675

C.1680-1720

C.1700

C.1725

BASES

C.1675

C.1700

C.1725

RIMS

C.1675

C.1700

C.1725

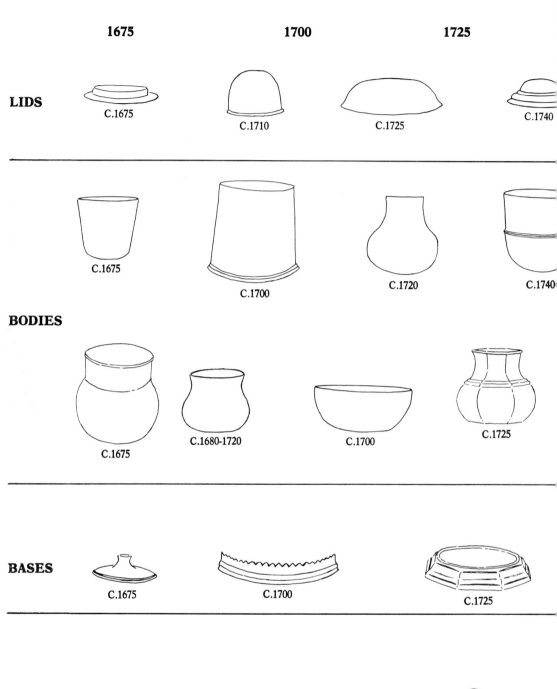

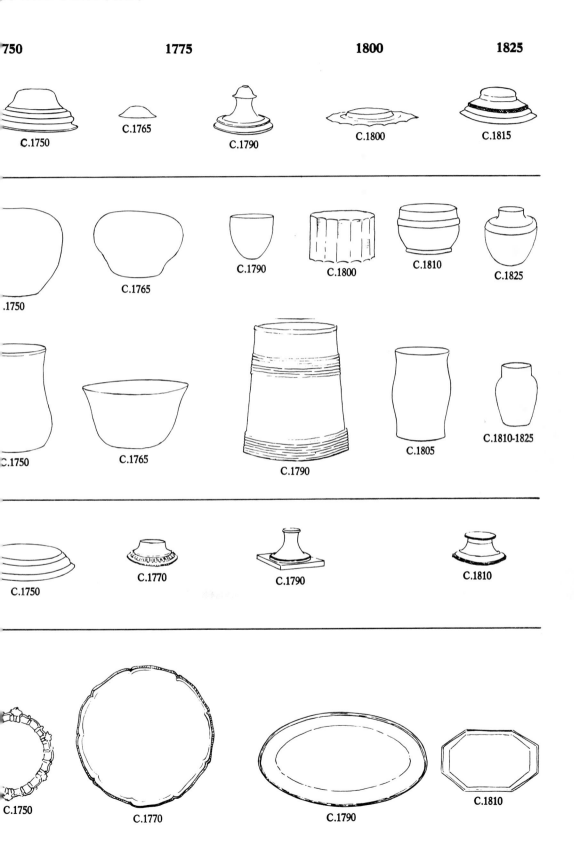

1750   1775   1800   1825

C.1750

C.1765

C.1790

C.1800

C.1815

C.1765

.1750

C.1790

C.1800

C.1810

C.1825

C.1750

C.1765

C.1790

C.1805

C.1810-1825

C.1750

C.1770

C.1790

C.1810

C.1750

C.1770

C.1790

C.1810

[231] Covered pitcher, by William Gale (w. 1816–1823), New York, 1823. Presented on the occasion of the first voyage through the Western Canal and Hudson River by the Manufacturers of Flour to the owners of the boat *Mary & Hannah*. Height: 12¾". *Courtesy, Albany Institute of History and Art. Photograph courtesy, Newark Museum*

Bibliography

It was not until 1888 that the first discussion of American silver appeared in print. Written by J. H. Buck, it was titled simply *Old Plate*. This was followed by Theodore Woolsey's article "Old Silver" in *Harper's Magazine* in 1896. Only in the twentieth century, however, did American silver begin to receive serious attention.

The first exhibition entirely devoted to American silver was held in Boston at the Museum of Fine Arts in 1906, and resulted in the publication of a catalogue that is a landmark in the description of early American examples of silver. The first major exhibition of American decorative arts was held in 1909 at the Metropolitan Museum of Art for the Hudson-Fulton celebration, and the catalogue of the silver included is impressive. This was followed in 1911 by an exhibition at the Boston Museum of Fine Arts called American Church Silver of the Seventeenth and Eighteenth Centuries. The catalogue for the exhibition contained examples of domestic silver as well as a glossary and a long introductory chapter by George M. Curtis on Connecticut silver, the first discussion of the silver of any one state.

From this time on the subject was established, and while there were still not many publications for several decades, those which appeared were of major significance. E. Alfred Jones's *The Old Silver of American Churches*, published by the Colonial Dames of America in 1913, probably will be forever the finest book produced on American silver because of its complete descriptions of over sixteen hundred American examples, the inclusion of facsimiles of marks for almost every object, the number of pieces illustrated, the historical documentation, and the quality of the printing. In the same year Curtis published a book on the *Early Silver of Connecticut*, which not only discussed the silver of that state but also provided for the first time extensive biographical information on the men who made silver.

309

The next big year was 1917, which saw the appearance of the first general book on American silver, Francis Hill Bigelow's *Historic Silver of the Colonies;* it included English silver owned in Colonial America as well as that made here. Hollis French published a glossary with his *List of Early American Silversmiths,* the first list of identified maker's marks. In 1920 Maurice Brix published a checklist of Philadelphia silversmiths which has still not been superceded.

It was in the 1930s, however, that real progress was made in the literature, beginning with C. Louise Avery's *Early American Silver,* which remains today one of the finest general books on the subject. While single biographies of silversmiths can be traced back to 1891, and Goss's *Life of Colonel Paul Revere,* and Wroth's *Abel Buell* appeared in 1926, it was in the thirties that full-scale biographies with checklists of silver were produced for Coney, Dummer, and the Hurds, and in 1940 for John Hull.

With a brief hiatus during the war years, the literature on American silver has been increasing annually to the extent that it is now necessary to make selective listings of the material available. In addition there are sources that, while usually not listed in bibliographies, are worth noting. For instance, the Yale Fine Arts *Bulletin,* the Metropolitan Museum *Bulletin,* and the publications of other museums with major collections of American silver often contain articles of significance. Outstanding in this category are the articles in the *Bulletin of the Museum of Fine Arts,* Boston, written by Kathryn C. Buhler, for many years a member of the staff of the Museum's Decorative Arts department and present-day doyenne of the field of American silver.

Another source of information apt to be overlooked is the series of articles which appeared in the *New York Sun* from about 1938 to 1945. Written by Helen Burr Smith on a variety of subjects, these brief articles contain the results of her original research. *Art Quarterly* is useful for an occasional review of a silver exhibition or an article, but even more for its periodic reporting of recent museum acquisitions. Worth noting also is the vast amount of information which is available about American silver and silversmiths in local histories, directories and genealogies, travel accounts, and early newspapers. Similarly rewarding and largely untapped to date are original records such as family papers and probate records, and other public records such as deeds and criminal court proceedings.

One of the most difficult areas to find information about is that of prices of silver. Wenham's *Practical Book of American Silver* makes some reference to prices current at the time of its publication in 1949. Early issues of *Antiques* note some prices at sales or in advertisements. However, such guides are only partially helpful, as prices fluctuate daily, sometimes radically. The asking price in a dealer's shop or the most recent price list from an auction of silver at Parke-Bernet Galleries in New York is probably the best source of information available.

There are certain bibliographical aids that should be utilized in searching for further information about any aspect of American silver. *Antiques* magazine, since its first issue in 1922, has carried some of the most important information about American silver and individual silversmiths. There is an index for the magazine, but few people realize that in January 1947, on pages 61–64, *Antiques* published a listing of all the articles on silver that had appeared in the magazine over the preceeding twenty-five years. For the beginner in the field, such a listing is invaluable.

Art Index is another helpful reference source for magazine articles, and includes *Antiques* (1929–1960) and museum bulletins as well as other art publications such as the British *Connoisseur,* which occasionally has articles relating to American silver. *The Reader's Guide to Periodical Literature* sometimes provides references that would not be found in *Art Index* and is worth consulting for specific subjects. Another bibliographical source is the book by Ralph M. and Terry H. Kovel, *A Directory of American Silver, Pewter and Silver Plate* (New York: 1961), since with the name of each silversmith it gives keys to the publications that mention that particular name.

Another listing not widely known or used is the bibliography prepared in honor of John Marshall Phillips after his death and published by the *Bulletin of the Associates in Fine Arts at Yale University* as Volume 21, No. 1, in October 1953. Because of his scholarship and preeminence in the field, every article, book, and catalogue written by Mr. Phillips and listed therein is of special importance.

More recently, Charles F. Montgomery and Catherine H. Maxwell have published a brief history of collectors and collections of early American silver with a remarkable list of exhibitions and writings on the subject. This appeared in *The Walpole Society Notebook, 1968,* a limited edition, but it is hoped that the article will be expanded and published with greater circulation in the future.

With this brief discussion of the bibliographical aids and the general development of the literature on American silver as an introduction, a selective listing is given with occasional annotations. Its purpose is twofold. It is to supply the crucial information about the best sources of material for those interested in pursuing the subject. At the same time, it is to acknowledge the major sources used in the writing of this book. For greater clarity, the listing is divided into subject headings. In a few instances a source may be listed more than once if it is especially helpful in more than one category, but in most cases the books that cover a broad range of information are listed under *General.*

General
Avery, C. Louise, *Early American Silver* (New York: The Century Company, 1930; reprinted New York: Russell and Russell, 1968 with new preface and bibliography).
Bigelow, Francis Hill, *Historic Silver of the Colonies and its Makers* (New York: The Macmillan Co., 1917; reissued [New York: Tudor Publishing Co.,] 1948).

Buhler, Kathryn C., *American Silver* (Cleveland and New York: The World Publishing Co., 1950).

————, "Silver, 1640–1820," *The Concise Encyclopedia of American Antiques, I* (New York: Hawthorn Books, Inc., 1958), pp. 79–93.

Davidson, Marshall, *The American Heritage History of Colonial Antiques* (The American Heritage Publishing Co., Inc., 1967).

Jones, E. Alfred, *The Old Silver of American Churches* (Letchworth, England: National Society of Colonial Dames of America, 1913).

Klapthor, Margaret Brown, *Presentation Pieces in the Museum of History and Technology, Smithsonian Institution* (Washington, D.C.: Smithsonian Institution, 1965).

McClinton, Katharine Morrison, *Collecting American 19th Century Silver* (New York: Charles Scribner's Sons, 1968).

Phillips, John Marshall, *American Silver* (New York: Chanticleer Press, 1949).

————, "The Hundred Masterpieces of American Silver in Public Collections," *Antiques, 54* (December 1948), 55 (February, April, 1949), 56 (July 1949).

Wenham, Edward, *The Practical Book of American Silver* (Philadelphia and New York: J. B. Lippincott, 1949).

Regional

Avery, C. Louise, *An Exhibition of Early New York Silver* (New York: Metropolitan Museum of Art, 1931).

Belknap, Henry Wyckoff, *Artists & Craftsmen of Essex County, Massachusetts* (Salem, Mass.: The Essex Institute, 1927).

Brix, Maurice, *List of Philadelphia Silversmiths and Allied Artificers from 1682 to 1850* (Philadelphia: Privately printed 1920).

Burton, E. Milby, *Charleston Silver, 1690–1860* (Charleston, S.C.: The Charleston Museum, 1942; reprinted 1968).

Carpenter, Ralph E., Jr., *The Arts and Crafts of Newport, Rhode Island* (Newport: The Preservation Society of Newport County, 1954).

Crosby, Everett Uberto, *95% Perfect* (Nantucket Island, Mass.: Tetaukimmo Press, 1953).

Curtis, George Munson, *Early Silver of Connecticut and Makers* (Meriden, Conn.: International Silver Co., 1913).

Cutten, George Barton, *The Silversmiths of Georgia, together with Watchmakers & Jewelers, 1733 to 1850* (Savannah, Ga.: The Pigeonhole Press, 1958).

————, *Silversmiths, Watchmakers and Jewelers of the State of New York Outside New York City* (Hamilton, N.Y.: Privately printed 1939).

————, *Ten Silversmith Families of New York State* (Albany, N.Y.: New York History, 1946).

————, *Silversmiths of Northampton, Massachusetts and Vicinity down to 1850* (Hamilton, N.Y.: Colgate University Library, 1939, pamphlet).

————, *The Silversmiths of North Carolina* (Raleigh, N.C.: State Department of Archives and History, 1948).

Cutten, George Barton, *The Silversmiths of Virginia from 1694 to 1850* (Richmond, Va.: Dietz Press, 1952).

———, and Cutten, Minnie Warren, *Silversmiths of Utica* (Hamilton, N.Y.: Privately printed 1936).

Dresser, Louisa, "Worcester Silversmiths and the Examples of Their Work in the Collections of the Museum," *Worcester Art Museum Annual*, Vol. I. (Worcester, Mass.: 1935–36).

Goldsborough, Jennifer F., *An Exhibition of New London Silver 1700–1835* (New London, Conn.: Lyman Allyn Museum, 1969).

Harrington, Jessie, *Silversmiths of Delaware 1700–1850* (Delaware: National Society of Colonial Dames of America in the State of Delaware, 1939).

Hennessey, William G., "Silversmiths of Portsmouth," *New Hampshire Profiles IV* (Portsmouth, N.H.: Feb., Mar., Apr., May, 1955).

Hiatt, Noble W., and Hiatt, Lucy F., *The Silversmiths of Kentucky* (Louisville, Ky.: Standard Print Co., 1954).

Hindes, Ruthanna, "Delaware Silversmiths 1700–1850," *Delaware History*, *XII* (Oct. 1967). (Wilmington, Del.: 1967).

Hoitsma, Muriel Cutten, *Early Cleveland Silversmiths* (Cleveland, Ohio: Privately printed 1953).

Johnson, J. Stewart, *Silver in Newark*, an exhibition catalogue with photographs of marks and biographies of silversmiths (Newark, N.J.: Newark Museum, 1967).

"Kentucky Silversmiths before 1850," *Filson Club History Quarterly*, *XVI* (April 1942), pp. 111–126.

Knittle, Rhea Mansfield, *Early Ohio Silversmiths and Pewterers 1787–1847* (Cleveland, Ohio: Calvert-Hatch Co., 1943).

Miller, V. Isabelle, *Silver by New York Makers, Late Seventeenth Century to 1900* (New York: Museum of the City of New York, 1937).

———, *New York Silversmiths of the Seventeenth Century* (New York: Museum of the City of New York, 1963).

Miller, William Davis, *The Silversmiths of Little Rest, Rhode Island* (Kingstown, R.I.: D. B. Updike, 1928).

New Haven Colony Historical Society, *An Exhibition of Early Silver by New Haven Silversmiths*, illustrated and with facsimiles of marks (Meridien, Conn.: New Haven Colony Historical Society, 1967).

Philadelphia Museum of Art, *Philadelphia Silver*, an exhibition catalogue (Philadelphia: 1956).

Phillips, John Marshall, *Early Connecticut Silver 1700–1830*, an exhibition catalogue (New Haven, Conn.: Gallery of Fine Arts, Yale University, 1935).

Pleasants, J. Hall, and Sill, Howard, *Maryland Silversmiths 1715–1830* (Baltimore: Privately printed 1930).

Prime, Mrs. Alfred Coxe, *Three Centuries of Historic Silver*, an exhibition catalogue with biographies of silversmiths and a few photographs of marks (Philadelphia: Pennsylvania Society of the Colonial Dames of America, 1938).

Rhode Island School of Design, *Catalog of An Exhibition of Paintings by*

Gilbert Stuart, Furniture by the Goddards and Townsends, Silver by Rhode Island Silversmiths (Providence, R.I.: 1936).

Rice, Norman S., *Albany Silver,* an exhibition catalogue with photographs of marks and biographies of silversmiths (Albany, N.Y.: Albany Institute of History and Art, 1964).

Starshak, Joseph B., "Dining in Deerfield: A Cultural Index," manuscript (Deerfield, Mass.: Heritage Foundation).

Warren, David B., *Southern Silver,* an extensively illustrated exhibition catalogue (Houston, Texas: The Museum of Fine Arts, 1968).

Williams, Carl M., *Silversmiths of New Jersey, 1700–1825* (Philadelphia: George S. MacManus Co., 1949).

Worcester Art Museum, *Old Silver Owned in Worcester County* (Worcester, Mass.: 1913).

Individual Silversmiths

Beasley, Ellen, "Samuel Williamson, Philadelphia Silversmith, 1794–1813," unpublished Masters dissertation (June 1964: University of Delaware).

Buhler, Kathryn C., *Paul Revere, Goldsmith, 1735–1818* (Boston: Museum of Fine Arts, 1956).

Clarke, Hermann Frederick, *John Coney, Silversmith, 1655–1722* (Boston: Houghton Mifflin Co., 1932).

———, *John Hull, A Builder of the Bay Colony.* Also includes information about Hull's partner Robert Sanderson (Portland, Maine: The Southworth Anthoensen Press, 1940).

———, and Foote, Henry Wilder, *Jeremiah Dummer, Colonial Craftsman & Merchant, 1645–1718* (Boston: Houghton Mifflin Co., 1935).

Forbes, Esther, *Paul Revere & The World He Lived In* (Boston: Houghton Mifflin Co., 1942).

French, Hollis, *Jacob Hurd and His Sons, Nathaniel & Benjamin, Silversmiths, 1702–1781* (The Walpole Society, Cambridge, Mass.: Riverside Press, 1939).

Gandy, Martha Lou, "Joseph Richardson, Quaker Silversmith," unpublished Masters dissertation (University of Delaware: June 1954).

Goss, Elbridge Henry, *The Life of Colonel Paul Revere,* 2 Vols. (Boston: Howard W. Spurr, 1891).

Hoopes, Penrose R., *Shop Records of Daniel Burnap Clockmaker* (Hartford, Conn.: The Connecticut Historical Society, 1958).

Rosenbaum, Jeanette W., *Myer Myers, Goldsmith, 1723–1795,* with technical notes on Myers' silver by Kathryn C. Buhler (Philadelphia: Jewish Publication Society of America, 1954).

Schwartz, Marvin D., *Elias Pelletreau* (Brooklyn, N.Y.: Brooklyn Museum, 1959).

Wroth, Lawrence C., *Abel Buell of Connecticut: Silversmith, Type Founder & Engraver* (Middletown, Conn.: Wesleyan University Press, 1958; first printed New Haven: Yale University Press, 1926).

Published Business Accounts

Buhler, Kathryn C., "The Ledgers of Paul Revere," *Bulletin of the Museum of Fine Arts* (Boston) *34* (1936), pp. 38–45.

"Excerpts from the Day Book of Joseph Richardson, Silversmith of Philadelphia, 1733–1740," *Pennsylvania Magazine of History and Biography, 29* (1905), pp. 121–122.

Tapley, Harriet S., "The Ledger of Edward Lang, Silversmith, of Salem," Essex Institute *Historical Collections, 66* (1930), pp. 325–29.

Background

Bannister, Judith, *Old English Silver* (New York: G. P. Putnam's Sons, 1965).

Dennis, Faith, *Three Centuries of French Domestic Silver*, 2 vols. (New York: Metropolitan Museum of Art, 1960).

Frederiks, J. W., *Dutch Silver*, 2 vols. (Den Haag: Martinus Nÿhoff's, 1952, 1958).

Jackson, Sir Charles J., *Illustrated History of English Plate*, 2 vols. (London: B. T. Batsford, 1911).

———, *English Goldsmiths and Their Marks* (London: 1921, reprinted London: B. T. Batsford, 1949).

Jones, E. Alfred, *Old Silver of Europe and America* (Philadelphia: B. T. Batsford, Ltd., 1928).

Langdon, John Emerson, *Canadian Silversmiths 1700–1900* (Lunenberg, Vt.: The Stinehour Press, 1960).

Oman, Charles, *English Domestic Silver* (London: Adam and Charles Black, 1959; fifth edition, 1962).

Taylor, Gerald, *Silver* (Penguin Books Ltd., 1956).

Source Material

Craig, James H., *The Arts and Crafts in North Carolina 1699–1840* (Winston-Salem, N.C.: Old Salem, Inc., 1965).

Cummings, Abbott Lowell, ed., *Rural Household Inventories (1675–1775)* (Boston: The Society for the Preservation of New England Antiquities, 1964).

Dow, George Francis, *The Arts & Crafts in New England, 1704–1775* (Topsfield, Mass.: The Wayside Press, 1927).

Essex Institute, *Probate Records of Essex County, Mass.: 1635–1664* (Salem, Mass.: The Essex Institute, 1916); *1665–1674* (Salem, Mass.: The Essex Institute, 1917); *1675–1681* (Salem, Mass.: The Essex Institute, 1920).

Gottesman, Rita Susswein, *The Arts and Crafts in New York: 1726–1776* (New York: The New-York Historical Society, 1938); *1777–1799* (New York: The New-York Historical Society, 1954); *1800–1804* (New York: The New-York Historical Society, 1965).

Prime, Alfred Coxe, *The Arts & Crafts in Philadelphia, Maryland, and South Carolina. First Series, 1721–1785* (The Walpole Society: The Wayside Press,

1929); *Second Series, 1786–1800* (The Walpole Society: Topsfield, Mass.: 1932).

Allied Crafts

Bedini, Silvio A., *Early American Scientific Instruments and Their Makers* (Washington, D.C.: Museum of History and Technology, Smithsonian Institution, 1964).

Brigham, Clarence S., *Paul Revere's Engravings* (Worcester, Mass.: American Antiquarian Society, 1954).

Britten's Old Clocks and Watches and Their Makers, ed. Baillie, G. H., Clutton, C., and Ilbert, C. A. (New York: E. P. Dutton & Co., Inc., 1956; seventh edition).

Groce, George C., and Wallace, David H., *The New-York Historical Society's Dictionary of Artists in America* (New Haven: Yale University Press, 1957).

Laughlin, Ledlie I., *Pewter in America*, 2 vols. (Boston: Houghton Mifflin Co., 1940. Revised edition 1 vol. Barre, Mass.: Barre Publishers, 1969).

Loubat, J. F., *The Medallic History of the United States of America, 1776–1876;* 2 vols. (New York: Reprinted 1967 N. Flayderman & Co., Inc., 1878).

Peterson, Harold L., *The American Sword 1775–1945* (Philadelphia: Ray Riling Arms Books Company, 1965).

Thieme-Becker (Ulrich Thieme and Felix Becker), *Allgemeines Lexikon der bildenden Kunstler* . . . (Leipzig: Wilhelm Engelmann, 1907).

Heraldry

Guillim, John, *A Display of Heraldry* (London: Printed by T. W., 1724).

Bolton, Charles Knowles, *Bolton's American Armory* (Boston: 1927. Reprinted Baltimore: Heraldic Book Company, 1964).

Marks

Board of Trade, *Report of the Departmental Committee on Hallmarking* (London: Her Majesty's Stationery Office, 1959).

Currier, Ernest M., ed. by Kathryn C. Buhler, *Marks of Early American Silversmiths* . . . , *List of New York City Silversmiths 1815–1841* (Portland, Maine, and London: The Southworth-Anthoensen Press, 1938).

Darling Foundation, *New York State Silversmiths* (New York: 1964).

Ensko, Stephen G. C., *American Silversmiths and Their Marks, III* (New York: 1948; Privately printed. Supercedes *I*, published in 1927, and *II*, in 1937).

Flynt, Henry N., and Fales, Martha G., *The Heritage Foundation Collection of Silver with Biographical Sketches of New England Silversmiths, 1625–1825* (Old Deerfield, Mass.: The Heritage Foundation, 1968).

French, Hollis, *A List of Early American Silversmiths and Their Marks;* includes also a glossary of terms (New York: The Walpole Society, 1917; reprinted New York: Da Capo Press, 1967).

Rainwater, Dorothy T., *American Silver Manufacturers* (Hanover, Pa.: Everybodys Press, 1966).

The Metal and Manufacture

Abbey, Staton, *The Goldsmiths and Silversmiths Handbook* (New York: Technical Press Ltd., 1952).

Cuzner, Bernard, *A Silversmith's Manual* (London: N.A.G. Press Ltd., 1949; first published, 1935).

De Matteo, William, *The Silversmith in Eighteenth-Century Williamsburg* (Williamsburg, Va.: Colonial Williamsburg, Inc., 1956).

Wilson, H., *Silverwork and Jewellery* (London: Sir Isaac Pitman & Sons, Ltd., 1951; originally published in 1902).

Technical

Fales, Martha G., "Some Forged Richardson Silver," *Antiques*, 79 (May 1961), pp. 466–69.

———, "The Care of Antique Silver," *History News*, 22 (February 1967); technical Leaflet, No. 40.

Kernan, John D., "The Dating of Early American Silver," *The Art Quarterly*, 25 (Spring 1962), pp. 54–66.

Phillips, John Marshall, "Faked American Silver," Chapter XII in Ruth Webb Lee, *Antique Fakes and Reproductions* (Northborough, Mass.: Privately printed 1950; second edition), pp. 244–252.

Plenderleith, H. J., *The Conservation of Antiquities and Works of Art*, Chapter X (London: Oxford University Press, 1957).

Savage, George, *Forgeries, Fakes and Reproductions* (New York: F. A. Praeger, 1963).

Catalogues of Important Exhibitions (Not listed elsewhere)

Avery, Clara Louise, "New York Metropolitan Museum of Art, Exhibition of Early American Silver," *Metropolitan Museum of Art Bulletin* (December: 1931).

Bohan, Peter J., *American Gold 1700–1860*, loan exhibition at Yale University Art Gallery (New Haven: Gallery of Fine Arts, Yale University, 1963).

(Buhler, Kathryn C.), *Colonial Silversmiths, Masters and Apprentices*, loan exhibition at the Museum of Fine Arts, Boston, of the outstanding examples of American silver from the various centers of colonial silversmithing (Boston: Museum of Fine Arts, 1956).

Chicago Art Institute, *From Colony to Nation*, exhibition of silver in conjunction with other major and minor arts (Chicago: Art Institute of Chicago, 1949).

The English-Speaking Unions of the Commonwealth and of the United States. *American Silver and Art Treasures. An Exhibition* (London: 1960).

Halsey, R. T. Haines, *New York Metropolitan Museum Catalogue of Exhibition of Silver Used in New York, New Jersey, and the South* (New York: Metropolitan Museum of Art, 1911).

Kent, Henry Watson, and Levy, Florence N., *Catalogue of an Exhibition of American Paintings, Furniture, Silver and Other Objects of Art*, Vol. II,

Part III: American Silver (New York: Metropolitan Museum of Art, 1909).

Museum of Fine Arts, Boston, *American Silver, the Work of Seventeenth and Eighteenth Centuries*, Introduction by R. T. Haines Halsey (Boston: 1906).

Newark Museum, *Classical America 1815–1845*, loan exhibition of decorative arts and fine arts (Newark, N.J.: 1963).

(Phillips, John Marshall), *Masterpieces of New England Silver 1650–1800*, loan exhibition. (New Haven: Gallery of Fine Arts, Yale University, 1939).

The Virginia Museum of Fine Arts, *Masterpieces of American Silver;* extensive introductory essay by Kathryn C. Buhler (Richmond: 1960).

Published Collections

Avery, C. Louise, *American Silver of the 17th and 18th Century* (Clearwater Collection), (New York: Metropolitan Museum of Art, 1920).

Biddle, James, *American Art from American Collections*, exhibition. Silver illustrated Fig. 95–132 and described pp. 51–63 (New York: Metropolitan Museum of Art, 1963).

Buhler, Kathryn C., *Massachusetts Silver in the Frank L. and Louise C. Harrington Collection;* Introduction gives a history of the collecting of American silver (Worcester, Mass.: Barre Publishers, 1965).

———, *Mount Vernon Silver* (Mount Vernon, Va.: Mount Vernon Ladies Association of the Union, 1957).

Comstock, Helen, "The John Marshall Phillips Collection of Silver," *The Connoisseur Year Book* (London: 1957), pp. 28–33.

Davis, John D., "The Silver," *Antiques* at Colonial Williamsburg, *LCV* (January 1969), pp. 134–137.

Fales, Martha G. *American Silver in the Henry Francis du Pont Winterthur Museum* (Winterthur, Del.: The Henry Francis du Pont Winterthur Museum, 1958).

———, and Flynt, Henry N., *The Heritage Foundation Collection of Silver* (Old Deerfield, Mass.: The Heritage Foundation, 1968).

Ford Museum, "The Silver," *Antiques*, 73 (February 1958), pp. 174–76.

Hammerslough, Philip H., *American Silver;* 3 vols. (Hartford, Conn.: Privately printed 1958, 1960, 1965).

Hipkiss, Edwin J., *The Philip Leffingwell Spalding Collection of Early American Silver* (Cambridge, Mass.: Harvard University Press, 1943).

———, *Eighteenth-Century American Arts*, the M. and M. Karolik Collection (Cambridge, Mass.: Harvard University Press, 1941).

Metropolitan Museum of Art, *Early American Silver*, picture book with notes by Vincent D. Andrus (New York: 1955).

Newton College of the Sacred Heart, *Exhibition of Early American Silver from the Collection of Mr. Cornelius C. Moore, Newport, R.I.* Catalogue listing form and maker. (Newton, Mass.: Privately printed 1963).

Norman-Wilcox, Gregor, "American Silver at the Los Angeles County Museum (the Marble Collection)," *The Connoisseur Year Book* (London: 1956), pp. 62–70.

Phillips, John Marshall, *Early American Silver Selected from The Mabel*

Brady Garvan Collection. Yale University Art Gallery; posthumously published with editing, introduction, and notes by Meyric R. Rogers (New Haven, Conn.: Yale University Art Gallery, 1960).

————, and others (eds.). *The Waldron Phoenix Belknap, Jr. Collection of Portraits and Silver.* (Cambridge, Mass.: Harvard University Press, 1955).

Smith College Museum of Art, *Early New England Silver lent from the Mark Bortman Collection,* an exhibition (Northampton, Mass.: 1958).

Important Public Collections of American Silver

Albany, New York	Albany Institute of History and Art
Baltimore, Md.	The Baltimore Museum of Art
	Maryland Historical Society
Boston, Mass.	Museum of Fine Arts
Cambridge, Mass.	Fogg Art Museum, Harvard University
Charleston, S.C.	The Charleston Museum
Chicago, Ill.	The Art Institute of Chicago
Cincinnati, Ohio	Cincinnati Art Museum
Cleveland, Ohio	The Cleveland Museum of Art
Dearborn, Mich.	The Henry Ford Museum and Greenfield Village
Deerfield, Mass.	The Heritage Foundation Collection
Detroit, Mich.	The Detroit Institute of Arts
Hartford, Conn.	Connecticut Historical Society
	Wadsworth Atheneum (Hammerslough Collection)
Los Angeles, Calif.	Los Angeles County Museum of Art (Marble Collection)
Minneapolis, Minn.	Minneapolis Institute of Arts
New Haven, Conn.	Yale University Art Gallery (Garvan and Phillips Collections)
New York, N.Y.	The Metropolitan Museum of Art
	Museum of the City of New York
	The New-York Historical Society
Philadelphia, Pa.	The Historical Society of Pennsylvania
	Philadelphia Museum of Art
Providence, R.I.	Rhode Island School of Design, Museum of Art
St. Louis, Mo.	City Art Museum
Washington, D.C.	Smithsonian Institution (Division of Cultural History)
Wilmington, Del.	The Henry Francis du Pont Winterthur Museum
Williamsburg, Va.	Colonial Williamsburg, Inc.
Williamstown, Mass.	Sterling and Francine Clark Art Institute
Worcester, Mass.	Worcester Art Museum

Recently Published Books

Bohan, Peter, and Hammerslough, Philip, *Early Connecticut Silver* (Middletown, Connecticut: Wesleyan University Press, 1970).

Buhler, Kathryn C., *American Silver 1655–1825 in the Museum of Fine Arts Boston*, 2 vols. (Greenwich, Connecticut: distributed by New York Graphic Society, 1972).

Buhler, Kathryn C., and Hood, Graham, *American Silver, Garvan and Other Collections in the Yale University Art Gallery*, 2 vols. (New Haven and London: Yale University Press, 1970).

Carlisle, Lilian Baker, *Vermont Clock and Watchmakers, Silversmiths and Jewelers 1778–1878* (Burlington, Vermont: privately printed, 1970).

Clayton, Michael, *The Collector's Dictionary of the Silver and Gold of Great Britain and North America* (New York and Cleveland: The World Publishing Company, 1971).

Farham, Katharine Gross, and Efird, Callie Huger, "Georgia Collects American Silver, 1780–1870," *High Museum Antiques Show Catalogue* (Atlanta, Georgia, 1970), pp. 57–88.

Gerstell, Vivian S., *Silversmiths of Lancaster, Pennsylvania 1730–1850* (Lancaster, Pennsylvania: Lancaster County Historical Society, 1972).

Holland, Margaret, *English Provincial Silver* (New York: Arco Publishing Company Inc., 1971).

Hood, Graham, *American Silver: A History of Style, 1650–1900* (New York: Praeger Publishers, 1971).

Hyde, Bryden Bordley, *Bermuda's Antique Furniture and Silver* (Norwich, England: Fletcher & Son Ltd., 1971), distributed in North America by the Maryland Historical Society.

Munson-Williams-Proctor Institute, *Utica Silver* (Utica, New York: Widtman Press, Inc., 1972), exhibition catalogue with list of Utica silversmiths.

Pleasants, J. Hall, and Sill, Howard, *Maryland Silversmiths 1715–1830* (Baltimore Maryland, 1930), reprinted by Robert Alan Green (Harrison, New York, 1972) with publisher's foreword.

Rainwater, Dorothy T., and Felger, Donna H., *American Spoons, Souvenir and Historical* (Camden, New Jersey: Thomas Nelson and Sons, 1968).

Wilkinson, Wynyard R. T., *Indian Colonial Silver* (London: Argent Press, 1973).

Index

This is an index to the text and captions. The Glossary and Bibliography should be consulted separately. Page numbers in the references precede illustration numbers, the latter being indicated by boldface type.